Exiles and Ironists

North American Studies in Nineteenth-Century German Literature

Jeffrey L. Sammons
General Editor

Vol. 1

PETER LANG
New York · Bern · Frankfurt am Main · Paris

Ursula Franklin

Exiles and Ironists
Essays on the Kinship
of Heine and Laforgue

PETER LANG
New York · Bern · Frankfurt am Main · Paris

Library of Congress Cataloging-in-Publication Data

Franklin, Ursula.
Exiles and ironists.

(North American studies in nineteenth-century German
literature ; vol. 1)
Bibliography: p.
1. Laforgue, Jules, 1860–1887—Criticism and inter-
pretation. 2. Heine, Heinrich, 1797–1856—Influence—
Laforgue. 3. Literature, Comparative—French and
German. 4. Literature, Comparative—German and French.
I. Title. II. Series.
PQ2323.L8Z67   1988   841'.8   87-21522
ISBN 0-8204-0559-0
ISSN 0891-4109

CIP – Titelaufnahme der Deutschen Bibliothek

Franklin, Ursula:
Exiles and ironists : essays on the kinship of
Heine and Laforgue / Ursula Franklin. – New
York; Bern; Frankfurt am Main; Paris: Lang,
1988.
(North American Studies in Nineteenth-Cen-
tury German Literature; Vol. 1)
ISBN 0-8204-0599-0

NE: GT

PQ
2323
. L8
Z 67
1988

Printed by Weihert-Druck GmbH, Darmstadt, West Germany

In Memory of my Friend and Teacher
John A. Yunck

Contents

Introduction 1

I. Heinean Inspirations in Laforgue's Early Literary
  Journalism. 11

II. Reverberations of Heine's *Lyrisches Intermezzo* in
  the Lyrics of Laforgue 41

III. Counterparts: Heine and Laforgue and the Theater 73

IV. Heine's Shakespeare and Laforgue's 107

V. The Poets on the Performing Arts 137

VI. Heine's *Französische Maler* 165

VII. Laforgue on French and German Art and Aesthetic
  Theories. 201

Postscript 237

List of Works Cited 255

Preface

There exists to date no full comparative study of Heine and Laforgue, though numerous are the books concerning Heine's influence on French poets. Moreover, virtually every commentator on Laforgue's sources mentions Heinrich Heine in vague or general terms, since Laforgue himself repeatedly paid tribute to his German master. Thus, while the intertextual link between the two poets has become a critical commonplace, no one has so far undertaken a precise, documented examination of the sedimentation of Heine's influence in Laforgue's textual universe. With this group of essays on the Exiles and Ironists, I have attempted to contribute the first thorough, if not exhaustive comparison suggested by so many commentators over the years.

I am deeply grateful for a Guggenheim Fellowship which permitted me to spend a year in Paris to do the research for this study, and I gratefully acknowledge the assistance of M. François Chapon of the Bibliothèque littéraire Jacques Doucet and the special collections curators of the Bibliothèque Nationale for granting me access to documents crucial in its preparation. I thank Mrs. Laurel Balkema, Interlibrary Loan Librarian, and Professor Howard Stein, Director of Research and Development, at Grand Valley State University for their tireless assistance.

I thank the editors of *Comparative Literature* and the *Canadian Review of Comparative Literature* for their kind permission to use material which first appeared in their journals.

The work of many scholars, too numerous to mention here,

has informed and inspired mine. I will always be indebted to Robert Greer Cohn, and I wish to express my special gratitude for both guidance and encouragement to Professors Lilian R. Furst, Jeffrey L. Sammons, and John A. Yunck, who read the manuscript and gave generously of their time and invaluable advice.

Introduction

This group of essays is intended to examine the literary and intellectual kinship between Heinrich Heine (1797–1856), who wrote most of his mature work in France, and Jules Laforgue (1860–1887), who wrote most of his poetry and prose in Germany. Both expatriate poets mark the end of literary traditions which they revolutionized: Heine transformed German Romantic, Laforgue French Symbolist poetry; and their innovative voices were to have repercussions far beyond their own times and national traditions. Thus Heinean echoes reverberate in Laforgue, and even Apollinaire from our own century, while Laforgue's influence on modern American poets like Allen Tate, Hart Crane, Ezra Pound, and T.S. Eliot is a commonplace of the history of comparative literature.

Both writers chose to spend the greater part of their creative lives in exile; but the self-imposed exile of the young German Jewish poet was soon to be legally reinforced by the German authorities under the pressures of Metternich, while that of Laforgue was, in fact, enforced by the material circumstances of his existence, his simple need to earn a living. Yet neither lost his cultural roots to become integrated into his new environment: Heine became one of the greatest German poets of his time while living in Paris; Laforgue became a great French poet while living in Berlin. They remained exiles. One aim of these essays is to show how this existential situation of exile in Heine and Laforgue not merely influenced their work, in which it became a recurrent theme, but also created the very mask through which these texts speak, in their characteristic mode of irony: in their poetry, for example, that of the Heinean rejected lover and the Laforguean Pierrot; in their prose that of the alien observer.

Other parallels also invite a deeper study of affinities between Heine and Laforgue; the paradox, for example, that while both poets amplified traditional and "popular" art forms—Heine with his celebration of the "Lied," Laforgue in elaborating the "complainte"—both revolutionized contemporary prosody. Further, Laforgue's famous "logopoeia" ("éternullité," "sexciproque(s)"), which was to set a trend in modern poetry and even prose—the most famous example, Joyce's *Finnegan's Wake*—was certainly indebted to the ironic wordplay and neologisms ("famillionär," "aristokrätzig") throughout Heine's poetry and prose. Both poets, moreover, attempted novels (*Der Rabbi von Bacherach, Aus den Memoiren des Herren von Schnabelewopski, Stéphane Vassiliew*), attempts which disappointed them, and each tried his pen unsuccessfully at drama; in fact, their fascination with the theater constitutes one of the most remarkable affinities between them. But their distinctive ironic voices attained some of their richest orchestrations in their mature prose, especially in their journalism.

That Laforgue read Heine at least partly in German is evident from occasional quotations by him in that language. However, Heine's standard works were available in French translation in the numerous volumes of the Michel Lévy edition of his *Oeuvres complètes* (1855), which supplemented an earlier (1834) edition. Laforgue expressed his preference for the German poet, even over his great French contemporaries, in one of his earliest poems:

> * Je prends
> Sainte-Beuve et Théo, Banville, Baudelaire,
> Leconte, Heine enfin, qu'aux plus grands je préfère,
> "Ce bouffon de génie", a dit Schopenhauer,
> Qui sanglote et sourit, mais d'un sourire amer!

* I take Sainte-Beuve and Théo, Banville, Baudelaire, Leconte, and finally Heine whom I prefer over the greatest. "That eternal buffoon," said Schopenhauer, who weeps and smiles, but with a bitter smile.

Laforgue's generous tributes to Heine, both poetic and infor-
mal, have suggested an intertextual link acknowledged by most
of their commentators, but critically examined by none.
Both Heine and Laforgue ventured into art criticism and
engaged in that literary journalism which Heine raised to a
distinguished literary genre—before Baudelaire and Mallarmé.
Thus we shall see how Laforgue's *Berlin: la Cour et la ville*
appears sometimes almost to echo Heine's *Briefe aus Berlin*.
And while Heine had become one of Germany's greatest literary
journalists during his life in France, Laforgue became one of the
most brilliant French art critics of his time while living in
Germany.

Heine used this powerful new instrument of literary journalism in the service of his self-imposed mission of combatting
contemporary German francophobia, and to bring about a
greater mutual understanding of two of Europe's great cultural
and literary traditions. Here we recall texts like *Französische
Maler*, *Französische Zustände*, *Über die französische Bühne*,
Lutetia—De l'Allemagne, *L'Ecole romantique*, some of which I
shall discuss in the following essays. Heine expressed his task in
a letter of 1833 written from Paris to a German friend: ''I shall in
this journal (*L'Europe littéraire*) do everything possible to
acquaint the French with the intellectual life of the Germans:
this is now my lifework, and perhaps it is my specific mission to
draw the countries closer . . . I am thus cosmopolitan incar-
nate.'' That the pen of this cosmopolitan pacifist became one of
the most feared weapons of his time is the paradox of the great
ironist in exile.

Much has been written on Heine's irony, one of the most
recent studies being Ursula Lehmann's *Polularisierung und
Ironie im Werk Heinrich Heines*.[1] Two recent theses on irony in
Laforgue—in which Heine is hardly mentioned—are José
Melim's *Another Study of the Irony of Jules Laforgue*[2] and Eilen
Sakari's excellent *Prophète et Pierrot: Thèmes et attitudes
ironiques dans l'oeuvre de Jules Laforgue*.[3] The most significant
study on the theme remains Warren Ramsey's *Jules Laforgue
and the Ironic Inheritance*.[4] The theme of exile in Heine has

been treated by A.I. Sandor, who links it to the poet's technique: *Exile of the Gods: Interpretation of a Theme, a Theory and a Technique in the Work of Heinrich Heine*.[5] There is no full comparative study on Heine and Laforgue, though studies on Heine's influence on French poets are numerous, such as Friedrich Hirth's *Heinrich Heine und seine französischen Freunde*,[6] Kurt Weinberg's Yale thesis on the poet and some of the French Symbolists, *Henri Heine "Romantique défroqué" héraut du symbolisme français*,[7] and most recently a German thesis by Oliver Boeck, *Heines Nachwirkung und Heine-Parallelen in der französischen Dichtung*,[8] which contains a brief chapter on Heinean repercussions in Laforgue. Hanna Geldrich's *Heine und der spanisch-amerikanische Modernismo*,[9] while tracing Heine's influence on the Latin American innovators at the end of the nineteenth century, throws light also on his influence on those French authors (Nerval, Gautier, Sand, the Parnassians and Symbolists) who contributed to his transmission to Latin America.

Virtually every commentator on Laforgue's sources mentions Heinrich Heine in vague or general terms, so that the intertextual link between the two poets has become a critical commonplace. Yet no one has attempted a precise, documented examination of the sedimentation of Heine's influence in Laforgue's textual universe.[10]

If "the ironic tone is central to modern literature,"[11] exile is the existential predicament shared by some of its greatest representatives today, like Joyce, Mann, Ionesco and Beckett, to name but a few modern ironists.[12] And we recall that isolation and alienation, whose ultimate degree is exile, characterized irony from the outset, from the low and "foxy" Eiron of Greek comedy,[13] to the lofty and wise Socrates, ostracized from the city. The Ciceronian figure—dissimilatio—and the Quintilian trope then elevated Irony formally into the arsenal of rhetorical and literary arms.[14] And it has always remained a weapon, bloody in the pen of a Swift, teasing in Sterne and his descendants,[15] finally a weapon against poetic *Begeisterung* and the creative spirit itself in the reflections of its great Romantic theoretician, Friedrich Schlegel.[16]

The view has frequently been expressed that any major artist and truly creative spirit is a foreigner in his own country, "that, by being different, strange, non-conformist, all essential criteria of the creative spirit, he *exiles himself* from the world of common sense. . . . classic examples are the *poètes maudits*— the Americans Edgar Allen Poe and Hart Crane, the Frenchmen Baudelaire, Verlaine and Rimbaud."[17] And to these we might add Hölderlin, Nietzsche, Lautréamont, Artaud, and others who went from alienation to madness. Examples of this inner exile, of being outcasts within one's own country and finally from the human community, have depressingly multiplied of late, with the increasing alienation of the human being in a civilization which evolves more rapidly than its creator.

Heine and Laforgue were compelled to leave homelands which had no place for them, due to forces economic for the one, political and psychological for the other. And for poets and writers exile is especially laden with problems, as it severs them from the cultural and linguistic seedbed of their work. Yet, the more recent exodus of German writers like Mann and Brecht from Nazi Germany confirms that the tragic separation need not necessarily be negative in its literary effect, because "in exile a poetic style can be developed to 'classic' height, which possesses an intellectual reflective attitude toward language, able to create out of that very distance from the native language an artistic means or *Kunstmittel*".[18] And has this not been confirmed, also, by the twentieth-century American and Irish expatriate writers in Paris? Heine and Laforgue became consummate masters of their characteristic styles in exile. They became ironists, because for them irony and wit were weapons for survival, both literary and existential.

While toward the end of his life Heine, totally crippled and disabled by his lifelong illness, had become one of Europe's most feared writers—an irony whose bitterness he tasted to the end—, the younger poet had also *wept* his exile:

* Oh Deutschland, meine ferne Liebe,
Gedenk ich deiner, wein ich fast!
Das muntre Frankreich scheint mir trübe,
Das leichte Volk wird mir zur Last.[19]

Laforgue, Pierrot with "his Hamletic soul,"[20] in the beginning also wept his exile, even if he later repudiated the poems of *Le Sanglot de la Terre*. The young Schopenhauerian had felt himself born into exile, "sur la terre d'exil," exiled into life:

† Aux flots de l'éternel et vaste écoulement,
L'Univers continue et toujours cette terre
Aux déserts du silence, épave solitaire,
Avec ses exilés roule stupidement.[21]

The following group of essays is not still another examination of irony in Heine and Laforgue; nor is it a thematic study of exile in the poets. Rather, its efforts to delineate the fundamental affinities between them center specifically on those aspects of their work and those texts which to me most clearly reveal their literary kinship.

Thus, we find Heinean inspirations already in some of Laforgue's earliest texts, his contributions to *La Guêpe* and *L'Enfer* which predate *Les Complaintes*, and to which I have devoted the first essay. These early attempts at literary journalism, apparently inspired at least in part by Heine's own early journalistic texts, *Briefe aus Berlin*, also contain some of Laforgue's first poems, one of which patently pays tribute to the German poet. My second study, on the reverberations of Heine's *Lyrisches Intermezzo* in the lyrics of Laforgue, addresses what has been called "a deep-seated relationship between the work of the great German ironist and the verse of

---

* Oh Germany, my distant love; when I think of you, I almost weep. Gay France seems sad, and the light people becomes burdensome to me.

† To the tides of the vast and eternal flow, the universe continues, and this earth, solitary flotsam, rolls ever on to deserts of silence with its exiles, stupidly.

Laforgue."[22] The poets' affinities and endeavors in the theater are explored in the following chapter. And their fascination with Shakespeare, a strong intertextual link between them, is the subject of a separate chapter. The following essay deals with the poets' journalistic texts on the performing arts, informed by Heine's observations in Paris and Laforgue's in Berlin. The two concluding pieces deal with art criticism, Heine's *Salon* of 1831, and Laforgue's German-inspired aesthetic theories, applied to the French Impressionists and also—in a Heinean vein—to contemporary German art. All these diverse facets of their textual cosmos reveal the deep-seated relationship between Heine and Laforgue in its complex and manifold manifestations.

This study of influence and affinity must somewhat curtail a major Heinean dimension, not reflected in his disciple, that of his political engagement which has fascinated the greater part of the overwhelming corpus of contemporary Heine scholarship. And while we see this facet reflected in most of the texts discussed, from the early *Briefe aus Berlin* to Heine's mature commentary on the performing arts, down to the very forging of his neologisms, it becomes so predominant in his art criticism that here my examination bifurcates from a study of influence to one of contrasts. Thus Heine and Laforgue as art critics had to be accommodated in separate chapters. For while Laforgue drew from all of the above, he did so with a difference: his texts, as well as his "word-monsters," lack the master's political edge.

Throughout these essays the translations from the French and German are my own, unless otherwise indicated in the notes. And I must regretfully admit that much of that special Heinean and Laforguean ironic savor had perforce to be sacrificed in the process. But one of the aims of this volume of essays is to acquaint the American student of nineteenth-century European literature with two of its major representatives, with an open invitation, of course, to explore their worlds by way of the wealth of their original texts. I have reproduced the verse in the original, with my prose translations at the bottom of the pages.[23]

8   Introduction

Notes

[1] (Frankfurt: Peter Lang, 1976). Much less significant is Vera Debluë's *Anima naturaliter ironica: Die Ironie im Wesen und Werk Heinrich Heines* (Bern: Verlag Herbert Lang & Cie., 1970).

[2] (unpublished, University of Oregon, 1966, University Microfilm International 67-1869).

[3] (Finland: University of Jyväskylä, 1974).

[4] (New York: Oxford University Press, 1953).

[5] (The Hague: Mouton, 1967).

[6] (Mainz: Kupferberg, 1949).

[7] (Paris: Presses Universitaires de France, 1964).

[8] (Göppingen: Kümmerle, 1972). This study disparages the authors Heine influenced for not having rightly understood the German poet's "progressive committment." Cf. Jeffrey L. Sammons' commentary in his *Heinrich Heine: A Selected Critical Bibliography of Secondary Literature, 1956–1980* (New York: Garland Publishing, Inc., 1982), 145.

[9] (Bern & Frankfurt: Verlag Peter Lang, 1971).

[10] Thus, for example Ramsey in his magistral *The Ironic Inheritance* limits himself to generalities like the following: "There is a deep-seated relation between the work of the great German ironist and the verse that Laforgue was preparing to write" (p. 40). J.L. Debauve, in *Laforgue et son temps* (Neuchatel: Baconnière, 1972), points to Heinean affinities, too, in general terms; of the *Moralités légendaires* he says: "Avec plus de couleur mais moins de causticité, c'est l'esprit de Heine" (p. 224). Léon Guichard, in *Jules Laforgue et ses poésies* (Paris: Nizet, 1977), briefly mentions Heine's famous neologisms as likely inspiration for Laforgue's (p. 95). Eilen Sakari refers frequently to Heine in *Prophète et Pierrot*. Her comments remain mostly general, like the following: "Aussi Laforgue peut-il avoir recours à la technique du désillusionnement, pour corriger des propos trop subjectifs, procédé typique d'Henri Heine qui se sert de l'ironie pour dégonfler le pathos" (p. 23). She discusses in more detail, however, the Heinean technique, frequently adopted by Laforgue, of the "queue de poisson," (p. 111) the ironically deflating final line of poems, a technique which I shall discuss in the poetry chapter (II) of this study.

[11] Northrup Frye, "The Road of Excess" in *Myth and Symbol* (Lincoln: University of Nebraska Press, 1963) 11.

[12] Charles Glicksberg, *The Ironic Vision in Modern Literature* (The Hague: Nijhoff, 1969), 193–241 specifically on these authors.

[13] Norman Knox, *The Word Irony and its Context, 1500–1755* (Durham: Duke University Press, 1961), 3–7. Also Francis Macdonald Cornford, *The Origin of Attic Comedy* (New York: Anchor Books, 1961), 119–20. Also Wilhelm Büchner, "Über den Begriff der Eironeia," *Hermes*, 76 (1941): 339–58.

[14] Ernst Behler, *Klassische Ironie, Romantische Ironie, Tragische Ironie: zum Ursprung dieser Begriffe* (Darmstadt: Wissenschaftliche Buchgesellschaft, 1972), 15–30.

[15] Cf. Lilian R. Furst's important new study, *Fictions of Romantic Irony* (Cambridge: Harvard Studies in Comparative Literature, 1984).

[16] Helmut Prang, *Die Romantische Ironie* (Darmstadt: Wissenschaftliche Buchgesellschaft, 1972), 5–15. The most extensive study on the subject is Ingrid Strohschneider-Kohrs, *Die Romantische Ironie in Theorie und Gestaltung* (Tübingen: Max Niemeyer Verlag, 1960), 7–91. The most recent study on theories of irony is Uwe Japp, *Theorie der Ironie* (Frankfurt: Klostermann, 1983).

[17] Paul Tabori, *The Anatomy of Exile: A Semantic and Historical Study* (London: Harrap, 1972) 32.

[18] Joachim Radkau, *Die deutsche Emigration in den USA. Ihr Einfluß auf die amerikanische Europapolitik 1933–1945* (Düsseldorf: Bertelsmann Universitätsverlag, 1971), 114ff., quoted in *Exil und innere Emigration* (Frankfurt: Athenäum Verlag, 1973, ed. Peter Uwe Hohendahl und Egon Schwarz), 101.

[19] Heinrich Heine, *Historisch-kritische Gesamtausgabe der Werke*, ed. Manfred Windfuhr (Hamburg: Hoffmann und Campe, 1973–), II, 80. I shall henceforth refer to this edition with the letters DA, unless otherwise indicated.

[20] Jules Laforgue, *Moralités légendaires*, ed. Daniel Grojnowski (Genève-Paris: Droz, 1980), 45.

[21] Jules Laforgue, *Les Complaintes et les premiers poèmes*, ed. Pascal Pia (Paris: Gallimard, 1970 and 1979), 173 and 191.

[22] Cf. Note 10 above.

[23] An excellent translation into English of Heine's poetry, as well as the plays *Almansor* and *William Ratcliff*, is Hal Draper's verse translation, *The Complete Poems of Heinrich Heine*: A Modern English Version (Boston: Suhrkamp/Insel Publishers Boston, Inc., 1982). A small selection of Laforgue's verse has been translated into English by Patricia Terry, *Poems of Jules Laforgue* (Berkeley: University of California Press, 1958).

I

Heinean Inspirations in Laforgue's Early Literary Journalism

In 1969, J.L. Debauve published a critical edition of the pieces Laforgue wrote for *La Guêpe* and *L'Enfer*, along with a history of the texts and the reviews in which they appeared.[1] Debauve, too, points to Laforgue's Heinean "sympathies," which the poet himself, moreover, acknowledges explicitly in one of these early texts.[2] Before considering some of the individual pieces that comprise the group of twelve poems, twenty-six *Parisian Chronicles* and nine other pieces (the twenty-one annotated humorous sketches lie beyond the focus of our discussion), we should note that the poet presented all of them as literary journalism. While only one issue of *L'Enfer* (*Hell*) appeared, in the summer of 1879, *La Guêpe* (*The Wasp*), a "weekly scientific and literary journal," appeared, though irregularly, from May of 1879 until February of 1880; and Laforgue was one of its principal, perhaps even remunerated, contributors.[3]

Throughout his creative career, the poet was to supplement his income by journalistic writing, such as his reportages of the Salon of Berlin of 1883 for the *Gazette des Beaux-Arts*, his articles about the German court destined for *L'Illustration* (published posthumously in the volume *En Allemagne: Berlin, la Cour et la ville*),[4] his contributions to *La Vogue*, *Le Décadent* and *Le Symboliste*,[5] and finally the seven *Chroniques parisiennes* written in 1887, shortly before his death, for the *Revue Indépendante*.[6]

The poet who had raised literary journalism to an art, and become its unparalleled master, was Heine, who had written his

most distinguished contributions to the genre in Paris. Laforgue
had easy access to these texts, in both the original and French
versions. The articles Heine wrote from France from December
1831, shortly after his arrival in Paris, until September 1832 for
the *Augsburger Allgemeine Zeitung*, including his reportages of
the Paris Salon of 1831, were available in French in the volume
De la France as early as 1833; and his series of journalistic
"letters" written for the same periodical from 1840 until 1843
were first published in French in 1855 in the volume *Lutèce*.[7]
The popularity of these two volumes is documented by their
many reprintings.[8]

But in connection with Laforgue's earliest products of literary
journalism, I would like to draw attention to a less-known group
of Heinean texts which constitute his own beginnings in the
genre, the *Briefe aus Berlin* written in 1822 for the *Rheinisch-
Westfälischer Anzeiger*, and which first appeared in French in
1867.[9] The best-known of Heine's poetry appeared in French in
the volume *Poèmes et légendes* as early as 1855; the volume of
Poésies inédites came out in 1885.[10] Laforgue's translation of a
fragment from the "Nachlese zum Lyrischen Intermezzo"
("Supplement to the Lyric Intermezzo") shows us that he was
familiar with at least some of the German poet's verse in the
original.[11]

The two pieces that Laforgue contributed to the sole number
of *L'Enfer* are a poem, "La Chanson des morts," subtitled
"Fragment d'un poème: *Un Amour dans les tombes*," signed
with the pseudonym "Ouraphle" and dated "Paris, février
1878;" and a prose composition, "Chronique stygianopolitaine," signed "Ouralphe" and dated "Paris, 30 juillet
1879."[12] The poem constitutes the earliest verse by Laforgue so
far known, with the exception of a play in alexandrines which I
shall discuss in the third essay; it is an exercise in the *danse
macabre* motif, celebrated in medieval iconography (e.g.
Amiens, Angers, Dijon, Rouen, Paris) and resuscitated by
German Romanticism. It is, therefore, not surprising that Heine
should have picked up the topos in one of his earliest collections,
the "Traumbilder" ("Dream Visions") (#8) of *Junge Leiden*

(*Young Sorrows*) (1817–1821). The French version of this "dream vision" is entitled "Le Cimetière" and forms part of the group of "Nocturnes" of the volume *Poèmes et légendes*; it is one of the two poems of this group of ten, moreover, that were translated by a great French poet, Heine's friend Gérard de Nerval.[13]

Heine's poem, framed by the persona's dream of passing by the cemetery on his way home from his mistress' house at midnight, is a "Moritat," a burlesque morality, sung by the ghost of a wandering street musician sitting on his tombstone and calling forth from their graves the ghosts of six other victims of "Liebestod." Accompanied by the player and lead-singer, they first bemoan their common fate together. Then each of them—a tailor's apprentice, a thief, an actor, a student, a rich man's servant, and a hunter—turns "Bänkelsänger" (street minstrel) to tell his story (death by a broken heart, death in jail, suicides, death by hanging, and death by beheading), each tale of horror closed off by the refrain of the other ghosts' happy approbation: "Da lachten die Geister im lustigen Chor."* But at the stroke of one hour after midnight, the song and dance of the dead ends, and they must scramble back into their graves. The poem is a masterpiece of the genre; one of its most remarkable features is Heine's finesse in the handling of rhythmic shifts, from the ballad-like opening quatrain in couplet rhymes to the increased tempo and free rhythms of the "Spielman's" wild song which drives the dead out of their graves:

> † "Bravo! bravo! immer toll!
> Seid willkommen!
> Habt vernommen,
> Daß mein Zauberwort erscholl!
> . . . .

* "Now the ghosts laughed in a happy chorus."

† "Bravo, bravo! mad as ever! Welcome all! You have heard my magic word resound! . . . . Today we shall not lack entertainment. Everybody here shall faithfully relate what has erstwhile brought him here, how he was chased and torn to pieces by the mad pursuit of love."

> Kurzweil kann uns heut nicht fehlen,
> Jeder soll hier treu erzählen,
> Was ihn weiland hergebracht,
> Wie gehetzt,
> Wie zerfetzt
> Ihn die tolle Liebesjagd'' (DA, I: 43).

Laforgue's "Chanson des morts" is much shorter than Heine's and is unfinished, as its subtitle suggests: "Fragment d'un poème: *Un Amour dans les tombes.*" The subtitle's second half clearly relates the piece to Heine's in linking love and the tombs. The opening frame, moreover, resembles that of Heine: the first-person persona is walking alone in a dark, cold night to arrive, toward midnight, at the graveyard:

> * Devant moi s'étalait l'immense cimetière . . .
> . . . .
> . . . Quand je vis tout à coup, légion vagabonde,
> Se prendre par la main des squelettes glacés.
> On commence, et tandis que tournoyait leur ronde,
> Ils glapissent en coeur [sic], l'hymne des trépassés:

The author's suspension points mark the fragmentary state of the poem, but the scene presented to and by the persona surely resembles Heine's; the ghosts (not surprisingly in the form of skeletons in Laforgue, who was so fond of sketching them in his notes!) dancing and intoning their song. In Laforgue, too, a rhythmic and strophic shift sets off the five numbered songs, each of them, too, closed off by a refrain:

> Ils hurlent en sifflant et l'ardente rafale
> Emporte les éclats de leur voix sépulcrale.

* Before me stretched the vast cemetery . . . . . When I suddenly saw a vagabond legion, frozen skeletons grab each other by the hand. They begin, and their round dance whirling, in unison they shriek the hymn of the departed: They howl and wheeze, and the scorching gust sweeps away the screams of their sepulchral voices.

But Laforgue's dead sing their distress in unison, rather than each telling his own tale of woe. And the theme of love, announced in the title, is never developed in the unfinished piece; instead the ghosts anathematize all the living that forget them so soon, and the God who allows it. Finally, the Laforguean ghosts, like those of Heine, precipitate themselves back into their graves. Whereupon Laforgue closes the poem with a typically Heinean device, the "queue de poisson," the ironically deflating final line which, in this case, undercuts the horror of the macabre scene:

> * Et moi pétrifié de ces clameurs funèbres,
> De mon gosier en feu sort un cri de terreur;
> Et je les vis soudain dans l'ombre et les ténèbres
> Qui fuyaient en tumulte harcelés par la peur,
> Puis tout se tût [sic] bientôt. De nouveau le silence
> Commençait à régner, quand j'ouïs tout à coup
> L'un d'eux fureter comme un spectre en démence
> Et hurler en pleurant "on m'a volé mon trou"!

In the "Chanson's" opening, Laforgue employs another Heinean device, the *Doppelgänger* motif (the double); as the persona walks on the lonely street toward the cemetery, he feels pursued by his double:

> † Derrière moi sans cesse il me semblait entendre
> Un pas qui me suivait et des ricanements! . . .[12]

Laforgue surely recalled Heine's most elaborate development of this motif in "Deutschland, ein Wintermärchen" ("Germany, a Winter's Tale"), Caput VI:

* And I, petrified by this funereal clamor, a cry of terror comes from my burning throat. And suddenly I saw them in the dark, the shades that were fleeing in an uproar, tormented by fear. Then soon everything was quiet. Silence began to reign again, when I suddenly heard one of them, ferreting about like a demented ghost, howl in tears "they've stolen my hole"!

† Behind me without cease I seemed to hear a step that followed me and derisive laughter! . . .

> * Ich schlenderte sinnend die Straßen entlang,
> Da sah ich ihn hinter mir gehen,
> Als ob er mein Schatten wäre, und stand
> Ich still, so blieb er stehen (B, VI: 590).[14]

Thus, Laforgue's earliest known poem appears to be indeed inspired by Heine.

The "Chronique stygianopolitaine," an obvious parody of the *Chroniques parisiennes*, is a burlesque report from the capital of hell, appropriate for the "literary, satirical and diabolical journal" entitled *L'Enfer*, thoroughly Heinean in tone. The very title of the piece contains one of Laforgue's first neologisms, recalling the older poet's famous examples. The setting of the city of the dead permits Laforgue to indulge in his cherished anachronisms, as the ruling family of Pluto and Proserpina and her lover Acalaphes mix with the English and the Zulus, and an Athenian orator, Isocrates, with a Roman one, Cicero. The poets Boileau and Delille court royalty like "his too Christian majesty, Louis XIV," while "François Ier . . . debauches all Stygianopolis," and Henri IV is on the lookout for tender young girls, "the pretty slips of girls! . . ." Aeneas "is still whining here," and the local playhouse is presenting "the *Crepuscular Carrion*, putrefaction in six phases" by Baudelaire, a play much applauded by Napoleon. Lamartine runs a bowling alley, Graziella a tobacco shop, and Demosthenes, still chewing pebbles, is in charge of a merry-go-round!

This early parody of classical mythology foreshadows already the accomplished *Moralités légendaires*, while it also recalls Heine's burlesque revivals of those gone to hell, or heaven. I am recalling here the "Unterwelt" poems of *Neue Gedichte*, in which Pluto bemoans his unhappy marriage to Proserpina:

> † Stets vergeblich, stets nach Frieden
> Ring ich. Hier im Schattenreich
> Kein Verdammter ist mir gleich!

* I strolled pensively along the streets, when I saw him walk behind me, as though he were my shadow; and when I stopped, he stopped walking too.

† Always in vain I strive for peace. Here in the realm of shades none of the damned resembles me! I envy Sisyphus and the noble Danaides.

Ich beneide Sisyphus
Und die edlen Danaiden (DA, II: 96).[15]

The Danaides became Laforgue's favorite mythical figures. But Heine's most elaborate poetic assembly of famous dead occurs in *Atta Troll*'s Wild Hunt. And the most memorable ghosts of this procession are three beautiful women, the classical Diana-Artemis, the Celtic fairy-princess Abunde, and, above all, Herodias, who inspired so many Symbolist writers, from Laforgue to Mallarmé.[16]

Before turning to the *Chroniques parisiennes*, we must consider Laforgue's verse contributions to *La Guêpe*, the first of which was "Idylle," a twenty-six line satirical piece in alexandrines and *rime plate*, celebrating the then popular comic soldier figure Dumanet and his love, Justine.[17] Though this little poem—"True! Coppée would paint a good picture of it!"—is obviously anchored in the contemporary French intertext, the theme of low-life soldier love recalls such Heinean poems as the "Lied der Marketenderin" ("Song of the Camp-follower"), or the Second Song of "Wünnebergiade," a mock-heroic "epic in two cantos."[18]

Laforgue appropriately dedicated his second poem for *La Guêpe*, "Excuse macabre," to "Hamlet, prince of Denmark," as its persona addresses the skull of "Margaretha, my well-beloved" in a burlesque pastiche of Hamlet's monologue to Horatio about "poor Yorick."[19] Does "Margaretha," the Germanization of "Marguerite," which was the name of the poet's first love,[20] merely pay tribute to German Romanticism and its legacy of Shakespeare enthusiasm; or might it possibly reflect an echo from Heine's *Shakespeares Mädchen und Frauen?*[21] The text, which Heine wrote in 1838 for an art editor to accompany a series of engravings of these heroines, and which I shall discuss in the fourth essay of this volume, is divided into "Tragödien" and "Komödien," and among the former the most charming of the twenty-four brief essays is devoted to "Ophelia (Hamlet)." Of the other pieces, two are devoted to the dark woman Laforgue might have remembered: "Margareta (King

Henry VI, First Part)'' and "Queen Margareta (Henry VI, Second and Third Part).'' Suffolk's lover, Henry's adulterous Queen, is painted in the most macabre colors, and Heine's portrayal of the Shakespearean Margareta might well have helped inspire Laforgue's burlesque rendition of the macabre Shakespearean monologue:

> * Margaretha, ma bien-aimée, or donc voici
> Ton crâne. Quel poli! l'on dirait de l'ivoire.
> (Je le savonne assez, chaque jour, Dieu merci,
> Et me permets d'ailleurs fort rarement d'y boire.)
> Te voilà! . . . Dans ces deux trous, deux beaux yeux jadis,
> Miroirs de ton âme enrhumée,
> Rêvaient . . . Las! où sont tes belles tresses d'or, dis,
> Margaretha, ma bien-aimée?[19]

"La Femme est une malade" (Woman is an Invalid"), under the epigraph "(Michelet),"[22] owes nothing to Heine but the ironic narrative mode in which it alludes to Michelet's *La Femme* of 1859; and the theme, like that of the preceding poem, is one congenial to the young misogynist.

"Au lieu de songer à se créer une position" ("Instead of thinking about getting ahead"),[23] the fourth poem Laforgue contributed to *La Guêpe*, under the epigraph "Oh! fi fi this world. (Hamlet)," is a mock *Sturm und Drang* piece, celebrating the theme of evasion—into cosmic spheres—from bourgeois constraints such as suggested in the title. With its lugubrious evocation of a blond-tressed lost love named Lotte, it intimates the sorrows of the young Goethe rather than those of Heine, but in the latter's manner: ". . . la tombe d'ivoire / Où, depuis

---

* Margaretha, my beloved, now here's your skull. What polish! Like ivory. (I wash it enough with soap each day, thank God, and permit myself, moreover, very rarely to drink of it.) There you are! . . . In these two holes, formerly two beautiful eyes, mirrors of your soul with its bad cold, used to dream . . . Alas! Where are your beautiful golden tresses, say, Margaretha, my beloved?

quinze jours,—si j'ai bonne mémoire,— / Pourrit la bien-aimée
aux longues tresses d'or. / —Pauvre Lotte! Ah! misère!—. . ."*
  In the following poem, "Ce qu'aime le gros Fritz" ("What Fat
Fritz Loves"),²⁴ Laforgue caricatures his own infatuation with
things German, from the soul to the stomach, the first of the four
quatrains evoking Hegel, the second again Goethe, the third
Heine, and the last sauerkraut and beer! I have elsewhere
discussed Laforgue's intertextual links with German philosophy;²⁵ we know that he was familiar with Hegel's *Asthetik*,
available in French before 1875, but that he did not concern
himself with the bulk of Hegel's philosophy. Rather, the
Hegelian traces in his poetry, to begin with the poem under
discussion, reflect both Schopenhauer's anti-Hegelianism and
Heine's frequent mocking allusions to his former teacher. Our
poem's opening stanza:

> † Oui, j'aime à promener ma belle âme allemande
> A travers l'Esthétique et les brouillards d'Hegel;
> Un nuage en bouteille est tout ce que demande
> L'âme éprise de vague et d'immatériel,

recalls Heinean poetic utterances like the following that might
have helped inspire it:

> ‡ Ich rief den Teufel, und er kam,
> Und ich sah ihn mit Verwundrung an.
> . . . .
> Blaß ist er etwas, doch ist es kein Wunder,
> Sanskrit und Hegel studiert er jetztunder (DA, I: 246).²⁶

* . . . the ivory tomb in which for two weeks, if I remember correctly, the
beloved with the long gold tresses has been going to rot.—Poor Lotte! Ah!
Misery!
  † Yes, I love to take out my beautiful German soul through Hegel's
Aesthetics and misty fogs; a cloud in a bottle is all that is asked for by the soul
in love with the vague and the immaterial.
  ‡ I called the devil, and he came; and I beheld him with astonishment. . . . .
He is somewhat pale, but that is no wonder, as he is studying Hegel and
Sanskrit now.

The first line of the third stanza of "Ce qu'aime le gros Fritz" echoes the poem's opening, as we pass from fat Fritz's German *Schöngeistigkeit* (appreciation of things of the mind) to his German hearing, from Hegelian fogginess to the "gothic accents" of the organ of Cologne cathedral, which arouses the old legend of the Willis' dance of his (German) heart:

> * J'aime à charmer aussi mon ouïe allemande
> Quand l'orgue de Cologne, aux gothiques accents,
> Eveille dans mon coeur quelque vieille légende
> Où passent des Willis dans des rayons flottants.

The choice of Cologne cathedral is certainly not coincidental, as it recalls Heine's frequent allusions to the edifice which had remained unfinished since the Reformation. Heine never tired of mocking the efforts that were made in the first half of the nineteenth century to complete the cathedral, as in "Bei des Nachtwächters Ankunft zu Paris" ("The Nightwatchman's Arrival in Paris") of *Neue Gedichte*,[27] or his most lengthy and outspoken attack on the project in *Deutschland, ein Wintermärchen*, Caput IV.[28] The dance of the Willis—the ghosts of brides that died before their wedding night—on moonlit country roads at midnight is a legend of Austrian folklore, resurrected and retold by Heine in *Elementargeister* (*Elemental Spirits*).[29] He also mentions the Willis in the second of the *Florentinische Nächte* (*Florentine Nights*),[30] and Heine's version of the legend was the source for the ballet *Giselle*, one of whose librettists was his friend Théophile Gautier. The closing stanza celebrates fat Fritz's beloved sauerkraut and beer, not without alluding, moreover, to the French clocks confiscated by the Germans in the Franco-Prussian war.[31]

Laforgue's "gros Fritz" is a caricature in the best Heinean satirical manner, and the young poet pays explicit homage to the master in the following poem, whose very title, "Epi-

---

* I love to charm also my German ear when the organ of Cologne, with its Gothic accents, arouses in my heart some old legend where Willis pass in floating moonbeams.

curéisme,''[32] announces the early-Heinean theme of this-world-liness and contempt for the hereafter. The mocking scepticism of its opening lines:

> * Je suis heureux gratis!—Il est bon ici-bas
> De faire, s'il se peut, son paradis, en cas
> Que celui de là-haut soit une balançoire,
> Comme il est, après tout, bien permis de le croire,

echoes Heine's:

> † Freilich, ein ungläub'ger Thomas,
> Glaub ich an den Himmel nicht
> Den die Kirchenlehre Romas
> Und Jerusalems verspricht (DA, II: 108).[33]

But epicureanism, while suggesting a hedonistic ethics, funda-mentally points to pleasures intellectual; it is these that the persona, whom one cannot fail to identify with Laforgue, enumerates:

> ‡ A la bibliothèque ensuite je me rends.
> —C'est la plus belle au monde!—Asseyons-nous. Je prends
> Sainte-Beuve, et Théo, Banville, Baudelaire,
> Leconte, Heine, enfin, qu'aux plus grands je préfère,
> "Ce bouffon de génie," a dit Schopenhauer,
> Qui sanglote et sourit, mais d'un sourire amer!

These lines reflect Laforgue's life in Paris around the time he composed the poem, evoking the Bibliothèque Nationale and the Bibliothèque Sainte-Geneviève, both of which he visited assid-

---

* I am happy gratis!—It is good to make, if possible, one's paradise down here below, in case the one on high is a hoax, as it is, after all, indeed permissible to believe.

† To be sure, a doubting Thomas, I do not believe in the heaven promised by the doctrine of Rome and Jerusalem.

‡ Then I go to the library.—It is the most beautiful one in the world!—Let's sit down. I take Sainte-Beuve and Théo, Banville, Baudelaire, Leconte, and finally Heine whom I prefer over the greatest. "That genial buffoon," said Schopenhauer, who weeps and smiles, but with a bitter smile!

uously at that period. One of his poems, "Derniers Soupirs d'un
Parnassien" ("Last Sighs of a Parnassian"),[34] is even signed
"Bibliothèque Sainte-Geneviève, 21 avril, 1880," and another,
"Memento Sonnet triste" ("Memento Sad Sonnet"),[35] is signed
"Jules Laforgue-Mouni." Our Buddhist monk lived his ascetic
existence in the two great libraries in which he frequented his
German friends: Heine, Schopenhauer, and later von Hartmann.
Laforgue had read Schopenhauer's remark on Heine, quoted in
"Epicuréisme," in Paul Janet's article on the philosopher,[36] in a
paragraph which also reinforced his opinion about Hegel:

> Let's come back to his judgments about the philosophers or the more or
> less famous writers of his time. He would say about Heine: "Heine is a
> buffoon, but a buffoon of genius . . ." . . . about Feuerbach: "what a
> gross and brutish machine! . . . There's the fruit of hegelatry (*die
> Hegelei*). . . ." (p. 283).

Laforgue's reference to Théophile Gautier ("Théo") recalls that
poet's friendship with Heine, documented in his essay on the
German poet which prefaced the 1856 edition of the famous
Tableaux de Voyage and all its successive reprintings. Of all the
writers mentioned, it is Heine who receives the greatest tribute
here, by a young French poet for whom he outshines even
Baudelaire!

The following two pieces from the group of twelve poems in
La Guêpe, entitled "Intérieur (I)" and "Intérieur (II),"[37] are
exercises in Realism whose irony does not hide the most abject
human misery.[38] The ironic tone of these poems, the first a
tableau of city, the second of country life, recalls Heine.
Laforgue wrote a third "Intérieur" which was published posthumously,[39] in exactly the same form as "Intérieur (I)," but with
more pronounced underlying social criticism, again recalling
Heine. Both the tone and the final line of that piece are
incorporated into the first stanza of "Soleil couchant (II)" of the
group from *La Guêpe*.

"Soeil couchant (I)" and "Soleil couchant (II)" both paint
exotic sunsets, the first taking us to Africa, the second to Egypt.
Each picture is then totally deflated at the poem's ending by a
brusque shift to the contrasting banality of a Parisian scene.

Thus, the superb African lion's captured mate is "Dans sa cage à Paris exposée aux badauds, / Et qu'un bourgeois, peut-être, avec son parapluie / Taquine . . . ."* In the second poem, we leave "the banks of the Nile" at sunset for a more familiar world:

> † . . . à Paris, tout en prenant le thé,
> A sa fenêtre ouverte, un gros propriétaire,
> Repu, rit du bohème au jabot lesté,
> Tourne béatement ses pouces—et digère.[40]

This final quatrain recalls one by Heine, about the bourgeoisie of Hamburg:

> ‡ Sie essen gut, sie trinken gut,
> Erfreun sich ihres Maulwurfglücks,
> Und ihre Großmut ist so groß
> Als wie das Loch der Armenbüchs' (DA, II: 79).[41]

Laforgue's social criticism found its most unambiguous expression in the last, untitled, poem which he contributed to *La Guêpe*[42] under the epigraph of a quotation from Chamfort which sounds as if it could have been written by Heine: "Society can be divided into those who have more food than appetite and those who have more appetite than food." The "defeated of this life" are painted in the manner of a Baudelairean "tableau parisien," their misery not even clothed in irony, so that in this final text of the group it is not the manner, but the message that recalls the young Laforgue's favorite poet.

* * *

In his twenty-six *Chroniques parisiennes*, which appeared in *La Guêpe*[43] from May 4 to November 23, 1879, the nineteen-

---

* In its cage in Paris, exposed to idle strollers, and which a bourgeois perhaps teases with his umbrella.

† . . . in Paris, taking tea at his open window, a fat landlord, well-fed, laughs about the skinny bohemian, turns his thumbs complacently—and digests.

‡ They eat well, they drink well and enjoy their happiness of a mole. And their generosity is as big as the poorbox' hole.

year-old Laforgue reported to his home town almost exclusively on the capital's literary, theatrical and art news, with an occasional reference to the (bad) weather, or the awkward British tourists invading the city deserted by its own during the summer months. The twenty-four-year-old Heine[44] had addressed his reports from the Prussian capital to the readers of his native Rhineland in the form of three long letters, dated January 26, March 16 and June 7, 1822, which the *Rheinisch-Westfälischer Anzeiger* published in ten installments.[45] The range of coverage of the *Briefe aus Berlin* is much wider than that of the *Chroniques parisiennes*, as Heine aimed at giving as comprehensive an image as possible of the cultural and social life of Germany's newest and largest metropolis. His letters which, in contrast to Laforgue's chronicles, addressed themselves to the general readership of an established paper, deal with the Prussian Court, Berlin society and its amusements, the city's newest buildings, its theater and opera, its university, its finest restaurants, and also its literary novelties. The young poet, who was already gaining recognition, participated, moreover, in the life he described, while Laforgue, barely out of the *lycée*, was still an outsider to the literary Paris on which he reported for a very limited audience of young readers.

In the opening of the first two letters, Heine addresses himself directly to the editor of the paper for which he is writing, recalling personal memories and friends, and thereby stressing his own integration into the social environment for and about which he writes. Then he raises the question of what, or rather on what not, to report, as he will omit material—such as news about the theater, or what Spontini wore at some social event—with which his readers are already familiar from other journalistic sources. In this he is already pointing to one of the major themes of the "Briefe," the politically loaded quarrel over the relative merits of Spontini and Weber. And one of the most fundamental differences between Heine and Laforgue's early journalism becomes manifest: Heine's is already *engagé*, while Laforgue's is politically innocent. Then Heine explains his method, or rather his lack of method: "Just don't ask me to be systematic; that is the angel of death of all correspondence. Association of ideas must always prevail.'' Heine's characteristic ''impressionistic technique'' is already taking shape: he will not ''paint,'' but merely ''intimate,'' the inner and outer life of Berlin, ''merely suggest, not describe. But where do I begin with this mass of materials? A French rule is helpful here: *Commencez par le commencement*.''[46]

After these preliminaries, the first letter assumes the form of a *flânerie*, a stroll through the city. Laforgue places his first chronicle in a similar form, except that he begins his ''Revue parisienne'' of May 4 *in medias res*, as it were: ''It was the other night. I was strolling along the boulevards with my characteristic gait.''[47] Eight o'clock strikes from the Sorbonne, and Paris bathes in the light of a new moon, which intrigues the future poet of *L'Imitation de Notre-Dame la Lune* (*The Imitation of Our Lady the Moon*), but ''Pooh! . . . everybody has his little lunacies . . .'' And then the lunar reverie is brusquely interrupted as three breathless harbingers almost run the *flâneur* down with ''Zola! . . . the Brochure! . . . Zola! . . . *Revue réaliste*! . . .; Zola! Hugo! . . . in the Voltaire!,'' brimming over with the news: Zola's brochure, *La République et la littérature*, an event in the evolution of Naturalism, which fills the first chronicle. At its conclusion, the reporter salutes his reader: ''May heaven keep you in bliss!''[48]

Heine gradually shifts from addressing his editor, to the reader to whom he continues to speak directly and whom he takes along on his city walk: ''We are standing on the Long Bridge. You are wondering, 'But it is not very long?' It is irony, my dear fellow.'' And a few steps farther, ''We can go through the castle and are immediately in the *Lustgarten*. 'But where is the garden?' you ask. Good heavens! Don't you realize, that's irony again. It is a four-cornered square enclosed by a double row of poplars.''[49] Irony characterizes not merely the style of the ''Briefe,'' but the very world they describe! Heine leads his reader through famous streets, to the stock exchange—'' there haggle those professing the Old and the New Testaments''—then to the University whose fraternities had just been outlawed by the government,

and to the "Brandenburg Gate" with its Victoria—"the good
woman has had her troubles too"—, finally into the famous
"Café Royal," meeting place of elegant and cultivated society,
where we meet E.T.A. Hoffmann and other famous literary
figures of the day. Then, at the end of his first letter, Heine
resorts to the device of the (fictional) "Kammermusikus," that
strange little chamber musician who will supply him with all the
news Westphalia might want: "The chamber musician, he
knows lots of news, doesn't he? We will rely on him. He shall
provide Westphalia with news, and what he doesn't know,
Westphalia does not need to know either."

Heine's "Briefe" are indeed much more complex, not merely
in coverage, but also in technique, in reader manipulation and
strategy, than Laforgue's brief "Chroniques." The constant,
barely veiled, political allusions are but a part of this complexity.[50] Laforgue approaches a political subject only once in his
twenty-six chronicles, but drops it immediately and turns to
other matters. This occurs in the second paragraph of the
twenty-third report, where he mentions the Russian ambassador
and foreign minister: "Prince Gortschakoff . . . Ah, no politics.
Beware of the penalty!"[51] Here we also see Laforgue addressing
his reader directly in the Heinean manner, more so than in most
of the other installments. And in this particular chronicle, he
succeeds, moreover, in creating the effect of the "décousu," the
rambling, free association of ideas-topics that gives Heine's
reportage its light and entertaining allure. Thus Laforgue continues: "But you make me lose my train of thought. Don't
interrupt me anymore. The Palais Royal has just given its
end-of-the-year revue. P. Alexis, a *beginner*, has opened at the
Gymnase this week, . . . At the Comédie-Française, twice a
week, toward midnight—the hour of crime!—Hernani and Doña
Sol . . . . . . Touching, very touching, the chapter of brief news
items . . . ," and then he relates a spectacular contemporary
crime of murder and dismemberment of the victim. Heine, too,
intersperses his reportage with this type of information, in
passing to other, frequently literary news; thus toward the end of
the first letter: "The boy who killed his mother with a hammer

was mad. The mystic agitations in Pomerania are making a great stir. Hoffmann is presently publishing, with Wilmann's in Frankfurt, a novel entitled 'The Flea,' which is supposed to contain many political gibes.''[52] *Meister Floh*, in fact, lost entire paragraphs through censorship before it could be published (DA, VI: 413); and Heine's "Zweiter Brief" was itself mutilated by the censors.

Heine opened his second letter by answering his own editor's reprimands about having too freely named certain public figures—"I shall strive to comply with your gently hinted wish not to let certain individuals stand out too much"[53]—before turning to the central episode of the "Jungfernkranz." This reportage about the all too popular song from Weber's *Freischütz*, sung by all Berlin, and driving the poet mad, brings to mind Laforgue's fifteenth chronicle, in which he complains about the immoderate vogue of the "Marseillaise," heard everywhere in Paris.[54] But Heine's development of the theme is much more elaborate than Laforgue's; it had, moreover, already been foreshadowed, as we saw, in the first letter in which Spontini was mentioned, and it was to be echoed in the third, where his operas would be referred to again.

Spontini, patronized and protected by the Prussian king, served the regime with his noisy "grand spectacle" productions. But despite the strong "spontinische Partei," Carl Maria von Weber, his rival, took the public by storm with his new Romantic operas, the greatest of which, *Der Freischütz*, had its debut in 1821. And Heine reflects its immense success in his "Jungfernkranz" episode:

> Haven't you heard about Maria von Weber's *Freischütz* yet? No? Unfortunate man! But haven't you at least heard the "Song of the Bridesmaids" or the "Wreath of the Maidens" from this opera? No? Fortunate man! . . . but the "Song of the Bridesmaids" is permanent; . . . it rings out to me from every house; everybody whistles it with his own variations; indeed, I almost believe the dogs are barking it in the streets.[55]

The poet's point is, of course, that even the king of Prussia cannot dictate public taste. But as he, Heine, is a "layman in the domain of the musical arts,'' he will merely relate what the two parties, "die spontinische Partei" and the "anti-spontinische Partei," say about the matter. For the former, the composer is "a great man, he is a genius, he is a god!" For the latter, "the greater part see in his music only drum- and trumpet-spectacle, resounding bombast and pompous monstrosity. Add to this the indignation of many—.''[56] And it is at this point that Heine's "Zweiter Brief" was cut by the censors.[57] Bearing in mind that Heine is reporting not a political, but rather an artistic subject, in Prussia too politically loaded, nevertheless, for free public discussion, one realizes that his *Briefe aus Berlin* are indeed much less innocent than most of their contemporary readers had understood them to be. The young poet's irony had already developed well beyond a mere literary strategy to capture and entertain the reader; Heine was already beginning to forge a weapon.

Laforgue's "Chronique IV," which deals, after all, not with some air from a contemporary opera, but with the French national anthem, is almost boisterous in tone, and its irony still lacks the suavity that conceals the Heinean edge. Its opening paragraph is, moreover, indebted to Heine for more than the style:

> If this good Rouget de Lisle has not been rotting in his coffin for thirty-six years, as I am inclined to believe, but if, on the contrary, his great shade is still rambling in Paradise or the Elysian Fields, or some other abode of delight invented by those jokers who, according to Hegel's saying, need to believe that after their death they will get a gratuity for not having poisoned their brother and for having cared for her ladyship their mother in her last illness, I imagine that he must have become very important lately among the crowd of shades. Never before, I believe, has the hymn that made him famous been so in vogue.[58]

Laforgue is indebted to Heine for this "mot d'Hegel," which he could have read in *De l'Allemagne* II,[59] or in the *Revue des Deux Mondes* in which Heine's "Geständnisse" ("Confessions") had appeared under the title "Aveux de l'auteur" in 1854. Reminiscing some twenty years later (in 1854 when he wrote his "Geständnisse" for the volume *De l'Allemagne*) about his student days in Berlin where he had attended some of Hegel's colloquia, during the very period in which he had written the *Briefe aus Berlin*, Heine recalls his famous teacher:

> One beautiful starry evening we were standing next to each other, and I, a twenty-two-year-old young man, had just dined well and had had my coffee, and I spoke with rapture of the stars and called them the abode of the blessed. But the master grumbled: "the stars, hum! hum! the stars are only shiny scabs on the sky."—"Heaven forbid"—I exclaimed— "then there is no happy place above to reward virtue after death?" But he said sharply, staring at me with his pale eyes: "So you still want a gratuity for having cared for your sick mother and not poisoned your brother?" (DA, XV: 34)

In his thirteenth chronicle, Laforgue reports in a very Heinean tone on the prizes of virtue awarded by the French Academy:

> The review of the prizes of virtue awarded by the Académie Française will not be able to amuse us either . . . . I have always wondered what that could amount to, virtue, in this life or anywhere else. In the end, does not everybody take his pleasures where he finds them?[60]

And this subject leads him to Gautier—Heine's friend, we recall—with whose doctrine of the separation of art and morality he is in full agreement: "make way for the *Fleurs du mal*, for *Mlle de Maupin* . . ."; and then the poet interpolates some lines from a Gautier poem before passing on to the project of the erection of a monument to honor the poet:

> By the way, there is talk about erecting a statue to Gautier . . . As far as I am concerned, I'm ready to sell, with enthusiasm, what is left of my classical books to contribute to the erection of a monument to one of the writers who have done the most for the French language.

Heine devotes several paragraphs of the second letter to a similar project, the city of Frankfurt's attempts to erect a monument to Goethe by subscription. The poet had already written a sonnet expressing his unambiguous contempt for the enterprise, which he inserted in the "Brief:"

* O laßt dem Dichter seine Lorbeerreiser,
　Ihr Handelsherrn! Behaltet euer Geld.
　Ein Denkmal hat sich Goethe selbst gesetzt (DA, VI: 29).[61]

Yet, Heine does not hide his ambiguous attitude toward the great man; in the young poet's opinion, Goethe owed at least some of his fame to compromising with the aristocratic regime: "Goethe is a great man in a silken vest." But then he applauds him wholeheartedly for having put a stop to the Frankfurters' not entirely disinterested efforts:

> The great man made an end to all discussion, as is well known, in returning the Frankfurt citizenship to the Frankfurters, explaining that "he was not a Frankfurter at all."
> The latter [the Frankfurt citizenship] is supposed to have fallen—to speak Frankfurtish—ninety-nine percent in value, and the Frankfurt Jews now have better prospects for this beautiful acquisition.

Again, the most severe socio-political criticism is barely hidden under the light ironic cover; and this confers on the *Briefe aus Berlin* a dimension totally lacking in the *Chroniques parisiennes*.

Toward the end of the second letter, Heine reports on Berlin's social life and the various professions' elegant balls, as well as those of the Prussian Court, all modeled after the Parisian ones. The most outstanding of these is the masked "Opernball," which may be watched by the common people for a small entry charge: "The lower class pays a small admission fee and can look down from the gallery at all this splendor. In the big royal box one can see the Court, for the most part unmasked."[62] This topic was taken up again in the third letter, whose central theme is a royal wedding, that of Princess Alexandrine and the Grand Duke of Mecklenburg-Schwerin.

Laforgue does not describe anything similar in his *Chroniques parisiennes*, but he was to describe almost exactly the same thing(s) a few years later, when he had himself become part of the Prussian Court as the French reader of the Empress Au-

---

* O leave the poet his laurels, you commercial lords! Keep your money. Goethe has built his monument himself.

gusta. In his articles about *Berlin, la Cour et la ville*, destined for
l'Illustration, he devotes, among others, special reports to "La
Cour," "L'Empereur," "L'Impératrice," a "Bal de gala," and
"Le Bal de l'Opéra."[63] Between the 1820's—Heine's Berlin—
and the 1880's—Laforgue's—the city had been transformed
from a royal to an imperial residence, and, according to the
poets' accounts, the dominant Prussian military and aristocratic
society had become even more oppressive. As Heine had
described the "niedrige Volksklasse' paying to see some of the
annual glamor of the "Opernball," so Laforgue describes the
poor people, some sixty years later, outside the "Bal de
l'Opéra":

> As on all similar occasions, in this good Berlin where one lives in a
> minor state of siege, the environs of the Opera are that evening carefully
> swept clear by the mounted police, and, as always, too, one sees on the
> curb that hedge of the poor, of pale complexion and flaxen hair, staring,
> flabbergasted, and not dreaming of permitting themselves the least word,
> the least banter.[64]

But to return to his early reports in *La Guêpe*, in his fifth
chronicle, of June 19, 1879, after deploring the absence of the
Comédie-Française (on tour in London) and the closing of the
theaters for the summer months, Laforgue turns to the art
critics, the sometimes powerful and frequently poorly qualified
judges of the Salons:

> It is true that people who have never undertaken special studies set
> about, with fabulous self-assurance, to put in writing their opinions about
> our artists. There is not the least literary greenhorn who does not have at
> least one Salon on his conscience, and such as have never preoccupied
> themselves with anything but getting Arthur and Denise married in the
> fifth act of their vaudeville, say to themselves, one fine morning, while
> putting on their pants, "why don't I, too, do my little Salon"![65]

Journalistic art criticism was of special interest to Laforgue
who, in 1881, was to take Taine's courses on aesthetics at the
Ecole des Beaux-Arts and visited the museums as assiduously as
the libraries.[66] Shortly before leaving for Berlin, he became

part-time secretary to the future director of the *Gazette des Beaux-Arts*, Charles Ephrussi, who helped him obtain the position at the Prussian Court. To write salons was one of Laforgue's ambitions,[67] and we find his earliest attempt in the genre, a humorous version, in *La Guêpe*, to which he contributed under the heading of "Variétés" a "Salon de 1879" (in May, one month before the above chronicle).[68] The witty, brief reportage is indeed a very unorthodox salon, as its author fails to mention a single painter or work represented, but concentrates instead on some of the visitors he encounters: "Let's go visit the Salon, for what else is there to do in Paris in the month of May, except visit the Salon? . . . Let's enter.—What characters!"[69] Of this "attroupement," the funniest is "the worthy M. Romuald, followed by his numerous and very honorable family," a kind of Gumpelino-and-family who recalls Heinean portrayals of the "bourgeois gentilhomme."[70]

Heine did not include art criticism in his *Briefe aus Berlin*, but he was to write his own salon, the series of articles on the *Gemäldeausstellung in Paris 1831*, published by Cotta in the *Morgenblatt für gebildete Stände* from October 27 to November 16 of that year.[71] I shall discuss this group of texts in detail in the sixth chapter of this volume. This was Heine's first journalistic production after his arrival in Paris, and it is not surprising that the former student of Schlegel and Hegel should be interested in this self-imposed assignment; that he was, moreover, not unqualified for it is evident from the product.[72] Heine republished these articles, with a few modifications and a "Postscript" under the title *Französische Maler* shortly afterward, and as they appeared in French as "Salon de 1831" in *De la France* in 1833,[73] it is almost certain that Baudelaire, Laforgue's other master, had read them by the time he wrote his own first salon in 1845. In that text, moreover, Baudelaire discusses works by four painters, some of whose pictures Heine had discussed in his *Salon de 1831* (Decamps, Delacroix, Schnetz, and Vernet). And in one instance he even quotes Heine: "M. Borget's pictures make us regret that China where the wind itself, says M. Heine, takes on a comic sound as it passes through the bellflowers,—

and where nature and man cannot look at each other without laughing.''[74] It is not unlikely that Laforgue's ambition to distinguish himself in the genre was nourished by those two masters, Heine and Baudelaire, the latter having himself been inspired by the former.

Laforgue's remaining contributions to *La Guêpe* all deal with literature; for example a "Revue bibliographique," of August 21, reporting on Charles Cros who had just been awarded the "prix Juglar" by the Académie Française for his *Coffret de santal* (*Little Box of Sandalwood*). In November, Laforgue contributed three rather conventional essays devoted to Emile Zola, Alphonse Daudet, and Henri Martin. With the reservation that "it's not in a few lines that one discusses as controversial a thesis as *Naturalism*," Laforgue clearly professes his admiration for Zola, "a critic of earnest sincerity," some of whose traits could apply to Heine: "He 'scoffs at the great centuries,' that is at all literary dogma, at any ideal in matters of criticism. Let a work be the manifestation of a strong personality, let it live abundantly of the life of our age." And he adds, "Everybody agrees on this today, except the gentlemen of the bourgeoisie. But the gentlemen of the bourgeoisie are dismissed to tend to their digestion."[75]

It was a major document in the development of Naturalism, we recall, that was reported in the first "Chronique parisienne," and that literary movement constitutes the *matière* also of three open letters Laforgue published in *La Guêpe* in October under the heading "Du Naturalisme." The first two are addressed to "M. Ego;" the other is subtitled "Response to M.F. Lacoste."

In the first piece, of October 2, Laforgue responds to an article entitled "Du Naturalisme," signed "Ego," which had appeared in *La Guêpe* on September 25. Needless to say, the poet opposes the views expressed in the article; what interests us, however, is not so much the ensuing argument, as Laforgue's polemical manner, apparent in the opening paragraph:

> Your article, *Naturalism*, has upset all my ideas about this much disputed theory. And as I do not want to abandon them, except when

> more legitimate ones than those which you are presenting to us seem to
> me to be able to replace them, I hasten to submit my objections to you,
> in the hope that, taking my conversion to heart, you will come back with
> better arms.[76]

This invitation to armed journalistic combat again recalls Heine, whose most notorious challenges to fight by pen (and sometimes arms!) were almost as famous as his poetry. We recall here but three of the best-known incidents, his attack on the poet Count August von Platen-Hallermünde in *Die Bäder von Lucca* (*The Baths of Lucca*),[77] his essay "Über den Denunzianten" ("About the Denouncer") challenging Wolfgang Menzel,[78] and his most famous, controversial, and extensive polemical text, "Ludwig Börne, eine Denkschrift" ("Ludwig Börne, a Memorial").[79] I surely do not intend to compare Laforgue's rather youthfully boisterous and harmless open letters against "M. Ego" with Heine's weighty and dangerous combats. But the young poet's polemical tendency manifest in these texts might well have been nourished by the example of his favorite writer. In both writers, moreover, the weapon owes its edge to irony, as in the conclusion of Laforgue's first letter:

> . . . You wanted to laugh, did you not? Come on, confess it. Or did I
> misinterpret your thought? Then take the pen and pulverize the objec-
> tions of your servant.

The second letter, Laforgue's response to "M. Ego's" answer to his first letter, continues in the same tone. In "Du Naturalisme III," Laforgue responds to M.F. Lacoste, who had published in *La Guêpe* an article on the subject in verse (90 alexandrines!), by a lengthy quotation from Zola's "Mes haines" ("My Aversions"),[80] a most appropriate choice in this journalistic squabble about the most controversial literary movement of the day.

It has been the purpose of this essay to demonstrate to what extent these earliest of Laforgue's texts were inspired, if not directly influenced, by the poet whom he admired the most at the time he wrote them. For although the importance of Heine's poetry, especially his early cycle *Lyrisches Intermezzo*, in the development of Laforgue's poetry has been generally—if vaguely—recognized, the echoes of Heine's prose in that of Laforgue have so far been overlooked. But our reading of Laforgue's contributions to *La Guêpe* and *L'Enfer* in the light of Heine's *Briefe aus Berlin* should redress the imbalance, as it has shown us how Heine's prose, too, influenced Laforgue who, like his master, was to distinguish himself as journalist and prose writer as well as poet. Laforgue's earliest contributions to literary journalism are both illuminated and overshadowed by the rich heritage from which they drew.

Notes

1 J.L. Debauve, Jules Laforgue, *Les pages de la Guêpe* (Paris: Nizet, 1969).

2 *Pages de la Guêpe*, 74: "Les sympathies avouées vont pour le moment à Baudelaire, Banville, Michelet et Heine 'qu'aux plus grands je préfère' (il le fera jusqu'à sa mort)."

3 *Pages de la Guêpe*, 45.

4 Jules Laforgue, *Oeuvres complètes*, VI, *En Allemagne: Berlin la Cour et la ville*, ed. Jean-Aubry (Paris: Mercure de France, 1922; Genève: Slatkine Reprints, 1979).

5 For a brief summary of these, see *Les Complaintes*, 29.

6 Jules Laforgue, *Chroniques parisiennes, ennuis non rimés*, ed. Malraux (Paris: La Connaissance, undated).

7 For *Französische Maler* and *Französische Zustände*, see DA, XII: 9–226; *De la France* par Henri Heine (Paris: E. Renduel, 1833) (successive editions by Calmann-Lévy Frères). For *Lutetia*, see *Heinrich Heine. Sämtliche Schriften*, ed. Klaus Briegleb (Munich: Carl Hanser Verlag, 1968–1976), V: 217–548. I shall henceforth refer to this edition with the letter B, unless otherwise indicated. *Lutèce* (Paris: Michel Lévy Frères, 1855). Full versions of *De la France* and *Lutèce* are included in *Heinrich Heine—Säkularausgabe*, eds. Nationale Forschungs—und Gedenkstätten der klassischen deutschen Literatur in Weimar and Centre National de la Recherhe Scientifique (Berlin and Paris: Akademie Verlag and CNRS, 1970–   ), XVIII–XIX. In this edition also *Poèmes et légendes* XIII; *Tableaux de voyage* I and II in XIV, XV; *De l'Allemagne* I and II in XVI, XVII. I shall refer to this edition with the letters HSA, unless otherwise indicated.

8 *De la France* was reprinted in 1857, 1860, 1863, 1867, 1884; *Lutèce* was reprinted in 1855 (2nd ed.), 1857, 1859, 1861, 1863, 1866, 1871.

9 DA, VI: 7–53. The French version in the volume *De tout un peu* (Paris: Michel Lévy Frères, 1867), 1–121.

[10] *Poèmes et légendes* (Paris: Michel Lévy Frères, 1855), reprinted in 1856, 1868, 1886. *Poésies inédites* (Paris: Calmann Lévy, 1885), reprinted in 1898.

[11] Cf. *Les Complaintes*, 203.

[12] *Pages de la Guêpe*, 86–89 and 161–63; "La Chanson des morts" also in *Les Complaintes*, 161–64.

[13] The translator(s) of the "Traumbilder" is not known: DA, I/2: 1099.

[14] The French version is in *Poèmes et légendes*, 217.

[15] In French in *Poésies inédites*, 215.

[16] B, IV: 540–47. In French in *Poèmes et légendes*, 51–57. For the evolution of the Herodias myth in the nineteenth century cf. Helen G. Zagona, *The Legend of Salomé and the Principle of Art for Art's Sake* (Paris: Minard, 1960).

[17] *Pages de la Guêpe*, 83–4; *Les Complaintes*, 165.

[18] B, VI: 311–12 and DA, I: 515–18. In French "La Chanson de la vivandière, "*Poésies et légendes*, 401–402.

[19] *Pages de la Guêpe*, 84–85; *Les Complaintes*, 168–69.

[20] *Les Complaintes*, 364.

[21] B, IV: 171–293. In French, *Les Héroines de Shakespeare*, in *De l'Angelterre* (Paris: Michel Lévy Frères, 1867).

[22] *Pages de la Guêpe*, 86–7; *Les Complaintes*, 166–67.

[23] *Pages de la Guêpe*, 89–91; *Les Complaintes*, 172–73.

[24] *Pages de la Guêpe*, 91; *Les Complaintes*, 177.

[25] Cf. my "Laforgue and His Philosophers, or the 'Paratext' in the Intertextual Maze," *Nineteenth-Century French Studies*, XIV (1886): 324–40.

[26] In French in *Drames et fantaisies* (Paris: Michel Lévy Frères, 1886), 246; in the *Revue des Deux Mondes*, October 1863.

[27] DA, II: 112–13. *Poèmes et légendes*, 190.

[28] B, IV: 583 and 585; *Poèmes et légendes*, 212. Cf. Jeffrey L. Sammons, *Heinrich Heine: A Modern Biography*, (Princeton University Press, Princeton: 1979), 273: ". . . it is not without interest that he [Heine] was a member of a Paris committee collecting money for the cathedral project. It was hoped that the liberals participating in this campaign would 'give it a different meaning than the indended one,' as one of the organizers wrote to Heine." Cf. also Eberhard Galley, "Heine und der Kölner Dom," *Deutsche Vierteljahrsschrift für Literaturwissenschaft und Geistesgeschichte*, 32 (1958): 99–110.

[29] B, III: 654–55. The French version is entitled "Traditions populaires" and in *De l'Allemagne* II (first published by Michel Lévy Frères in 1835), 60. Cf. Daniel A. de Graaf, "Quelques Rencontres avec Henri Heine dans la littérature française," *Les Langues Modernes* 59 (1956), 140: "En lisant la *Vénus d'Ille*, de Prosper Mérimée, on est frappé de la ressemblance que dénote ce récit avec les *Elementargeister* de Heine." Thus, *Elementargeister* had diverse echoes in French literature.

[30] B, I: 601. "Les Nuits florentines" was published in the *Revue des Deux Mondes* in April and May of 1836.

[31] *Les Complaintes*, 366.
[32] *Pages de la Guêpe*, 92–3; *Les Complaintes*, 178–79.
[33] *Poésies inédites*, 304.
[34] *Les Complaintes*, 202.
[35] *Les Complaintes*, 181.
[36] Paul Janet, "La Métaphysique en Europe depuis Hegel, un philosophe misanthrope," *Revue des Deux Mondes*, XXI. (1877): 269–86.
[37] *Pages de la Guêpe*, 93–4; *Les Complaintes*, 174 and 180.
[38] Cf. *Les Complaintes*, 366 for a discussion of the contemporary French intertext.
[39] *Les Complaintes*, 175.
[40] *Pages de la Guêpe*, 94–5; *Les Complaintes*, 182–83.
[41] Poèmes et légendes, 183.
[42] *Pages de la Guêpe*, 96; *Les Complaintes*, 184.
[43] *Pages de la Guêpe*, 97–155.
[44] Regarding the ambiguities surrounding Heine's birth date, cf. Sammons, *A Modern Biography*, 11–15.
[45] Cf. note 9 above, and DA, VI: 364.
[46] DA, VI: 9, *De tout un peu*, 3–4.
[47] *Pages de la Guêpe*, 97.
[48] *Pages de la Guêpe*, 99.
[49] DA, VI: 10ff. *De tout un peu*, 4ff.
[50] Yet, many of the political allusions might easily escape the hasty reader. For a recent assessment of Heine's mastery in manipulating them, cf. Jost Hermand, *Der frühe Heine: Ein Kommentar zu den "Reisebildern"* (Munich: Winkler Verlag, 1976), esp. 22–42, "Briefe aus Berlin."
[51] *Pages de la Guêpe*, 138.
[52] DA, VI: 18. *De tout un peu*, 27–8.
[53] DA, VI: 19. *De tout un peu*, 30.
[54] Here one also recalls Laforgue's complaints years later about the continual piano playing that pursued him relentlessly through the Paris streets. Cf. "Complainte des pianos qu'on entend dans les quartiers aisés" of *Les Complaintes*, 53–55; or the "Dimanche" poems of *Des Fleurs de bonne volonté* in *L'Imitation de Notre-Dame la Lune Des Fleurs de bonne volonté* (Paris: Gallimard, 1970), 98–9, 127, 156–7.
[55] DA, VI: 21 and 23. *De tout un peu*, 34–5 and 40–41.
[56] DA, VI: 25. *De tout un peu*, 45–6.
[57] DA, VI: 422–23 for background material on Prussian censorship of criticism of Spontini's work.
[58] *Pages de la Guêpe*, 131.
[59] *De l'Allemagne*, II: 293–94.
[60] *Pages de la Guêpe*, 127.

[61] Heine had published the poem, entitled "Das projektierte Denkmahl Göthes zu Frankfurt am Main" in 1821; Cf. DA, VI: 431.

[62] DA, VI: 36. *De tout un peu*, 76.

[63] *En Allemagne: Berlin la Cour et la ville*, 78–93, "Bal de gala;" 94–104, "Le Bal de l'Opéra."

[64] *En Allemagne: la Cour et la ville*, 96.

[65] *Pages de la Guêpe*, 109.

[66] Cf. *Les Complaintes*, 18.

[67] Cf. his letter to Ephrussi of May, 1822, from Baden, in which he says: "I can see that I am not capable yet of writing an article on art, and that, before thinking of writing a salon, I ought first to do one or two of them for myself as an exercise. And to think that last year, if I had been offered a salon to do for a paper, I would have boldly accepted." Jules Laforgue, *Oeuvres complètes*, IV, *Lettres-I (1881–1882)*, ed. G. Jean-Aubry (Genève: Slatkine Reprints, 1979), 158.

[68] *Pages de la Guêpe*, 157–60.

[69] Laforgue published a piece similar to the salon article of *La Guêpe* under a more appropriate title, "Le Public des dimanches au salon" in *La Vie moderne* in the May 21, 1881, issue. In 1883, he contributed a long article on the "Salon de Berlin" to the *Gazette des Beaux-Arts*. I shall discuss this text, as well as five other articles which Laforgue contributed to this journal from 1882 to 1886 in another chapter (VII) of this volume.

[70] The Marchese Christophoro di Gumpelino, alias Christian Gumpel, is one of the principal characters of *Die Bäder von Lucca*, a caricature of the Hamburg banker Lazarus Gumpel, who travels in Italy to study art and become a gentleman. We shall discuss the figure again in a following chapter (IV). B, II: 391–470. French version: "Les bains de Lucques" in *Tableaux de Voyage* (Paris: Michel Lévy Frères, 1856), II.

[71] DA, XII, 9–48. *De la France*, 324–83. The paintings Heine discussed in his *Salon* of 1831 are reproduced in DA, XII/2 (between 562 and 563), as well as in Irmgard Zepf's thorough study *Heinrich Heines Gemäldeausstellung zum Salon 1831* (Munich: Wilhelm Fink Verlag, 1980). They are all reproduced, some in color, in HSA, VII: 48–86.

[72] Cf. also Michael Mann's edition of these articles in *Heinrich Heines Zeitungsberichte über Musik und Malerei* (Frankfurt: Insel-Verlag, 1964), esp. 185–97 for an excellent discussion of the "Gemäldeausstellung in Paris 1831." This volume also includes reproductions of twelve of the paintings Heine discussed.

[73] Cf. note 7 above.

[74] Baudelaire, *Curiosités esthétiques, L'Art romantique*, ed. Henri Lemaitre (Paris: Classiques Garnier, 1962), 67. The quotation is annotated as follows: "Henri Heine, *Die romantische Schule*, III, I, i. Une traduction de ce texte avait paru en 1833 dans *l'Europe littéraire*, sous le titre *Etat actuel de la*

littérature en Allemagne; autre traduction dans les *Oeuvres* de Heine, publiées par Renduel en 1835 (tome IV, V^e partie). Baudelaire avait pu lire l'une ou l'autre."

[75] *Pages de la Guêpe*, 173–74.

[76] *Pages de la Guêpe*, 166–67.

[77] B, II: esp. 441–70. *Tableaux de Voyage*, II, "Les bains de Lucques."

[78] DA, XI: 154–68; Henri Heine, *Satires et portraits* (Paris: Calmann Lévy, 1884) (first ed. 1868), 206–37, "Le Dénonciateur."

[79] DA, XI: 9–132. *Satires et portraits*, 1–105.

[80] *Pages de la Guêpe*, 172.

II

Reverberations of Heine's *Lyrisches Intermezzo* in the Lyrics of Laforgue

In discussing the group of Heinean poems that most profoundly marked Laforgue, I shall attempt to trace that influence—both direct and mediated—in his verse.[1] None of Heine's lyric cycles enjoyed greater popularity in nineteenth-century France than *Lyrisches Intermezzo* (DA, I: 131–203). It was the *Intermezzo* along with another group of poems, *Die Nordsee* ("*La Mer du nord* et quelques *Romances*"), that Nerval translated into French prose in 1848. In 1857, Paul Ristelhuber furnished a verse translation of the cycle which appeared with Baudelaire's publisher, Poulet-Malassis, the same year as *Les Fleurs du mal.*[2] Another translation, by Albert Mérat and Léon Valade, was published by Lemerre in 1868; and after Laforgue's involvement with the poems, translations of the *Intermezzo* appeared in 1894, 1913, and surprisingly, in 1917!

Heine first published the poems, most of which (forty-six of the sixty-six pieces) had already appeared previously in various journals, together with his tragedies *William Ratcliff* and *Almansor*, in a volume entitled *Tragödien, nebst einem lyrischen Intermezzo* in 1823, a year and a half after the publication of his first book, *Gedichte*, in 1821. In 1827, the year after publication of the *Reisebilder* (*Tableaux de voyage*), Heine's most famous book for many years in both Germany and France, the poet published his *Buch der Lieder*, comprising most of his poetry written up to that time, including *Lyrisches Intermezzo.*[3] The principal mediator, or transmitter, of the cycle in France was its first translator, Gérard de Nerval.

The friendship of Heine and Nerval has been traced by Charles Dédéyan and Alfred Dubruck,[4] and it was most movingly recalled shortly after Nerval's untimely death by Heine himself in the preface to the French edition of his poems, *Poèmes et légendes* of 1855. Here Heine explains why he could not resist "the sorrowful pleasure of reprinting in this book the gracious pages which my late friend Gérard de Nerval wrote as preface to the 'Intermezzo' and the 'North Sea'." The German poet recalls

> . . . not without deep emotion the evenings in March of 1848, when the good and gentle Gérard used to come to see me daily in my retreat of the Barrière de la Santé to work quietly with me at the translation of my peaceful German day-dreams, while around us all political passions were clamoring and the old world was collapsing with a dreadful clash! (B, VI: 519).

He then goes on to recall that though Nerval did not have a perfect command of German, he was a *poet*, who "understood the meaning of poetry written in German better than those who had made of that idiom the study of their entire lives" (B, VI: 520).

Nerval had established himself as translator by his rendition of Goethe's *Faust* and a volume of *Poésies Allemandes*.[5] His essay "Les Poésies de Henri Heine," followed by translations of some of Heine's ballads, as well as another essay on his friend preceding his translation of the *Intermezzo*, appeared in the *Revue des Deux Mondes* in 1848,[6] and Heine included this version of the *Intermezzo* as well as Nerval's "gracious pages" of introduction in the French edition of his works.[7]

Nerval begins "Les Poésies de Henri Heine" with an apologia for poetry in troubled times, similar to Heine's own comments quoted above: "At a moment when Europe is aflame, it takes some courage perhaps to preoccupy oneself with mere poetry and translate a writer who has been the leader of the young Germany and exercised a great influence on the development of minds, not with his revolutionary songs, but with his most detached ballads, his most serene verse." The allusion to Heine's affiliation with the *Junge Deutschland* movement of the thirties evokes for Nerval's French readers the almost contemporary *Jeune France* excitement of their youth and its great "chef" and representative, Victor Hugo. Then Nerval links Heine to Voltaire and the spirit of the French eighteenth century and German Romanticism: "Heinrich Heine is, if we can couple these words, a picturesque and sentimental Voltaire, an eighteenth-century sceptic covered over with a layer of silver by the blue beams of German moonlight." He paints Heine as a man of contrasts, and adds that "if Prussia is the homeland of his body, France is the homeland of his spirit." He is both "cruel and tender, naive and treacherous, sceptic and credulous, lyric and prosaic, sentimental and scoffing, impassioned and glacial, witty and picturesque, antique and modern, medieval and revolutionary. . . . he is a man of contrasts." Needless to recall, again the implied reader must remember Hugo.

Heine is, moreover, featured as the creator of a new German idiom—after Goethe!—, for "he has transformed that dialect which only the Germans can write and speak, without, however, always understanding each other themselves, into a universal language." And then follows, in fact, a reference to Goethe whom, along with some other famous German poets, Heine has surpassed: "Appearing on the literary horizon a little later, but with no less brilliance, than the bright pleiad in which Wieland, Klopstock, Schiller and Goethe shone, he was able to avoid certain faults of his predecessors." In Nerval's summation, "nothing is stranger to us than this mind at once both so French and so German." Nerval concludes his first essay with an image of Heine as *poète-Pierrot*, a figure that was to fascinate the poetic and artistic imagination from Romanticism to Symbolism and finally modern art and poetry:

The power of the images and the sentiment of beauty have for some stanzas made our jester serious; but now he is making fun of his own emotions and passes his motley buffoon's sleeve over eyes filled with tears and makes his bells ring loudly and bursts out laughing in your face: you've been taken in; he has trapped you in a sentimental snare into which you have fallen like a simple Philistine.—That's what he says, but he is lying. He was moved himself, in fact, for everything is sincere in this multiple nature. Don't listen to him when he tells you not to believe in his laughter, nor his tears.

After the translation of several ballads, Nerval continues his discussion of Heine and of some of the individual poems. And some remarks regarding Heine the love poet must also have interested Laforgue: "There is always something suspicious and uneasy in Heinrich Heine's most amorous and indulgent poetry; for him love is a garden full of flowers and shades, but of poisonous flowers and deadly shades." As for women, "their grace is perfidious, beauty is fatal; all seduction deceives, all charm is a danger."

In the pages directly preceding the *Intermezzo*, Nerval stresses Heine's stylistic finesse and the plastic beauty of his verse: "his form is resplendent with beauty, he works and chisels it . . ." Then he describes the cycle he is presenting to the French reader: "The poem *Intermezzo* is, in our opinion, perhaps Heine's most original work. . . . All these disconnected stanzas have a unity,—love. . . . Neither the Greeks nor the Romans, nor Mimnermes whom antiquity considered superior to Homer, nor the great Tibullus, nor the ardent Propertius, nor the ingenious Ovid, nor Dante with his Platonism, nor Petrarch with his gallant *concetti*, have ever written anything like it." We can see why Heine "could not resist" reproducing his friend's "gracious pages" in his French edition. However, Nerval continues, the subject of the cycle, which he repeatedly calls a "poem," is the simplest and most fundamental of all love poetry: ". . . the subject of the 'Intermezzo'? A young girl, first loved by the poet, and who leaves him for a fiancé or some other rich or stupid lover. Nothing more, nothing less; it happens every day." And "this completely common theme . . . has become a wonderful poem in the hands of Heinrich Heine," full of "passion, sadness, irony."

Finally Nerval wonders whether his translation can do justice to the remarkable original: "will the translation preserve something of this intellectual figure [plastique intellectuelle]?" And, himself the most sensitive of poets, Nerval surely must have felt that his prose rendition was perforce condemned to betray the Heinean *Lied* to a considerable degree, as so much of its effect depends on its prosody, on Heine's mastery of rhyme and rhythm. Ironically, any poet after reading the Nerval translation, and with only the slightest knowledge of German, would be directed to the original—by the very introduction of the translator himself.

I have quoted at length from Nerval's prefatory pages, for I am convinced that this "paratext" played a vital role in the survival of the primary text, especially as concerns the Heinean legacy in Laforgue.[8] Laforgue's readers will recall the tributes to Heine in his earliest poems, like "Epicuréisme" which I discussed in the preceding chapter, or "L'Espérance."[9] Among those early poems is a piece entitled "Intermezzo," published posthumously, which has come down to us in two manuscripts, marked "traduit de Heine." Thus, Nerval's preface *did* lead Laforgue to the German *Intermezzo*. The piece which he chose to translate, moreover, is not among the poems of the Nervalian version; in fact, Heine himself had excluded it with some others from *Lyrisches Intermezzo* of the *Buch der Lieder*, and Laforgue gleaned it from the group of six numbered and appended poems, entitled "Zum 'Lyrischen Intermezzo'," of which it is the first:

> * Schöne, helle, goldne Sterne
> Grüßt die Liebste in der Ferne,
> Sagt, daß ich noch immer sei
> Herzekrank und bleich und treu.[10] (also in DA I: 462).

Laforgue's verse translation renders Heine's quatrain as a *sizain* by interpolating a second and fifth line:

> † Belles, claires étoiles d'or
> Dont la nuit est semée!
> Oh! saluez de loin ma bien-aimée!
> Dites lui que je suis encor
> Dites [lui] que je suis toujours
> Pâle et fidèle et malade d'amour (p. 203).

* Beautiful, bright, golden stars, greet the beloved far away. Say to her that I am still sick of heart and pale and faithful.

† Beautiful, bright stars of gold scattered in the night! Oh greet my beloved from afar! Tell her that I am still, tell her that I am always pale and faithful and sick from love.

A comparison with the prose translation (note 10) makes Laforgue's sensitivity to Heine's verse especially conspicuous. Laforgue might well have written this translation in the last year before his departure for Germany, when he was preoccupied with his other German friends, Schopenhauer and von Hartmann, as he tells Gustave Kahn in a letter of December 1880, and which he concludes by saying: "I leave you to reread my friend H. Heine."[11]

A letter written a year after the above, from Berlin, to his friend Charles Henry, shows that there, too, he continued to read Heine in the original, and specifically the *Lyrisches Intermezzo*. It is the poet's first winter at the Prussian Court, and he is already depressed in his gilded exile. He reads a lot and reports: "I am doing some German." He also tries to return to his poems: "I am going to get back to my poetry and try to paint these poor, feeble flowers up more sadly."[12] After quoting lines by Baudelaire, Laforgue continues: "my heart is dying with sadness" [pourri de tristesse], and then follow, under the salutation "Guten Abend," quotations from three pieces of *Lyrisches Intermezzo*, in German: "Lehn' deine Wang' an meine Wang'!," the first line of #6; "O schwöre nicht and küsse nur, / Ich glaube keinem Weiberschwur! . . . O schwöre, Liebchen immerfort," the first, second and seventh lines of #13; and "Und wüßten's die Blumen, die kleinen, / Wie tief verwundet mein Herz, / Sie würden mit mir weinen, / Zu heilen meinen Schmerz,"* the first quatrain of #22. These quotations are followed by "pourri, pourri de tristesse," which closes the letter.[13]

This document of Laforgue's state of mind at the close of 1881 marks the end of his "tragic" period, the time at which he wrote his autobiographical novel *Stéphane Vassiliew* and composed poems for the projected *Le Sanglot de la terre*. A little over a

---

* Press your cheek against my cheek! Oh do not swear and only kiss; I do not believe women's oaths! . . . Oh swear, beloved, evermore. And if the flowers knew how deeply wounded is my heart, they would weep with me to heal my sorrows.

year later, he wrote to Kahn: "Now my great desire is to . . .
enjoy things. Before, I was a tragic Buddhist, and now I am a
dilettante Buddhist."[14] And the fact the he chose as epigraph for
Le Sanglot de la terre (*The Sobs of the Earth*), his collection of
anguished metaphysical poems, the following two lines from one
of Heine's *Lazarus* poems,

> * De la santé et un supplément d'argent,
> Voilà, Seigneur, tout ce que je demande,[15]

already signals the beginnings of a change from Laforgue's early
and tragic stance toward the ironic mode.[16]

Recent European Heine scholarship has minutely traced the
Rezeptionsgeschichte of the *Buch der Lieder*,[17] showing that the
German reading public's understanding of Heine's deft irony in
that work developed only gradually over several generations.
Here I am reminded of a fundamental principle of embryology,
that ontogeny recapitulates phylogeny; for Laforgue's own
reading of Heine, and especially of the *Intermezzo* underwent an
almost identical evolution during the short years of his acquaintance with the German's poetry.

Heine was most interested, in the 1820's in establishing his
fame as lyric poet, thus writing for a broad public of the middle
class. But the *Buch der Lieder* was initially not as successful as
he had hoped, and, as his publisher Campe did not fail to remind
the poet frequently, sold poorly, at the beginning.[18] It has been
speculated that Heine's earliest readers, moreover, were pre-
dominantly members of the aristocracy or at any rate of the
higher social strata, and that only a later generation of his
readers was principally composed of the *bürgerliche* middle
class which, however, read the *Buch der Lieder* "sentimentally," using it as source of cheap emotionalism, "eine Quelle
von billigen Emotionen."[19] This larger readership appreciated
Heine the heart-broken love poet, his cliché images of nature,
conventionally associated with this poetic stereotype. The po-

---

* Health and a supplement of money, that's all, Lord, I ask.

ems' edge, their covert and even overt irony, were largely ignored. Love and nature were *the* lyric themes for these readers, and they preferred them rendered in the manner and tone of the *Volkslied,* popularized by Romantic poets like Eichendorff, by Arnim's great collection, *Des Knaben Wunderhorn,* and by Müller's *Gedichte,* to all of whom Heine was, moreover, indebted.[20]

Thus even after the *Buch der Lieder* had gained a large readership, Heine's poetic innovations—the inclusion of everyday language, sudden breaks of mood and ironic undercutting, the pointed brevity of the epigram, as well as unprecedented liberties of erotic expression—were either ignored or aroused offense. The general reading public, as well as some of the critics, preferred what they were used to: traditional romantically-sentimental poetry, even after the hour of Romanticism. The unprecedented number of musical renditions, by some of the greatest composers, proves that Heine brilliantly succeeded in responding to the popular demand, while at the same time writing a new poetry.[21] S.S. Prawer discusses Heine's literary strategy at length: ''. . . paradoxical in this as in everything else, it was for this society which he satirized with all the resources of his superb mimic gift, that Heine wrote his works. He had no other audience. . . . In a Germany of triumphant Philistinism, Heine became the most widely read poet of the day, whose volumes of verse (notably the *Buch der Lieder* itself) sold more copies than any before. . . . It is this paradox which helps to explain the curiously double-edged nature of so many of Heine's poems. He is trying at once to do justice to his own complex and ironic nature and to please an audience that demands sentimentalities and that at heart he despises.''[22]

Heine even gained a readership of women, the ''Damenwelt,'' for whom expurgated editions of his poetry were published; but he did have a relatively small group of enlightened enthusiasts, the (all male) students of Germany's universities, whose favorite poet he remained throughout the second half of the nineteenth century, until the Hölderlin cult replaced Heine at the turn of the century.[23]

In my opinion, Laforgue's reading of Heine, too, underwent

an evolution, and the poet of the early poems of the projected *Sanglot de la terre* probably read his Heine "sentimentally." For example in the letter to Henry in which he described his heart "pourri de tristesse" and quoted from *Lyrisches Intermezzo*, Laforgue included the following lines:

> * Mon Coeur, prière (suite)
> Qu'il fasse tout pur, à travers l'azur,
>   Et, mordu d'un cilice,
> Qu'il marche vers Vous, déchiré de tous,
>   Et brûle et resplendisse,
> Au seuil des grands cieux, dans un radieux
>   Ecroulement de roses
> Ardent reposoir où monte, le soir,
>   L'encens triste des choses. . . .[24]

These appear closely related in both form and *matière* to "Apothéose," one of the early poems concluding with an elaborate image of the bleeding heart:

> † Un Coeur ruisselant, un Coeur tout en sang
>   Qui, du soir à l'aurore,
> Saigne, sans espoir, de ne pas pouvoir
> Saigner, oh! saigner plus encore (p. 199)![25]

The following piece of the "Premiers poèmes," entitled "Désolation," again develops the image: "Mon Coeur saigne d'amour et se fond en douceur" and ends in a paroxism of hemorrhaging: "Je veux saigner pour tout, saigner, toujours, encor . . ."‡ (pp. 200–201).

Jean-Pierre Richard has examined this recurrent Laforguean imagery in "Les Complaintes," and finds that "une angoisse d'hémorragie pénètre ces poèmes."[26] But no commentator, to

---

* My Heart, prayer (continuation) May it be all pure, across the azure, and, tormented by a shirt of hair, let it walk toward You, torn asunder by all, and burn and shine at the threshold of the great skies, in a radiant downpour of roses, ardent repository where, in the evening, rises the sad incense of things . . .

† A streaming Heart, a Heart all bloody which, from evening to dawn, bleeds, without hope, for not being able to bleed, oh bleed, still more.

‡ My heart bleeds with love and dissolves in sweetness.
  I want to bleed for everything, bleed, always, again.

my knowledge, has ever suggested that one of the sources of Laforgue's "obsession hématique," which we can trace through all his poetry and even the *Moralités légendaires*, might well be Heine.

The image of the bleeding heart, of the "zerrissene Herz" (the "heart torn to pieces"), and of bleeding to death recurs in the *Buch der Lieder*. In the *Intermezzo* alone, there are images of serpents feeding on the beloved's heart, as in #18: "Und sah die Nacht in deines Herzens Raum. / Und sah die Schlang', die dir am Herzen frißt—''* (DA, I: 151); or serpents in the lover's heart, #51: "Ich trage im Herzen viel Schlangen, / Und dich, Geliebte mein" (DA, I: 185). The beloved has torn the lover's heart asunder, in #22: "Sie hat ja selbst zerrissen, 11 / Zerrissen mir das Herz" (DA, I: 155). In #34, the poet's heart speaks: "Ach wenn ich nur das Kisschen wär', / Wo sie die Nadeln steckt hinein! / Und stäche sie mich noch so sehr, / Ich wollte mich der Stiche freun"† (DA I: 165). In the following piece, the lover's heart breaks: "Fast vor Weh das Herz mir bricht"‡ (DA, I:167), and the long penultimate piece of the *Intermezzo* ends in a paroxism of bleeding which awakens the poet from his dream:

> * Mein Lieb, ich kann nicht aufstehn,
> Noch blutet's immerfort,
> Wo du ins Herz mich stachest
> Mit einem spitz'gen Wort.

* And saw the night in your heart, and saw the serpent which feeds on your heart.

† I carry in my heart many serpents, and you my beloved.
For she herself has torn to pieces, torn to pieces my heart.
Oh if I only were the cushion into which she sticks her needles! And however much she pierced me, I should be glad of the stabs.

‡ My heart is almost breaking with pain.

* My love, I cannot rise, it is still bleeding steadily where you stabbed my heart with a sharp word. "Very gently, Heinrich, I lay my hand upon your heart. Then it will bleed no longer, and healed is all its pain." My love, I cannot rise, my head is bleeding too; for I shot myself (in the head) when you were stolen from me. "With my own curls, Heinrich, I stop the bleeding of the wound and force back the bloodstream and heal your head." Then the wounds burst open, and the bloodstream gushed forth with wild force from head and breast, and lo!—I awoke.

"Ganz leise leg ich, Heinrich,
Dir mein Hand auf's Herz;
Dann wird es nicht mehr bluten,
Geheilt is all' sein Schmerz."

Mein Lieb, ich kann nicht aufstehn,
Es blutet auch mein Haupt;
Hab ja hineingeschossen,
Als du mir wurdest geraubt.

"Mit meinen Locken, Heinrich,
Stopf ich des Hauptes Wund',
Und dräng zurück den Blutstrom
Und mache dein Haupt gesund."
. . . .
Da brachen auf die Wunden,
Da stürzt' mit wilder Macht
Aus Kopf und Brust der Blutstrom,
Und sieh! —ich bin erwacht (DA, I: 199–201).

Elsewhere in the *Buch der Lieder*, we find the same images, as in the last tercet of sonnett III, with its characteristic Heinean point:

* Und wenn das Herz im Leibe ist zerrissen,
Zerrissen, und zerschnitten, und zerstochen—
Dann bleibt uns doch das schöne gelle Lachen (DA, I: 122).

The fifth sonnet describes blood gushing from the heart's old wound: "Und Blut entquillt der alten Herzenswunde.† (DA, I: 124), while in sonnet VII, the lover exclaims: "Könnt ich dich and die glühenden Lippen pressen, / Und könnt mein Herz verbluten unterdessen"‡ (DA, I, 127). In sonnet VIII, serpents again attack the lover's heart, blood gushing from his thousand wounds: "Wie gift'ge Schlangen un mein Herz sich ringeln; / Du

* And when the heart is torn to pieces in the breast, torn to pieces and cut and pierced—then there remains to us, however, beautiful shrill laughter.

† And blood gushes forth from the old wound of the heart.

‡ Oh could I only press those glowing lips while my heart was bleeding to death.

sahest mein Blut aus tausend Wunden sprudeln"* (DA I: 129). And we could find many more examples of Heine's obsessive blood imagery which, I am convinced, marked—not to say stained—Laforgue's poetry.

The early, sentimental and anguished Laforgue of the "philosophical" poems read his Heine as a sentimental and anguished poet. Thus Pascal Pia notes that Laforgue's poem "L'Angoisse sincère" (pp. 220–222), dated "Nuit du 4 juin" [1880], bore on two of the four extant drafts, entitled "La Grande Angoisse," the name H. Heine as signature of an epigraph which was not filled in.[27] Here the association of Heine with this moment of Laforgue's poetic expression is again borne out.

However, Laforgue learned to read his favorite poet and thus learned from him how to defend himself against bleeding to death; he learned "das schöne gelle Lachen," and the irony that has become his characteristic trait and for which his master was famous—or infamous, according to his enemies. Small wonder, then, that Laforgue was soon to reject his early poetic stance. Thus already in February of 1881, as he reports to Kahn on the progress of his projected collection, *Le Sanglot de la terre*, Laforgue writes: "I have 1,800 lines in my volume. But I am beginning to dislike it at times."[28] And two years later, the evolution is completed, as he writes in May of 1883 in an oft-quoted letter to his sister: "I find it stupid to proclaim big words and make a display of eloquence. Today, as I am more sceptical and get less easily carried away and as, on the other hand, I am in possession of my language in a more meticulous and more clownish way, I am writing little poems of fantasy, having only one aim: to do something original, at any cost. I have the *firm intention* of publishing a very small volume (handsome edition), . . . title: *Some Complaints of Life.* . . . I already have about twenty of these complaints." Farther on in the letter, we seem to be hearing Heine himself, as Laforgue continues that "it is, in fact, the coarseness of life that must put

---

* How poisonous serpents wind around my heart; you saw my blood gush forth from a thousand wounds.

a humorous melancholy into our verse," and adds "let's say things in a subtle way. Poetry ought not to be an exact description (like a novel), but bathed in dreams."[29]

As Heine had cultivated the popular art form of the *Lied*, so Laforgue, too, "is now turning toward a form conceived as popular, turned up from the Collective Unconscious, the *Volkstum* . . ." And, as with Heine, it was partly inspired by the literary tradition. Reboul continues: "Literary life in the cafés and elsewhere had given him the example: what complaints in Richepin! What falsely popular and gross songs in all this living literature of minuscule groups." Then Reboul recalls how the inauguration of the Lion of Belfort on September 10, 1880, helped inspire Laforgue to write the *complainte*.[30] In a posthumously published prose fragment, Laforgue describes the popular festivity that was to partially inspire his new poetry, *Les Complaintes*: "Night festivity. inaugurat. of the lion of Belfort— poor—sad—. . . fairground festivity. . . . two women in faded jerseys walking around on the stage, yelling. Musicians are making havoc with the dented brass .instruments dominated by the big drum, boom! boom!" And then appears a poor Pierrot: "A clown in huge pants reaching up to his neck and pulling on his ankles, . . . a red wig, pointed white hat, a mask of flour puckering and wrinkling when he swooned without conviction (this gentleman, this brother, has his successes like you and I— Strange!)."[31]

All that remains of the old *Sanglot* in *Les Complaintes* is the liminal piece, "Préludes autobiographiques," whose presence in the new volume Laforgue defended in a letter to Kahn of March, 1885: ". . . I would very much like to keep the prefatory poem. It is composed of former verse, it is full of clamor and tenderness—it is autobiographical. I have sacrificed a big volume of philosophical poetry of the past because it was manifestly bad, but in the end it was a stage; and I insist on saying (to the few to whom I shall send the volume), that before becoming a dilettante and Pierrot I sojourned in the Cosmic."[32] The poem is, moreover, overtly reminiscent, evoking "my great twenties." And a Heinean note is manifest in this distich:

* En attendant la mort mortelle, sans mystère,
Lors quoi l'usage vent qu'on nous cache sous terre (p. 40).

A Heinean characteristic of the entire *recueil* is the predominance of the theme of love in all its forms, from the crudest sexuality—shades of Schopenhauer—to the pastiche of sentimental love poetry, frequently both in the same poem. Thus, in the "Complainte de Notre-Dame des soirs," in which Laforgue rejects the life-sustaining sun for the sterile and virginal moon:

> † Eux sucent des plis dont le frou-frou les suffoque;
> Pour un regard, ils battraient du front les pavés;
> Puis s'affligent sur maint sein creux, mal abreuvés;
> Puis retournent à ces vendanges sexciproques.
> Et moi, moi je m'en moque!
> Oui, Notre-Dame des Soirs,
> J'en fais, paraît-il, peine à voir (p. 44).

Also reminiscent of Heine is the Laforguean neologism "sexciproque(s)," which the poet had, at one point, wished to "correct." Heine was, we recall, famous for his neologisms, such as "famillionär," "aristokrätzig," the two most celebrated of the many examples of ironic wordplay throughout his poetry and prose; I am convinced that it influenced Laforgue's "logopoeia," especially as Freud has explained this phenomenon and its ramifications in the unconscious.[33] It abounds, for example, in the "Complainte des Voix sous le Figuier boudhique" ("Complaint of the Voices Under a Buddhist Fig Tree") (pp. 46–50), a sort of mock dramatic poem of several voices, which Laforgue considered one of the most important of the *Complaintes*.[34] The voices heard are Schopenhauer's, von Hartmann's and that of the Buddha, disguised in the choruses of "Les Communiantes," "Les Voluptantes," "Les Paranymphes," "Les Jeunes Gens," and finally that of "Le

---

* Waiting for mortal death, without mystery, when, according to custom, they hide us in the earth.

† They suck on folds of dresses whose rustles suffocate them. For a glance, they'd kiss the ground. Then they grieve upon many a sunken bosom, poorly satisfied, then return to those sexiprocal harvests. And me, I couldn't care less! Yes, our Lady of the Evenings, I am, it seems, painful to behold.

Figuier." Thus classical antiquity ("paranymphes"), Christianity ("communiantes"), and Buddhism ("figuier") propose their wisdom to the young boys and girls, "Les Jeunes Gens," and "Les Voluptantes," a neologism which needs no Freudian comment. The latter, in the service of the Hartmannian "Inconscient," dream of the "nest furnished by the idolatrous male," evoking a scene that Heine also mocked in the *Intermezzo* #26:

> * Wir haben viel für einander gefühlt,
> Und dennoch uns gar vortrefflich vertragen.
> Wir haben oft "Mann und Frau" gespielt,
> Und dennoch uns nicht gerauft und geschlagen (DA, I: 157).

The "Voluptantes" see it this way:

> † C'est le nid meublé
> Par l'homme idolâtre;
> . . . .
> Presque pas de scènes;
> La vie est saine,
> Quand on sait s'arranger.
> O financé probe,
> Commandons ma robe!
> Hélas! le bonheur est là, mais lui se dérobe . . .

However, "les jeunes gens," who have read Schopenhauer, share the Heinean view of women:

> ‡ Bestiole à chignon, Nécessaire divin,
> Os de chatte, corps de lierre, chef-d'oeuvre vain!
> . . . .
> Mais, fausse soeur, fausse humaine, fausse mortelle,
> Nous t'écarlèterons de hontes sensuelles!

* We've felt a lot for each other, and yet got along very well. Often we played "husband and wife," and yet neither fought nor warred.

† It's the nest furnished by the idolatrous male; . . . Almost no scenes; life is sound when one knows how to get along. O upright fiancé, let's order my gown! Alas! Happiness is there, but he is slipping away . . .

‡ Little beast with your chignons, divine Necessity, bones of a cat, body of ivy, vain masterpiece! . . . But, false sister, false human being, false mortal, we'll put you on the rack of carnal shame!

The last word had read "sangsuelles" in the original edition, and Laforgue subsequently changed his neologism to "sensuelles." Again the fear of women is, as in Heine, associated with blood imagery, if but unconsciously.[35]

Laforgue begins the following piece, "Complainte de cette bonne lune," a dialogue between the stars and the moon, with a parody of a popular song:

> * *On entend les Etoiles*:
> Dans l'giron
> Du Patron,
> On y danse, on y danse,
> Dans l'giron,
> Du Patron,
> On y danse tous en rond (p. 51),

and continues the star's speech in that popular, low style: "— Let's see now, Miss Moon." The opening, of course echoes the song: "Sur le pont d'Avignon / On y danse, on y danse, / Sur le pont d'Avignon, / On y danse tous en rond." Heine had frequently used the same device, of evoking through parody a *Volkslied* known to all his readers. An example from *Lyrisches Intermezzo* is #53:

> Ich steh' auf des Berges Spitze,
> Und werde sentimental.
> "Wenn ich ein Vöglein wäre!"
> Seufz' ich vieltausendmal.

After recalling swallow and nightingale, the lover becomes in the final stanza a "Gimpel," the least intelligent of birds, and which also carries the secondary meaning of "einfältiger Mensch" (simple fellow):

* *One hears the Stars*: In the Master's lap, they are dancing, they are dancing. In the Master's lap, they are dancing round and round.

† I am standing on the top of the mountain and become sentimental. "If I were a lattle bird!" I sighed many thousand times.

> * Wenn ich ein Gimpel wäre,
> So flög'ich gleich an dein Herz;
> Du bist ja hold en Gimpeln,
> Und heilest Gimpelschmerz'' (DA, I:187).[36]

The threefold repetition forcefully makes his point. Heine's readers recall, of course, "Wenn ich ein Vöglein wär, / Und auch zwei Flüglein hätt, / Flög ich zu dir.'' The poet again uses this device in the fifteenth poem of *Die Heimkehr* (*The Return*), here with a more bitterly ironic intent. The *Volkslied*—"Da droben auf jenem Berge, / Da steht ein goldnes Haus, / Da schauen wohl alle Frühmorgen / Drei schöne Jungfraun heraus; / Die eine heißt Elisabeth, / Die andre Bernharda mein, / Die dritte, die will ich nicht nennen, / Die sollt mein eigen seyn,''† -singing the lover's one and only love, a pure maiden, becomes degraded to a celebration of the persona's amorous adventures with all three ladies of the house which has, ironically, become a "fine castle:''

> ‡ Da droben auf jenem Berge,
> Da steht ein feines Schloß,
> Da wohnen drei schöne Fräulein,
> Von denen ich Liebe genoß.
> Sonnabend küßte mich Jette,
> Und Sonntag die Julia,
> Und Montag die Kunigunde,
> Die hat mich erdrückt beinah (DA, I: 225).

Laforgue again utilized this strategy in the refrain of the following poem, "Complainte des Pianos qu'on entend dans les

---

* If I were a bullfinch, I would fly right to your heart; for you are kind to bullfinches and heal bullfinch pain.

† High up on that mountain, there stands a golden house, from which every early morning three beautiful maidens look out. One is named Elizabeth, the other is my Bernharda. The third I will not name for she will become my own.

‡ High up on that mountain, there stands a fine castle. There live three beautiful young ladies from whom I enjoyed favors of love. Saturday, Jette kissed me, and Sunday Julia did. And Monday it was Kunigunde who almost suffocated me.

quartiers aisés,''* again a piece of several voices, and in which young girls pass from innocence to motherhood; here the refrain:

> † "Tu t'en vas et tu nous laisses,
> Tu nous laiss's et tu t'en vas,
> Défaire et refaire ses tresses,
> Broder d'éternelles canevas,''

which turns more sinister in the finale:

> "Tu t'en vas et tu nous laisses,
> Tu nous laiss's et tu t'en vas.
> Que ne suis-je pas morte à la messe!
> Ô mois, ô linges, ô repas! (pp. 53–5),

evokes the popular song "Tu t'en vas et tu nous quittes.'' But Laforgue's most famous example is the opening of the "Complainte de Lord Pierrot'' (pp. 93–5), a close parody of "Au Clair de la lune, / Mon ami Pierrot,'' which undercuts the poem's lordly title, while substituting some mild blasphemy for the familiar words. Thus ‡ "Ma chandelle est morte, / Je n'ai plus de feu'' becomes "Ma cervelle est morte. / Que le Christ l'emporte!'', in a playful variation pointing to Pierrot's anti-intellectualism as well as his lack of faith, and ironically recalling the "Pour l'amour de Dieu'' of the original. The parodic opening octave closes with a striking visual image of the completely detached and passive Pierrot: "Béons à la lune, / La bouche en zéro,'' after which the "Complainte'' proper begins. Both Heine and Laforgue, famous for their irony, became masters of parody as well, in both their poetry and prose.

Throughout the *Complaintes*, there are parodies of sentimental love poetry in the Heinean manner, as for example in the "Complainte des Printemps'' (pp. 72–3), in which the lover-seducer addresses his beloved:

---

* "Complaint of the Pianos which One Hears in the Better Parts of Town.''
† You are going away and you leave us, you leave us and you go away, to undo and redo our tresses and embroider eternal stories. You are going away and you leave us, you leave us and go away. Why didn't I die at mass! Oh months, oh linens, oh repasts!
‡ My candle is dead, I have no fire left. My brain is dead. Let Christ take it away! Let's bay at the moon, our mouth a zero.

* Permettez, ô sirène
  Voici que votre haleine
  Embaume la verveine;
  C'est le printemps qui s'amène!

One recalls Heine's quatrains "In wunderschönen Monat Mai" ("In the lovely month of May") of the *Intermezzo*; but there is a second voice in Laforgue's complaint, which overtly undercuts the lover's flowery sentimentality:

† —Ce système, en effet, ramène le printemps.
  Avec son impudent cortège d'excitants,

and which also again evokes his bleeding:

—Mais vous saignez ainsi pour l'amour de l'exil!

This second sobering voice finally, too, bemoans the ways of nature and the universal loss of virginity: "Virgins of yesterday, today draggers of foetuses."

This spring poem is followed by a "Complainte de l'Automne monotone" (pp. 74–5), recalling the autumn pieces of the *Intermezzo*, like #57, "Das ist ein Brausen und Heulen, / Herbstnacht und Regen und Wind" ("That is a storming and howling, autumn night and rain and wind"), or #58, "Der Herbstwind rüttelt die Bäume, / Die Nacht ist feucht und kalt ("The autumn wind shakes the trees; the night is damp and cold") (DA, I: 191). The third stanza of Laforgue's autumnal complaint evokes the same scene:

‡ Le vent, la pluie, oh! le vent, la pluie!
  Antigone, écartez mon rideau!
  Cet ex-ciel tout suie,

* Permit, oh you siren, your breath here to embalm the verbena; that's springtime coming along!

† This system, in fact, brings back spring with its impudent train of stimulants.—But you are bleeding for the love of exile!

‡ The wind, the rain, oh! the wind, the rain! Antigone, draw open my curtain! This ex-sky, all soot, is it dissolving *decrescendo, statu quo, crescendo*? The wind is weary; is it turning the umbrellas inside out?

> Fond-il *descrescendo, statu quo, crescendo?*
> Le vent qui s'ennuie,
> Retourne-t-il bien les parapluies?

In the fourth line, the musical notations of *descrescendo* and *crescendo* are less surprising than the unpoetic and unmusical *statu quo*. That phrase occurs, to my knowledge, in only one other poem, Heine's *Lazarus* piece, two lines of which Laforgue had chosen as epigraph for his projected, and then abandoned, *Sanglot de la terre*. The two lines, we recall, (cf. note 16), which Laforgue had chosen were from the poem's closing quatrain:

> * Gesundheit nur und Geldzulage
> Verlang ich, Herr! O laß mich froh
> Hinleben noch viel schöne Tage
> Bei meiner Frau im statu quo!

After having evoked a hunting scene in his autumn complaint, autumnal landscapes and seascapes, and "Le soleil mort, tout nous abandonne" ("The sun dead, everything abandons us"), Laforgue added two distiches to the poem's original version, which close it in a distinctly Heinean tone:

> † —Allons, fumons une pipette de tabac,
> En feuilletant un de ces si vieux almanachs,
> En rêvant de la petite qui unirait
> Aux charmes de l'oeillet ceux du chardonneret.

Laforgue introduces several ballads in his *Complaintes*, in which the narrative element is of primary importance, as in some of Heine's "Romanzen" of the *Buch der Lieder*. For his ballad-complaints, Laforgue adopts an artfully "popular" manner. Under the title of "Complainte du pauvre jeune homme" (pp. 119–21), for example, the poet indicates "sur l'air populaire:

---

* Health and a supplement of money, that's all, oh Lord, I ask. Oh let me happily still live many beautiful days beside my wife in statu quo.

† —Well then, let's smoke a little pipe of tobacco while leafing through one of those old almanacs, dreaming of the little one who would join to the charms of the carnation those of the goldfinch.

'Quand le bonhomm' revint du bois' " ("To the popular tune: 'When the good man came back from the woods' "). And this macabre tale of the poor young man, thrown out by his mistress' husband and abandoned by his own wife, who finally kills himself, can indeed be sung, each stanza closing with the refrain: "Digue dondaine, digue dondon!" Another example of this form is the following piece, the "Complainte de l'Epoux out-ragé" ("Complaint of the Outraged Husband") (pp. 122–23), to be sung "sur l'air populaire: 'Qu'allais-tu faire à la fontaine?' " ("to the popular tune: 'What were you going to do at the fountain?' "). Here the story of an adulterous wife caught with her lover by her husband—in church—consists of a dialogue between the pair,

> * —Qu'alliez-vous faire à la Mad'leine,
>   Corbleu, ma moitié.
> Qu'alliez-vous faire à la Mad'leine?
>   —J'allais prier pour qu'un fils nous vienne,
>   Mon Dieu, mon ami;
> J'allais prier pour qu'un fils nous vienne,

and ends with an unconvinced husband killing his wife, who in dying sends her soul to her lover. The poem is reminiscent of Heine's "Gespräch auf der Paderborner Heide" ("Conversation on the Heath of Paderborn"), also a mock-ballad in dialogue form, in which the same events are seen from two different points of view:[37]

> † Hörst du nicht das Waldhorn blasen?
>   Jäger sich des Weidwerks freuen,
>   . . . .
>   "Ei, mein Freund, was du vernommen,
>   Ist kein Waldhorn, noch Schalmeie;

* What were you going to do at the Madeleine, by God, my spouse? What were you going to do at the Madeleine? I was going to pray for a son, my God, my friend; I was going to pray for a son.

† Do you not hear the blowing of the horn? Hunters delight in the chase, . . . "Why, my friend, what you have heard is neither hunting horn nor bell. I only see the swineherd coming, driving home his swine.

Nur den Sauhirt seh'ich kommen,
Heimwärts treibt er seine Säue (DA, I: 109–11).

The romantic "Waldhorn," ironically deflated by the poem's second voice, was an image which became dear to Laforgue. We recall the beloved of the "Complainte des formalités nuptiales" (pp. 84–7) and her "I would always like to listen to this hunting horn," "Look, one can no longer hear that horn; that horn, you know. . . .," and the importance of that motif in the *Derniers Vers*, the "Taïaut" Taïaut! et hallali!" ("Tally-ho! Tally-ho!" and flourish of the horn as the death blow is given) of "L'Hiver qui vient" ("Winter Approaching") and from the same piece the lines: "Les cors, les cors, les cors—mélancoliques! . . .," ("The horns, the horns, the melancholy horns!"), as well as the second poem, "Le Mystère des trois cors" of the same collection.[38]

Thematically there are many parallels between our poets, all connected with the principal theme they share, frustrated love. Thus, for example, both poet personas insist that their beloved appreciate their verse. In one of Heine's *Heimkehr* poems, #72, the poet lover tells his future wife:

* Und wenn du schiltst und wenn du tobst,
Ich werd' es geduldig leiden;
Doch wenn du meine Verse nicht lobst,
Laß ich mich von dir scheiden (DA, I: 287).

We recall with what violence the poet lover of the "Complainte des blackboulés" blackballs his unappreciative love; in fact, he wishes her tortured to death:

† Et voilà ce que moi, guéri, je vous souhaite,
   Coeur rose, pour
   Avoir un jour
Craché sur l'Art pur! sans compter le poète (pp. 88–9).

* And if you scold, and if you rage, I will patiently bear it; but if you don't praise my verse, I will get a divorce.
† And here is what I, cured, wish upon you, pink Heart, for having one day spit on pure Art! not to mention the poet.

Indian lore is a sub-theme manifest in both Heine's and Laforgue's poetry. But here we are dealing with affinity, rather than influence, as the poets became involved with the theme by different paths of the vast intertext. Laforgue became acquainted with it through his Buddhist studies, inspired by Schopenhauer, while Heine could not escape the widespread cult of India of the 1820's and 1830's in Germany.[39] We find its sedimentation in one of the *Intermezzo's* most famous poems, #9:

> * Auf den Flügeln des Gesanges,
> Herzliebchen, trag'ich dich fort,
> Fort nach den Fluren des Ganges,
> Dort weiß ich den schönsten Ort.
> Dort liegt ein rotblühender Garten
> Im stillen Mondenschein;
> Die Lotusblumen erwarten
> Ihr trautes Schwesterlein (DA, I: 141).[40]

The following piece of the *Intermezzo*, #10, again celebrates the Lotus flower, and her lover, the moon, thus establishing a Laforguean ambiance par excellence:

> † Die Lotusblume ängstigt
> Sich vor der Sonne Pracht,
> Und mit gesenktem Haupte
> Erwartet sie träumend die Nacht.
> Der Mond, der ist ihr Buhle,
> Er erweckt sie mit seinem Licht',
> Und ihm entschleiert sie freundlich
> Ihr frommes Blumengesicht (DA, I: 143).

In the "Heimkehr" cycle, the theme is elaborated in the fifth stanza of #7. We have already encountered the Indian-Buddhist

---

* On the wings of song, beloved, I carry you off to the plains of the Ganges. There I know the most beautiful spot. There lies a garden with red flowers blossoming in the still moonlight. The lotus flowers are awaiting their beloved little sister.

† The lotus flower fears the splendor of the sun, and with lowered head awaits dreaming the night. The moon is its lover, awakening it with its light. And for the moon it graciously unveils its pious flower face.

theme in the "Complainte des Voix sous le figuier boudhique," and find it alluded to in the title of the "Complainte des Mounis du Mont-Martre" (p. 132), "mounis" being Buddhist monks. The poet, moreover, signed one of his early poems, "Mémento Sonnet triste" (p. 181), "Jules Laforgue—Mouni," as I noted in the preceding chapter. Though affinity rather than influence, Laforgue's reading of the *Intermezzo* certainly must have encouraged his elaboration of the theme.

While Laforgue's persona frequently aspires to the Néant-Nirvana, with karmas and samsaras surpassed, he even more often deplores the obstacles to it, that other Buddhist-Hindu notion of Maya, the illusory world of the senses to which particularly women are enslaved. Thus the final stanza of the "Complainte des formalités nuptiales" predicts the beloved's fate:

> * Elle va perdre, lys pubère,
> Ses nuances si solitaires,
> Pour être à son tour,
> Dame d'atour
> de Maïa!
> Alleluia (p. 87)!

Man's appearance on earth, whose death is mourned in the "Marche funèbre pour la mort de la terre" (pp. 206–9), marks the end of that innocent illusion: "Mais l'être impur paraît! ce frêle révolté / De la sainte Maia déchire les beaux voiles / Et le sanglot des temps jaillit vers les étoiles . . ."† In the same piece, in which the poet with his characteristic anti-intellectual stance rejects Hegel and human reason, he calls on the Buddha and Christ; and both, along with other sages, including Heine, are also evoked in "L'Espérance:"

---

 * She is going to lose, pubescent lily, her so solitary nuances, in order to be, in her turn, tirewoman of Maya! Hallelujah!

 † But the impure being appears! that frail rebel of holy Maya tears the beautiful veils, and the sob of the ages gushes toward the stars.

* Et Bouddha méditant sous le figuier mystique,
Jésus criant vers Dieu son unique abandon,
Lucrèce désolé, Brutus calme et stoïque,
Caton, Léopardi, Henri Heine, Byron,
Tous les sages de l'Inde et tous ceux du Portique
Crurent-ils en mourant que tout était dit?—Non (p. 217).

Laforgue frequently blends Buddhism with Hinduism, and Buddhist-Hindu metempsychosis is alluded to in several early poems, like "Résignation" (p. 223), or one of the "Litanies nocturnes" (p. 245). Hindu ascetics are evoked in a piece dated "14 novembre 1880," evidently intended for *Le Sanglot de la terre*, and entitled "Le Sanglot universel," with "Ceux enfin où Maïa l'Illusion est morte, / Solitaires, muets, flagellés par les vents."† (p. 252). But the "bouddhiste tragique," we noted, was soon abandoned, and another Laforguean persona replaced him: Pierrot.

We first meet him in the "Complainte de Lord Pierrot" and "Autre Complainte de Lord Pierrot," and this figure dominates the *recueil L'Imitation de Notre-Dame la Lune*, which Laforgue published in November 1885. The rich literary heritage of the figure has been retraced by recent scholarship.[41] As Laforgue now comes into his own voice, and as thus other literary echoes, including the Heinean, are progressively left behind, his major persona, Pierrot, who in one of his "Locutions" exclaims

‡ Ah! tout le long du coeur
Un vieil ennui m'effleure. . .
M'est avis qu'il est l'heure
De renaître moqueur (p. 39),

* And Buddha meditating under the mystic fig tree, Jesus crying out his unique abandon to God, Lucretius desolate, Brutus calm and stoical, Cato, Leopardi, Heinrich Heine, Byron, all the sages of India and all those of the Portico, did they believe while dying that all had been said?—No.
† Those finally where Maya the Illusion has died, solitary, silent beings flagellated by the winds.
‡ Ah! all along my heart an old anxiety touches me lightly. . . My impression is that it's time to be reborn given to mockery.

is, however, indeed akin to Heine. Heine, too, frequently saw himself as harlequin.[42] We recall here, moreover, the magnificent portrait that Nerval had painted of his friend as *poète-Pierrot*, to the very tear in his eye!

The Buddhist-Hindu theme is now treated in the Heinean mode, the ironic and mocking tone of Pierrot, who in another of his "Locutions" professes:

> * Ainsi pour mes moeurs et mon art,
> C'est la période védique
>   . . . .
> C'est comme notre Bible hindoue
> Qui, tiens, m'amène à caresser,
> Avec ces yeux de cétacé,
> Ainsi, bien sans but, ta joue (p. 39).

In "La Lune est stérile" (p. 54), the romantic lotus becomes part of a violent invective against the very moon as collaborator with Nature's ways, in a total inversion of Romantic imagery:

> † Tu ne sais que la fleur des sanglantes chimies;
> Et perces nos rideaux, nous offrant le lotus
> Qui constipe les plus larges polygamies,
> Tout net, de l'excrément logique des foetus.

We note here the recurrence of the "obsession hématique;" similarly, in "La Vie qu'elles me font mener" ("The Life They Make Me Lead"), one of the poems of the posthumously published collection *Des Fleurs de bonne volonté* (*Flowers of Good Will*), the invective is directed against woman, the traditionally virginal lotus becoming a Flower of Evil.[43] In "Esthétique," of the same *recueil*, however, Pierrot—though still bleeding—takes his destiny more calmly:

---

* Thus for my manners and my art, it's the Vedic period. . . . It is like our Hindu Bible which, well, induces me to caress thus, with these eyes of a cetacean, aimlessly indeed, your cheek.

† You only know the flower of bloody chemistries, and pierce our curtains, offering us the lotus that constipates the greatest polygamies, to be blunt, with the logical excrement of foetuses.

> * Je le prends par la douceur, en Sage,
> Tout aux arts, au bon coeur, aux voyages . . .
> Et vais m'arlequinant des défroqués
> Des plus grands penseurs de chaque époque . . .
>
> Et saigne! en jurant que je me blinde
> Des rites végétatives de l'Inde . . . (p. 95).

Finally, then, his miseries have been reduced to manageable proportions, as in "Petites Misères de mai," whose opening once more recalls a former phase—"avant d'être dilettante et Pierrot, j'ai séjourné dans le Cosmique"—that of the "bouddhiste tragique" and of the sentimental poet, now surpassed: "On dit l'Express: Pour Bénarès / La Basilique / Des gens cosmiques! . . ." (p. 147).† In the following poem, significantly entitled "Petites Misères d'autommne," our love poet recalls how he had once bled:

> ‡ Ses boudoirs pluvieux mirent en sang
> Mon inutile coeur d'adolescent . . .
> Et j'en dormis. A l'aube je m'enfuis . . .
> Bien égal aujourd'hui (p. 150).

It is Heine who taught him how to heal his wounds and his art.

In Laforgue's late poetry, then, the direct Heinean echoes are few, even as the poet becomes a sort of French Heine of the *fin de siècle*. Moreover, as I have already noted, he never hesitated acknowledging his indebtedness to his master; and previous commentators have acknowledged those Laforguean tributes to Heine, without attempting to trace their origins. In our exploration of these origins, the reverberations of Heine's early poetry, and particularly *Lyrisches Intermezzo*, in Laforgue's early

---

* I am taking it calmly, like a sage, all given to the arts, to the good heart, to voyages . . . And I am going to clown it with the unfrocked of the greatest thinkers of each epoch . . . And bleed! swearing that I am arming myself with the vegetative rites of India.

† They say the Express for Benares, the basilica of the cosmic people.

‡ Her rainy boudoirs bloodied my useless heart of an adolescent . . . And I slept over it. At dawn I fled . . . Makes no difference today.

verse, we have touched on fundamental affinities between the two ironists who wrote most of their work in exile, attitudes which throw new light on a significant facet of Franco-German literary relations.

Notes

¹ For an excellent discussion of direct and mediated influence, cf. Claudio Guillén, *Literature as System* (Princeton: Princeton University Press, 1971), 17–57, "The Aesthetics of Literary Influence."

² Bibliothèque Nationale, *Intermezzo, poème de Henri Heine trad. en vers français par Paul Ristelhuber* (Paris: Poulet-Malassis, 1857). In-16, 88 pp. [Yh 2740].

³ For the history of the publication and reception of these volumes of poetry, cf. DA, I/2: 575ff. and 784ff.

⁴ Charles Dédéyan, *Gérard de Nerval et l'Allemagne* (Paris: SEDES, 1975), 2 Vols. Alfred Dubruck, *Gérard de Nerval and the German Heritage* (The Hague: Mouton, 1965).

⁵ Gérard de Nerval, *Faust, tragédie de Goethe: Nouvelle traduction complète en prose et en vers par Gérard* (Paris: Dondé-Dupré, 1828); *Poésies Allemandes: Klopstock, Goethe, Schiller, Bürger: morceaux choisis et traduits par Gérard* (Paris: Méquignon, Harvard, Bricon, 1830).

⁶ *Revue des Deux Mondes*, XXIII, (1848): 224–43 and 914–30. Regarding Nerval's Heine translations and his introduction and commentary, cf. Haskell M. Block's essay on "Heine and the French Symbolists" in *Creative Encounter: Festschrift for Herman Salinger*, ed. Leland R. Phelps (Chapel Hill: University of North Carolina Press, 1978), 26: "Recent study has shown that large sections of the introduction and commentary were actually written by Gautier and were then subjected to minor alterations by Nerval. This collaboration makes the introductory essay all the more interesting in the light of Gautier's importance for Baudelaire and his followers." That is, Nerval's "Les Poésies de Henri Heine" was written in collaboration with Gautier, while the second essay, preceding his translation of *Lyrisches Intermezzo*, was Nerval's own.

⁷ *Poèmes et légendes* (1868), 81–7, for Nerval's "Notice du traducteur."

⁸ For a definition of the "paratext," and its role in intertextuality, cf. Gérard Genette, *Palimpsestes* (Paris: Editions du Seuil, 1982), 9: ". . . la relation, généralement moins explicite et plus distante que, dans l'ensemble formé par une oeuvre littéraire, le texte proprement dit entretient avec ce que l'on ne peut guère nommer que son *paratexte*; titre, sous-titre, intertitres; préfaces, postfaces, avertissements, avant-propos, etc.; . . ." Genette, here, however, restricts "paratexte" to an author's own commentary on a text, citing as example Joyce's titles for sections of *Ulysses* published before the entire book

came out, and in which those "paratexts" were then omitted. He further includes "brouillons," sketches to works, abandoned by their author as he publishes the definitive text. For my definition of the "paratext," cf. "Laforgue and His Philosophers," (Cf. note 25, Chapter I).

⁹ *Les Complaintes*, 178–9 and 216–19. All quotations from Laforgue's early poetry and *Les Complaintes* will be from the Pascal Pia (Gallimard) edition, unless otherwise indicated, and marked by page number.

¹⁰ *Heinrich Heine Sämmtliche Werke*, Neue Ausgabe in zwölf Bäden, Erster Band (Hamburg: Hofmann und Campe, 1890), 182. The original Hoffmann und Campe edition of Heine's complete works (*Sämmtliche Werke*, Originalausgabe, Hamburg: 1861–69) was available to Laforgue at the Bibliothèque Nationale [8° Z50351–50372]. In the Calmann-Lévy edition of Heine's works in French the piece is reproduced in the volume *Poésies inédites* under "Intermède lyrique," not numbered and the seventh of eight. This prose version reads: "Belles et claires étoiles d'or, saluez ma bien-aimée en lointain pays; dites-lui que je suis toujours malade de coeur, et pâle, et fidèle." *Poésies inédites* (1898), 83. Nerval's version of "L'Intermezzo" appears in this edition in the volume *Poèmes et légendes*, cf. note 7 above.

¹¹ Jules Laforgue, *Lettres à un Ami* (1880–1886) (Paris: Mercure de France, 1941), 23.

¹² Laforgue, *Lettres* I: 75.

¹³ *Lettres*, I: 77–78.

¹⁴ *Lettres à un Ami*, 41.

¹⁵ Sakari, *Prophète et Pierrot*, 111.

¹⁶ The two Heinean lines are from "Zum Lazarus" #11, last stanza: "Gesundheit nur und Geldzulage / Verlang ich, Herr! O laß mich froh / Hinleben noch viel schöne Tage / Bei meiner Frau im statu quo" (B, VI: 208)! In the French Heine edition, *Poèmes et légendes*, 358, "Le Livre de Lazare," the translation reads as follows: "De la santé et un supplément d'argent, c'est tout ce que je te demande, Seigneur! Oh! laisse-moi vivre encore de beaux jours auprès de ma femme dans le *statu quo!*" The variant in Laforgue's epigraph suggests that it was his own translation.

¹⁷ For example, Erich Mayser, *H. Heines "Buch der Lieder" im 19. Jahrhundert* (Stuttgart: Akademischer Verlag Hans-Dieter Heinz, 1978); Alberto Destro, "Das *Buch der Lieder* und seine Leser: Die Prämissen einer mißlungenen Rezeption," in *Zu Heinrich Heine* (Stuttgart: Ernst Klett, 1981); Manfred Windfuhr, "Heinrich Heines deutsches Publikum (1820–1860). Vom Lieblingsautor des Adels zum Anreger der bürgerlichen Intelligenz" in *Literatur in der sozialen Bewegung. Aufsätze und Forschungsberichte zum 19. Jahrhundert* (Tübingen: Martino, 1977), 260–83.

¹⁸ Only after the 1830's did sales pick up, a fourth edition being printed in 1841, the fifth, *Ausgabe letzter Hand*, on which all modern editions are based, in 1844, the thirteenth coming out in 1855.

[19] Cf. Windfuhr, "Heinrich Heines deutsches Publikum." Also Destro, "Das *Buch der Lieder* und seine Leser," 16.

[20] Cf. Mayser, *Heines "Buch der Lieder" im 19. Jahrhundert*, 22–32.

[21] Walter A. Behrendson, "Heines 'Buch der Lieder,' Struktur- und Stilstudie" in *Heine-Jahrbuch* (1962), 30, reproduces the following report of Heine-*Vertonungen*: "Die meist vertonten Gedichte bis 1914 nach Ernst Challiers Liederkatalog sind:

Du bist wie eine Blume	222	Liedpublikationen
Ein Fichtenbaum	121	"
Ich hab im Traum geweinet	99	"
Mädchen mit dem roten Mündchen	88	"
Und wüßtens die Blumen	88	"
Im wunderschönen Monat Mai	83	"
Wenn ich in deine Augen seh	73	"
Ich will meine Seele tauchen	72	"
Ich stand in dunklen Träumen	69	"
Hör ich das Liedchen klingen	62	"

Von diesen meistkomponierten Liedern stehen 7 im 'Lyrschen Intermezzo,' drei in der 'Heimkehr,' 6 haben 8, 3 haben 12, nur eins hat 16 Zeilen."

[22] S. S. Prawer, *Heine: Buch der Lieder* (London: Edward Arnold Publishers Ltd., 1960), 18.

[23] Mayser, *Heines "Buch der Lieder" in 19. Jahrhundert*, 83.

[24] Laforgue, *Lettres* I: 76–77.

[25] Laforgue adapted these lines, with only minor variations, as final stanza of the "Complainte de la Vigie aux minuits polaires:" "Un coeur tout en sang, / Un bon coeur ruisselant, / Qui, du soir à l'aurore, / Et de l'aurore au soir, / Se meurt, de ne pouvoir / Saigner, ah! saigner plus encore!" (68–9).

[26] Jean-Pierre Richard, "Le sang de la complainte," *Poétique*, 40 (1979): 477–95.

[27] *Les Complaintes*, 220.

[28] *Lettres à un Ami*, 37.

[29] Laforgue, *Oeuvres complètes*, V, *Lettres-II (1883–1887)*, 20–21.

[30] Jules Laforgue, *Les Complaintes, L'Imitation de Notre-Dame la Lune texte présenté et commenté par Pierre Reboul* (Paris: Collection de l'Imprimerie Nationale, 1981), 15–16.

[31] *Posthumes de Laforgue*, "Feuilles volantes," in *La Revue blanche*, X, (1896): 370–71, #8 (Genève: Slatkine Reprints, 1968).

[32] *Lettres à un Ami*, 79.

[33] Sigmund Freud, *Der Witz und seine Beziehung zum Unbewußten* (Frankfurt: Fischer, 1958), esp. 13ff, "Die Technik des Witzes," a chapter which Freud opens with the Heinean example "famillionär," and in which he discusses other examples drawn from the poet's work. For a detailed discussion of the portmanteau word in Heine, cf. Almuth Grésillon, *La règle et le*

monstre: le mot-valise. Interrogation sur la langue, à partir d'un corpus de Heinrich Heine (Tübingen: Max Niemeyer Verlag, 1984). After carefully analyzing all forms of these neologisms, not merely in Heine, but also citing a few examples from Laforgue among many others, the author discusses their formation in relation to the Freudian notion of condensation (*Verdichtung*) and then concentrates on Heine's sixty-two forms of the phenomenon, "object de scandale." She concludes that for Heine the *mot-valise* is the privileged means of expressing the forbidden, "de donner corps à un non-dit devant lequel les mots usuels se révèlent insuffisants, sinon impuissants." But Heine's use of these "monsters" diverges sharply from those of Laforgue in that it is linked to the experience of political exile. And one of the most frequent modes "par lequel le mot-valise de Heine rend compte de l'insupportable situation politique consiste à opérer, dans l'artefact d'un mot en principe impossible et monstrueux, l'impossible fusion du pouvoir et du contre-pouvoir. . . . Face à l'impossibilité de mener le combat politique, Heine transfère le combat sur le terrain de la langue, il porte le scandale au corps même de la langue en transgressant les régularités de celle-ci. . . . Il mène le combat sur le terrain qui fut le sien, celui du langage" (126 and 130). For a study of Laforgue's vocabulary, cf. Madeleine Betts, *L'Univers de Laforgue à travers les mots* (Paris: La Pensée universelle, 1978).

   [34] In a letter to his publisher, Vanier, of February or March 1885, Laforgue writes about the poem: "You will see that I have added a lot to the piece *the voices etc.*, for me the most important (significant) in a sense of the volume— I have numbered the series of distiches in the order in which they will be placed.—I hope that the matter will be taken care of all right. An error in this piece would annoy me.—" Debauve, *Laforgue et son temps*, 95.

   [35] "For Heine love is a catastrophe, almost a vice," says Sammons. "It lures and excites, holding out promises it does not keep, ripping up the fabric of the self. Yet the desire for love is inextinguishable; the longing that it might somehow actually be what it feels like remains" (*A Modern Biography*, 61). Precisely this holds true for Laforgue as much as for Heine.

   [36] The "serin," incidentally, which translates the German "Gimpel," also has the secondary meaning of "niais, nigaud" (simple fool), so that the *Intermezzo* translation retains the irony for the French reader.

   [37] This piece is in the French edition in *Poésies inédites*, 49–50, under the general heading "Romances," and entitled "Dialogue dans la Lande de Paderborn."

   [38] Laforgue, *L'Imitation de Notre-Dame la Lune*, 182–5. All quotations from Laforgue's poetry from these collections, as well as his other late poetry, will refer to this (Pia-Gallimard) edition, unless otherwise indicated, and be marked by page number.

   [39] A. W. Schlegel, one of his professors at Bonn, held the Chair for Sanskrit there, while the great Franz Bopp held the first Chair for Sanskrit at Berlin, at

the time when Heine also visited Hegel's lectures there. Though Heine never passed, like Laforgue, through a Buddhist phase, his reading of Herder had exposed him to the Romantics' enthusiasm for Indian culture.

[40] Georg Forster's translation of the "Sakontala" furnished Heine's source for Indian "Blumenromantik." Cf. DA, I/2, 787.

[41] A very recent study of the theme is Louisa E. Jones's excellent *Sad Clowns and Pale Pierrots* (Kentucky: French Forum Publishers, 1984); cf. the chapter devoted to Laforgue, 225–31. The best-known work on the theme is Jean Starobinski's *Portrait de l'artiste en Saltimbanque* (Genève: Skira, 1970). Cf. Also A.C. Lehmann, "Pierrot et fin de siècle" in *Romantic Mythologies* (New York: Barnes and Noble, 1967), 209–23. Also, Robert F. Storey, *Pierrot: A Critical History of a Mask* (Princeton: Princeton University Press, 1978), esp. the chapter "Pierrot Fumiste: Jules Laforgue," 139–55. And most recently, by the same author, *Pierrots on the Stage of Desire* (Princeton: Princeton University Press, 1985).

[42] Cf. Jürgen Voigt, *Ritter, Henker, Harlekin: der junge Heine als romantischer Patriot und als Jude* (Frankfurt: Peter Lang, 1982). This study throws light on the emergence of the Harlequin figure especially in Heine's prose, in connection with his struggles as Jewish writer.

[43] I have pointed to the allusion to "Le Lotus de la bonne Loi," a major Buddhist text, which Laforgue might have had in mind, "Laforgue and His Philosophers" (Cf. note 25, Chapter I).

III

Counterparts: Heine and Laforgue and the Theater

This chapter stands under the sign of "counterparting," established by Lilian Furst in Franco-German Comparative Literature, for it is by counterparting that I shall examine the two poets' relation to the theater.[1] I shall be concerned here not merely with their endeavors and failures as playwrights, with their early plays and the dramatic sketches and scenarios that preoccupied them later in their careers, but also with some of the sedimentation that was to mark the famous lyric poetry of these dramatists *manqués*. Then, in counterparting Heine's Shakespeare and Laforgue's in the following essay, I shall examine the pivotal position which that poet, foreign to them both, occupied in their work, thus constituting a strong intertextual link between them. As literary journalists, moreover, Heine and Laforgue discussed theater critically, as well as other, related, performing arts, like music, opera, dance, and the circus. These too will be examined as part—as counterpart—of the theater in Heine and Laforgue, in a subsequent chapter.

We recall that the cycle of Heine's poems that enjoyed the greatest popularity in nineteenth-century France, and that most directly influenced Laforgue, was *Lyrisches Intermezzo*. He published it in 1823 in the same volume—*Tragödien nebst einem lyrischen Intermezzo*—as his tragedies *Almansor* and *William*

Ratcliff. He had already published some excerpts from *Alman-sor* under the title *Almansor. Fragments from a Dramatic Poem* in November of 1821 in the Berlin review *Der Gesellschaftler*.[2] And while *Almansor* never reappeared during Heine's lifetime, the poet published a French translation of *William Ratcliff*, entitled *William et Marie*, in 1840 in the Revue de Paris; he also included that tragedy in the third edition of *Neue Gedichte* in 1852.[3] Both plays appeared in the French edition of Heine's works in the volume *Drames et fantaisies* in 1864, preceded by a long preface of the translator, Saint René Taillandier,[4] who had published that same text as an article, interspersed with excerpts from *Almansor*, in the *Revue des Deux Mondes* in 1863.[5]

Heine began writing *Almansor* in the late summer of 1820, while vacationing in Beuel near Bonn; he had begun his law studies the previous year at the recently founded University of Bonn, where he also visited the colloquia of one of Germany's great Shakespeareans, August Wilhelm Schlegel. Schlegel encouraged his student's poetic efforts and deeply impressed him then, despite the highly satirical account of that experience which Heine was to leave later in *Die Romantische Schule*.[6] One of Heine's Bonn student friends, Johann Baptist Rousseau, recalls:

> Heine spent the fall of 1820 at Beuel, the friendly little village across from Bonn, and began his tragedy *Almansor* there in deepest seclusion. . . . He read it to me scene by scene, as it flowed from his pen, and at the same time gave me many a good lesson about the possible structures of the iambic pentameter which had become clear to him through his practice.[7]

In the fall, Heine moved to Göttingen to continue his studies, and on October 20, he reports to his friend that he has almost completed the third act of *Almansor*, continuing:

> I hope this winter also to finish the two remaining acts. Even if the play should not please, it will at least attract great attention. I have thrown my own self into this play, with all my paradoxes, my wisdom, my love, my hatred and all my madness. . . . I have completely adhered to Aristotle's comments and have conscientiously adopted his strictures with respect

to place, time and action.—I have further also sought to bring some
poetry into my tragedy . . . (HSA, XX: 29).

In February of the following year, Heine writes to another
friend, Friedrich Steinmann, that *Almansor* is almost finished, to
the last half of the fifth act. But now he doubts whether it even
merits the claim to be a tragedy, let alone a good one. There is,
Heine continues, much poetic beauty and originality in it;
however, he now feels that perhaps he simply has no dramatic
talent, or that he might have been unduly influenced by French
classical tragedy with its strict adherence to the three unities,
limited *dramatis personae*, and preciosity of expression, as in
Phèdre or *Zaïre*. And he concludes his long, discouraged discussion of *Almansor* by suggesting that it might experience the
same fate as Schlegel's *Ion*:

> . . . I have tried, in drama too, to combine the romantic spirit with strong
> plastic form. Therefore my tragedy will meet with the same fate as
> Schlegel's *Ion*. For the latter was likewise written with a polemical
> purpose (HSA, XX: 36–37).

In March 1821, Heine moved to Berlin, where he continued
his law studies and where he was to become the student of yet
another of Germany's most famous teachers, Hegel. It is here,
we recall, that Heine published excerpts from *Almansor* in the
Gesellschaftler, and where in three January days of 1822 he
wrote his other tragedy, *William Ratcliff*.[8]

Almansor takes place in late 15th-century Granada, the last
Moslem stronghold in Ferdinand and Isabella's christianized
Spain. Almansor, who had left his home with his parents,
Abdullah and Fatima, to escape conversion, returns after their
death in Africa to once more see Zuleima, the bride chosen for
him since their childhood days. Her father, Aly, had converted
to Christianity and changed his name to Don Gonzalvo, in order
to be able to remain in his homeland. He is presently preparing,
moreover, for the wedding of Zuleima, now Doña Clara, to a
certain Don Enrique, a false noble and crook who, driven by his
"servant," in reality Don Diego and a former jail companion,

wants to marry the girl for her fortune. Before the wedding, Aly explains to the groom—and us—that Doña Clara-Zuleima is really not his own daughter, but the child of Abdullah and Fatima, who had raised his own son, Almansor, each family thus adopting the future spouse of their child. But the close friendship of the two families was brusquely and violently broken by Aly's conversion and the flight of Abdullah, who had sworn to kill Almansor in revenge for his own daughter's and her foster father's conversion. The dramatic situation thus resembles that of *Romeo and Juliet*, with the children's love fated by their families' hostility.

Almansor arrives in Granada in the ruins of his father's abandoned castle the very night when the pre-wedding celebrations festively illuminate Aly's palace. He is intercepted by his father's former servant, Hassan, who had chosen to remain behind in Spain to lead a group of underground Moslems hidden in the hills around Granada, and who almost kills Almansor disguised in Spanish costume. When he embraces his master's son, he gives him—and us—a lengthy exposition of conditions in Granada, where Moslems fought and died for their creed, where others converted like Aly, and others still betrayed their brothers. Not only were the Moslems divided in the defeat, but the priests were the worst among them:

> * Gibt's irgendwo 'nen Glauben zu verschachern,
> So sind zuerst die Pfaffen bei der Hand (B, I: 284).

Then Almansor relates how they heard during their flight in Africa about the horrors of the Inquisition in Spain, of the burning of the sacred book by the horrible Great Inquisitor, "der furchtbare Ximenes," whereupon Hassan replies with the justly famous and tragically prophetic lines:

> † Das war ein Vorspiel nur, dort, wo man Bücher
> Verbrennt, verbrennt man auch am Ende Menschen (B, I: 284–85).

---

* If there's a faith to barter anywhere, the priests are first at hand.
† That was a prelude merely. Where they burn books, in the end they will also burn people.

An even more extensive exposition of the Moslem defeat in Spain is presented by a Chorus later in the play, in what constituted the third act, before Heine decided to omit the division into five acts for publication is 1823.

The tableau in which Almansor enters Aly's castle introduces the traditional comic figure in the domestic Pedrillo, formerly Hamahmah, who can't get used to swearing in Christian and tells Almansor how sadly things have changed:

> * Beim Barte des Propheten—ich wollte sagen
> Der heiligan Eli—Elisabeth—
> Das Schloß ist keine Herberg' mehr (B, I: 295).

When Almansor serenades Zuleima, she thinks she is in a dream, since she had believed him dead. His presence rekindles her love, and their lyric duet's blood imagery presages the tragic outcome:

> † Almansor: Und floß auch Blut schon aus Almansors Seele,
> Am Grab der Mutter und am Grab des Vaters,
> So muß sie hier doch ganz und gar verbluten,
> Hier an dem Grabe von Zuleimas Liebe.
> Zuleima: O schlimme Worte und noch schlimmre Kunden!
> Ihr bohrt euch schneidend ein in meine Brust,
> Und auch Zuleimas Seele muß verbluten (B, I: 303–4).

Then Zuleima pleads with Almansor to flee her father's wrath:

> ‡ Dich darf er nimmer schaun, entflieh! entflieh!
> Der Väter Feindschaft bringt den Kindern Tod (B, I: 307),

recalling Shakespeare's most famous lovers. And while Almansor invokes Medschûn and Leilâ, the lovers of Nisâmi's Persian

---

* By the beard of the Prophet—I meant of the holy Eli—Elizabeth—The castle is not longer any refuge.

† Almansor: And if blood already flowed from Almansor's soul on the mother's and the father's grave, so it must altogether bleed to death, here on the grave of Zuleima's love.

Zuleima: Oh awful words and still more awful tidings! You stab and cut my breast, and Zuleima's soul, too, must bleed to death.

‡ He must never see you, flee! flee! The fathers' hostility brings death to the children.

epic, Zuleima wants to sublimate their love to immortality in a Christian afterlife:

> * Die Erde ist ein großes Golgatha,
> Wo zwar die Liebe siegt, doch auch verblutet.
> . . . .
> Nimm hin dagegen Christi Lebenskuß (B, I: 313).

Almansor, though horrified by the images of the Christian martyrized god, and by the priests who in their ritual drink his blood, is ready to let himself be converted to his beloved's creed as price for their happiness. But when Zuleima reveals that in this life she is promised to another, Don Enrique, Almansor cries out in black—Romantic—despair. As he is about to kill himself, after Hamlet-like reflections on the worth of life and of death, Hassan, the valiant Moslem, entices him to live and steal his own, Zuleima, and flee with her:

> † Almansor: . . . Ich bin recht müd',
> Und krank, und kranker noch als krank, denn ach!
> Die allerschlimmste Krankheit ist das Leben;
> Und heilen kann sie nur der Tod. . . .
> . . . .
> Hassan: Nein, Sohn Abdullahs, feige ist der Schwächling,
> Der keine Kraft hat mit dem Schwert zu ringen,
> Und ihm den Nacken zeigt, und zaghaft von
> Des Lebens Kampfplatz flieht—steh auf, Almansor!

* The earth is a great Golgatha, where love indeed conquers, but where it also bleeds to death. . . . Instead accept Jesus' kiss of life.

† Almansor: I am quite tired, and sick, and sicker still than sick, for oh! the very worst of ills is life; and only death can heal it.

Hassan: No, son of Abdullah, cowardly is the weakling who has no strength to fight by the sword, and turns his back and faintheartedly flees life's battlefield—stand up, Almansor! Almansor: By whose fault does this fruit lie on the ground? Hassan: by wind and storm; first the worm gnaws the fibers, and then the storm easily throws down the fruit. Almansor: Thus must not man, the very weakest fruit, also fall to the ground, when the worm, the worst of worms, gnawed away the strength of life and he is shaken by the wild storm of despair?

Almansor, picking a chestnut from the ground:
    Durch wessen Schuld liegt diese Frucht zu Boden?
Hassen: Durch Wind und Sturm; Der Wurm zernagt die Fasern,
    Und leicht wirft dann der Sturm die Frucht herab.
Almansor: Soll nun der Mensch, die allerschwächste Frucht.
    Nicht auch zu Boden fallen, wenn der Wurm,
pointing to his heart,
    Der schlimmste Wurm die Lebenskraft zernagte,
    Und der Verzweiflung wilder Sturm ihn rüttelt (B, I:
    319–21)?

Hassen talks Almansor out of his philosophical despair into action. Together they storm Aly's castle and abduct the bride; and the final tableau shows us Almansor with the fainted Zuleima in his arms, high up on a cliff. As she awakens, she thinks she is already in heaven, reunited with her true love. But as Almansor hears Aly's men approaching, he precipitates himself from the cliff with Zuleima in his arms. Aly, who wanted to save his son, after the dying Hassan had told him that the intruding knight was Almansor, comes too late to unite his children in life, and calls on his new God in the face of their death:

    * Jetzt, Jesu Christ, bedarf ich deines Wortes,
    Und deines Gnadentrostes, und deines Beispiels.
    Der Allmacht Willen kann ich nicht begreifen,
    Doch Ahnung sagt mir: ausgereutet wird
    Die Lilie und die Myrte auf dem Weg,
    Worüber Gottes goldner Siegeswagen
    Hinrollen soll in stolzer Majestät (B, I: 337).

Thus the tragedy does indeed represent, as Heine himself had said, the spirit of Romanticism linked to classic form; and into it he had thrown all his wisdom, his love, his hatred and his madness! The piece was a total failure! It came to only one

---

* Now, Jesus Christ, I need your word and your merciful consolation, and your example. I cannot comprehend the will of the Almighty, but a foreboding tells me: the lily and the myrtle shall be exterminated on the way on which God's golden chariot of victory shall roll in proud majesty.

performance during Heine's lifetime, on August 20, 1823, in Braunschweig,[9] where it was hissed off the stage, allegedly because its author was mistaken for a detested local Jewish money changer of the same name. In 1899, the play was put on in Berlin, likewise without success.[10] As Heine had himself suggested, the piece was poetic, rather than dramatic, the play of a lyric poet not very familiar with the exigencies of the theater, who had read many French classics during his teens and some Shakespeare more recently, whose acquaintance with the theater was bookish, rather than practical. Thus, all his characters speak the same language of high style, their speeches often are of inordinate length, and Pedrillo-Hamahmah's humor appears a bit forced. In its first published form in *Der Gesellschaftler*, Heine called his composition a "dramatisches Gedicht;" he must have felt that it was a dramatic poem, rather than a poetic drama. This is further borne out by the fact that in the 1823 publication he omitted the division into acts, as well as a formal *dramatis personae*, although he still does call it "eine Tragödie." In the eight-line liminal poem, however, he refers to it as a "pretty song," "half epic and half drastic," i.e. dramatic:

> * Glaubt nicht, es sei so ganz und gar phantastisch
> Das hübsche Lied, das ich euch freundlich biete!
> Hört zu: es its halb episch und halb drastisch,
> Dazwischen blüht auch manche lyrisch zarte Blüte;
> Romantisch ist der Stoff, die Form ist plastisch,
> Das Ganze aber kam aus dem Gemüte:
> Es kämpften Christ und Moslem, Nord und Süden,
> Die Liebe kommt am End' und macht den Frieden (B, I: 276).

As Taillandier was quick to point out, Love did not come to make peace at the end: "it is not love that appeases everything in the end, but death and delirium."[11]

---

* Do not believe that it is entirely fantastic, the pretty song which I offer you graciously! Listen: it is half epic and half dramatic. In between also blossoms many a tender lyric bud. The material is Romantic, the form is plastic; the whole came from the soul. Christian and Moslem fought, North and South. Love comes in the end to make peace.

Heine's early critics read the play as a dramatic transposition of the young poet's unhappy love for his counsin Amalie, recognizing in Aly's hostile castle his uncle Salomon's Ottensen country house, later to be commemorated as "Affrontenburg" ("Castle of Affronts," B, VI: 199–201). Thus Mutzenbecher, who also points to the influence of Byron on *Almansor*—at the instigation of Schlegel at Bonn—, recalls Heine's later dedication of the tragedies to his uncle:

> * Meine Qual und meine Klagen
> Hab ich in dieses Buch gegossen,
> Und wenn Du es aufgeschlagen,
> Hat sich Dir mein Herz ergossen,

concluding "that the entire drama is animated and indeed carried by the unhappy love for his cousin Amalie Heine."[12]

Some contemporary critics had, however, already recognized the reflection of another of Heine's "Qualen" in *Almansor*, that of anti-Semitism, some even seeing anti-Christian tendencies in the play. Heine denied the latter, writing in April of 1823 to Immermann: "The local malicious coteries of vermin have now already accorded me their dirty tokens of attention, . . . as I hear, they want to impute a biased tenor to *Almansor* and in this way start rumors about it which fill me with sovereign disgust" (HSA, XX: 78). But when he offered the publisher Dümmler what was to become *Tragödien nebst einem Lyrischen Intermezzo*, Heine designated *Almansor* as "a longer dramatic poem, called *Almansor*, whose subject is religio-polemical, dealing with contemporary interests . . . (HSA, XX: 63).

One of the recent "Zeitinteressen" had been the Hep-Hep riots against the Jews in Hamburg and other German communities.[13] Sammons states that "*Almansor* is an early product of Heine's continuing fascination with medieval Spain and the tragic fate of its Moorish and Jewish populations. There can be little doubt that his Moors are an allegorical figuration of

---

* My pain and complaints I have poured into this book.
And when you've opened it, my heart is poured out before you.

oppressed Jewry."[14] At the end of his stay in Bonn, Heine wrote to his friend, Fritz von Beughem: "You cannot imagine, dear Fritz, how often and vividly I think of you. So much the more so as I am presently leading an extremely *sad, sickly*, and *solitary* life. To seek out new friendships is, under the present circumstances, a difficult and inadvisable business, and as concerns my old friends, I think I seem no longer good to them" (HSA, XX: 26). The letter, dated July 15, 1820, is from that summer in which Heine secluded himself at Beuel to work on *Almansor*, whose beginnings grew out of the very spirit reflected in the letter.

It is clearly not so much the famous story of the young poet's unhappy love for his cousin, as it is the infamous history of anti-Semitism experienced by Heine at that period of his life that is objectified in *Almansor* with its "religio-polemical purpose." Although transposed from Jews to Moslems, and placed back three centuries into the past, the tragedy reflects, according to Ludwig Rosenthal, first the recent repression of the Hamburg Jewish minority; secondly, Heine's ambiguous and rather contemptuous stance toward the assimilatory tendencies of Reform Judaism; finally, the poet's disdain for the baptized Jews, in the play the "Maurenchristen."[15] And, as Kircher points out, Heine's historical studies showed him that under Ferdinand and Isabella, the Inquisition in Spain persecuted the Jews almost as severely as the Moslems. This commentator also points out that the tragedy's protagonist, Almansor, is willing to let himself be baptized only to gain Zuleima, but that he never approaches the slightest conversion.[16] Surely, this protagonist might well reflect Heine himself who will shortly succumb to the pressures of German circumstances and become an unbelieving Christian merely to be able to earn his living in his own country.[17] There is, moreover, another reason Heine chose the setting of fifteenth-century Granada and its history for his first tragedy. Charlene A. Lea recalls that "during the years in which HEINE wrote ALMANSOR, he often hinted at a possible, but probably invented Sephardic origin of his own family. The Sephardic Jews of Spain and Portugal . . . were heirs to a highly sophisticated synthesis of Judaic and secular culture with which HEINE apparently wished to be identified."[18]

Heine had read enormously in preparation for his first play, as the record of the books he consulted at Bonn and Göttingen at that time reveals.[19] And Mounir Fendri, in his study on Heine's involvement with the Islamic Orient, shows how thoroughly the poet had familiarized himself with Islamic history and culture.[20] Not merely did Heine read numerous historical works about 15th-century Spain, about Islamic rule in Spain and particularly in Granada, but he also consulted histories of the Inquisition and Cardinal Ximenes, its leading figure. Walter Kanowsky's list of Heine's readings clearly points to the main thrust of *Almansor* as a historical play of religio-polemical intent, which reflects the poet's unhappy love merely incidentally. Heine had, moreover, also consulted Voss' Shakespeare translations as well as an English critical edition, most likely under Schlegel's influence; thus the Shakespearean echoes in Heine's first play.

I have discussed *Almansor* at considerable length, as the poet spent so much time and effort on it. *William Ratcliff*, on the contrary, was written very quickly and, taking place in his own time, needed no historical documentation. On the other hand, Heine had in Berlin gained some first-hand experience of the theater, which he visited assiduously, as reflected in the *Briefe aus Berlin*, written at that period.

William Ratcliff is a family tragedy, placed in northern Scotland, and also a story of ill-fated love. As the nobleman MacGregor is about to betroth his daughter Maria to Lord Douglas, the latter tells how, attacked by robbers on his way to the castle, he was saved by a mysterious horseman. The mysterious horseman turns out to be William Ratcliff, who will later try to kill Douglas, as he had killed Maria's previous fiancés, each time presenting the horrified bride with the slain groom's engagement ring on her wedding nights. From Maria's mad old nurse, Margarete, we learn that Maria's mother, Beautiful-Betty, had in her youth been courted by one Edward Ratcliff, whom she had rejected, marrying MacGregor instead. Thereupon Edward, too, married and had a son, William. But driven to his former love, Edward kept lurking about the MacGregor castle at night, until the jealous husband, Maria's father, had him murdered. Beautiful-Betty died of grief a few days later. But the lovers' ghosts are not at rest. We see them appear in the background of several scenes, two nebulous figures trying to embrace one another. They had haunted William's youth until one day, visiting MacGregor's castle, he recognized the ghostly woman's features in Maria, the girl he was fated to love. Her father, full of remorse, invited William to stay with them, and he courted Maria. When she refused him, afraid of his wild passion, William went to London vainly trying to forget her, wasted away his fortune there, and finally became a member of a gang of outlaws in the Scottish highlands. Thus we see a lengthy scene of the thieves' holdout, where Ratcliff, noble outlaw, plans his combat with Douglas, Maria's most recent fiancé. He summons him to the Schwarzenstein, but this time the ghostly couple does not help him in the fight as formerly; rather, Douglas is aided by the ghosts of the murdered suitors and overcomes William. In return for having saved him from the robbers, Douglas leaves him his life. The wounded William makes his way to the MacGregor castle to abduct Maria before she can become Douglas' wife. When Maria sees him wounded, her love for him returns, and she binds up his wounds with her bridal veil. But when William cannot talk her into fleeing with him, he kills her, and then her father, MacGregor, thus avenging his own father's murder. Then he kills himself, and when Douglas arrives on the scene, he finds it strewn with corpses, crazy Margarete once more evoking the bloody past: MacGregor's murder of Edward Ratcliff now avenged—with both sets of lovers, the ghosts of Edward and Beautiful-Betty, as well as their children, William and Maria, finally at rest.

Heine thus composed a typical Romantic "Schicksals-tragödie," whose protagonist is driven by his destiny, a dark, demonic force which he must blindly obey, and which frequently beckons him to avenge a murder. Such plays usually begin close to the denouement and tend thus to be very short; Heine's play is not divided into acts, but into seventeen scenes leading swiftly to the inevitable tragic outcome. One of Heine's models might well have been Grillparzer's *Ahnfrau*,[21] and the choice of Scotland was no doubt due to Heine's admiration for Sir Walter Scott, of whose great popularity he speaks at length in the second of his *Briefe aus Berlin* (DA, VI: 28).

Again in unrhymed iambic pentameter, *William Ratcliff* shows marked technical improvement over *Almansor*. Avoiding the poetic *longueurs* of his first play, Heine now moves the plot along more swiftly and hence more dramatically. Yet, to Heine's disappointment, *William Ratcliff* was as unsuccessful as *Almansor*, never even reaching the stage, though it was several times transformed into an opera after the poet's death, among others by César Cui and Pietro Mascagni.[22]

That Heine had indeed hoped to see *Ratcliff* performed is evident from the letter to his publisher from which I have quoted above, and in which he says: "I will transmit to you the little tragedy which I have destined for the stage, and which will surely also be produced, as soon as I find you not unfavorably inclined toward my offer." Later that year, he writes to an acquaintance: "I have not abandoned hope yet of seeing *Ratcliff* produced" (HSA, XX: 63 and 102). And many years later, in 1850, he was to ask his friend Heinrich Laube, by then director of the Burg Theater in Vienna, to read the play and "think about whether, with some changes, something could not be made of it for the stage" (HSA, XXIII: 27).

Thus Heine's early confidence, as he had expressed it to Immermann when he had sent him a copy of his book—"I am convinced of the value of this poem *Ratcliff* . . . because it is true, or I myself am a lie; everything else that I have written and will still write may perish" (HSA, XX: 78)—never completely abated. Heine's continued interest in this early work is demonstrated also by his publication of its French translation in 1840, as well as its inclusion in the third edition of *Neue Gedichte* in 1852. In the preface to that edition, Heine justifies its inclusion as follows: "I now concede to this tragedy or dramatic ballad with good reason a place in the collection of my poems, because it belongs as a significant document to the records of my creative life.'' One is reminded of Laforgue's defense of the inclusion of his "Préludes autobiographiques" in *Les Complaintes*. Heine adds that *Ratcliff* commemorates his "Sturm-und-Drang Periode which is revealed very incompletely in the *Young Sorrows* of the *Book of Songs*." In *William Ratcliff*, moreover, "bubbles already the great soup question" which will subsequently preoccupy the world. Heine alludes to the scene of the outlaws, which includes criminals like "honest Tom," driven to crime by a corrupt society. Thus the young poet's prophetic vision of "the oak-forests which still slumber in the acorn." And as Friedrich Schlegel had called the historian a prophet who looks back into the past, so one could say of the poet "that he is a historian whose eyes look toward the future" (B, I: 340).

Heine will plan one more tragedy, which he describes in June 1823 to a friend: "An all new tragedy in five acts and certainly original in every way stands dimly, but in its main outlines, in my mind." Two months later, he writes to Moser: "The tragedy is worked out in my mind. . . . It is becoming very deep and somber. . . . I read a lot about Italy." Then he begs his friend to send him anything he might find about Venice and the Venetian carnival. The following January, he tells his sister that he has not yet written a line of his tragedy, as he must devote his time to this law studies (HSA, XX: 101, 109, 135). Kanowsky's list of the books Heine consulted at the Göttingen University library in the spring of 1824 includes descriptions of Venice and Italy, which Heine probably utilized for his Italian *Reisebilder* after he had abandoned the tragedy.[23] No drafts of the play have come to light so far, and the poet's correspondence suggests that he finally lost interest in it and turned to other projects.

Heine's early ambition and attempts at drama have their counterpart in Laforgue in one of his earliest known texts, only recently come to light: *Tessa, comédie en deux actes et en vers*, dated "Batignolles 1877," published by David Arkell in 1980.[24] The play, written soon after his family had moved to Paris, transposes and transports his most recent preoccupations—his memory of an unhappy love, his fascination with Schopenhauer, and his admiration for Heine—into sixteenth-century Italy, the first act set in Florence, the second in Rome.[25]

In the opening scene, Lucrèce, a Florentine noble lady, arranges with her valet, Amilcar, a somewhat less naïve version of Heine's Pedrillo, to deceive her husband, Ser Girolamo, into believing that she is being courted by the young painter Guido— hero of the play—in order to shield her love affair with one Lorenzo. When Guido arrives to serenade Lucrèce before a promised rendezvous at night, he surprises the couple and over- hears their plot to use him. That fateful night, Guido also sees a poor orphan girl sleeping on the street and leaves some money beside her. When he confronts Lucrèce about having basely used his pure affection for her evil ends, she recalls their different stations in life and haughtily departs. Thereupon Ser Girolamo, the jealous husband, spurred on by Amilcar, casti- gates his wife's supposed lover, but verbally rather than by arms. Guido, henceforth banned from Florence, takes pity on the orphan girl and decides to take the seven-year-old Tessa along into exile. His friend, the bohemian poet Filippo, comes to cheer him up; and the three go away together.

At the beginning of the second act, ten years have passed, as in Guido's Roman studio Filippo consults with a very Molièrean physician, Onuphrius, about curing his friend Guido from de- pression and "la mi-san-thro-pie," induced by the unforgotten experience with the evil Lucrèce—ten years ago. As Filippo decides on the homeopathic cure,

> * Onuphrius: En latin similia similibus.
>   Filippo, apart:
>   Merci
>   (Haut) Ce système prendrait le grand nom que voici:
>   L'ho-me-o-pa-thie,

Onuphrius concurs for a sizeable fee. Thus, to cure love with love, Filippo plots to have Guido confess his love for his beautiful ward, Tessa now seventeen and in love with her benefactor. But Guido, in an amusing anachronism already

---

* Onuphrius: In Latin similia similibus. Filippo, aside: Thank you. (out loud): This system would take this great name: Ho-me-o-pa-thy.

presaging the *Moralités légendaires*, is a confirmed Schopenhauerian, armed besides with Heinean irony:

> * Guido: Sceptique en bonne humeur, cuirassé d'ironie,
>   Comme un indifférent je traverse la vie.
>   . . . .
>   Je suis sans passion, ma foi ais [sic] un beau sort,
>   Et je n'ai qu'un désir: arriver à la mort
>   Sans avoir essuyé les femmes et la peste!

Only by pretending to love Tessa himself and asking Guido for
her hand is Filippo able to shake his friend out of his apathy,
Tessa doing her part to bring about the happy ending. It is
through her, left alone in Guido's studio, that we discover the
obstacle to their happiness:

> (She leans her elbows on the table, pensive; her eyes fall on the book left
> open by Guido. . . . A word glanced strikes and awakens her; she reads
> more attentively what she had glanced at.)
>   Oh! quel livre!
> (She reads, stopping after each sentence to understand it well.)
>   Life is an evil. Salvation will be the end of the world, the deliverance
> of humanity. The value of continence is that it leads to this deliverance.
>
>   Love, therefore, is the enemy.
>   Oh!
>   Women are its accomplices.
>   Guido was reading this!
>
> The ascetic saves entire generations from life. He gives an example
> which has almost saved humanity two or three times. The women did not
> want it so, that is why I hate them.
>
>   † Oh! quel livre!

> *Guido: Sceptic in good spirits, armed with irony, I walk through life
> indifferently. . . . .I am without passion, indeed yes, have a good lot; and I
> have only one desire: to arrive at death wihout having suffered women and the
> plague!
>   † Oh! what a book! And this one . . . Guido: What? Tessa: We will burn it
> (him). Guido: On the altar of love. All systems pass, love is eternal!

If Guido has not read Schopenhauer, he has at least read Challemel-Lacour's important article about the philosopher, which appeared in the *Revue des Deux Mondes* in 1870![26]
But all turns out well in the end as Guido is disarmed by the innocent Tessa, his true love, who insists that Schopenhauer be burned on the altar of love:

> Tessa: —Et Celui-ci . . . (pointing to Schopenhauer.)
> Guido: Quoi?
>   Tessa, with a heavy voice,
>   Nous le brûlerons.
> Guido: Sur l'autel de l'amour. Tous les systèmes passent,
>   L'amour est éternel! (He kisses her.)

Filippo, the poet, promises to write a comedy about it all, which he will dedicate to the lovers.

Arkell considers Laforgue's unhappy experience in love as essential for understanding *Tessa*,[27] which recalls some of the earlier critical reaction to Heine's *Almansor*. Although in some of his posthumously published notes written years later, Laforgue remembers the blond Marguerite with whom he fell in love in Tarbes when he was fourteen years old, I doubt whether she was the principal occasion of his first play. A tragedy, rather than a comedy, would have been a more appropriate vehicle in which to objectify unhappy love, and the haughty patrician lady described by Guido as "a cold effigy of marble, / A great lady with an Olympian smile / A superb animal that appealed to my senses," would hardly reflect little Marguerite of Tarbes. The indications

> * Bridoison
>   Tessa
>   Deux femmes.
>   O Schopenhauer!
>   Un bienfait n'est jamais perdu,

---

* Bridoison Tessa Two women. Oh Schopenhauer! A good deed is never in vain.

placed between the title and *dramatis personae*, which may represent ideas for alternate sub-titles or epigraphs, point rather to the intertext than *le vécu*. "Bridoison" is a stock comic character, defined in Littré as "simpleton, fool, stupid," and "name of a character from Beaumarchais' comedy *The Marriage of Figaro*."[28] I have already noted the Schopenhauerian echoes in the text; and the proverb brings to mind Musset's comedies.[29]

Laforgue's manuscript contains a series of marginal comments in another handwriting, published appended to the text, along with Laforgue's corrections and, in one case, his refusal to change his wording, basing himself on Littré. Although the author of the comments is not known, they clearly indicate that the seventeen-year-old poet had presented his comedy to an elder for criticism. This, too, suggests that *Tessa* represents a literary exercise, rather than the objectification of past experience.

Both Heine and Laforgue had been ambitious early to become playwrights, Laforgue even almost during his adolescence. How intensely Laforgue was interested in the theater at that period is evident also from a group of texts he wrote less than two years later, and which we have examined, his *Chroniques parisiennes* for *La Guêpe*. Of the twenty-six numbered reportages, sixteen deal in part with the theater, and two specifically with "Les Jeunes," young playwrights and their overwhelming difficulties in trying to get their plays accepted, or even read, by theater directors. Only an aspiring playwright, one of "us, young writers, friends of art," could know their plight:

A young writer writes a play and presents it to the Comédie-Française. If his play is accepted, it goes, before being played, to sleep for five or six years on the shelves. I am not inventing, but stating the facts. And the author must not complain, . . .

Supposing that the play of this young writer, instead of being "accepted," is "accepted subject to corrections," that is to say, politely refused, where can he take it? To the Odéon, which is the second Théâtre Français? But the director of that house is in regard to young writers of a ferocity which has become proverbial with the public! To the third Théâtre Français? But everybody rushes there . . . . And outside of these three theaters, the others play light comedy, farce, vaudeville, operetta . . ., and the poet made up of enough Biblical candor to go knock on their doors would get a fine going over. What to do? Wait for things to happen; and the young writers wait.[30]

En attendant, Laforgue, like Heine, turned to other projects. Though in his published work there are no drafts of another formal play, we know that, like Heine, he planned to write an Italian drama. Gustave Kahn, who met Laforgue in 1880, recalls the poet's plans at that time: "he informed me that he wanted to devote himself to a history of art and was also considering a drama about Savonarola."[31] As there is no further mention of that drama in either notes or correspondence, it was probably abandoned like Heine's Venetian tragedy. But Laforgue's letters document his continued interest and efforts in the genre, as he writes to his brother a little over a year before his death, reminiscing about his beginnings: "I remember the times when I used to take plays, chapters of novels, and lots of verse to Bourget . . ."[32]

Toward the end of 1881, Laforgue went to Berlin to become the French reader of the Empress Augusta and, like Heine before him, regularly visited the capital's theaters. The following August, he writes to a friend that he has begun "a great play, Pierrot the joker [*Pierrot fumiste*], which gives me convulsions," and in December he reports to another correspondent that he has written "a comedy in one act, blacker than *The Ravens*," and then announces another one in the same sentence.[33] Two months later, we find Laforgue writing "minor verse and a one-act play which overflows with optimism;" and in March, "three scenes and my prose in one act is [sic] finished," and he adds: "I also have in mind a Faust in one act."[34] There are other mentions of "an already old play in one act," and, later that summer, the poet explains: "as concerns my play, which is neither a drama at all nor a comedy, but a play in one act: frankly, it now seems to me like an *exercise* in that genre with a good intention of doing something different from what is being done ordinarily, nothing more."[35] Of all these projects recorded in the published correspondence, only the *Pierrot fumiste* has come to light;[36] and in 1883, writing to Kahn, the poet says: "Still the passion for the theater, but I find nothing."[37]

Laforgue's "idea of a Faust in one act" has its counterpart in Heine's fascination with Faust, which dates back to the 1820's[38] and culminates in the *Tanzpoem* in five acts, *Der Doktor Faust* of 1847.[39]

This work had been commissioned by the London theater director Benjamin Lumley, and Heine wrote it in the first weeks of 1847, for a generous honorarium. Due to technical difficulties—Heine, of course, suspected intrigues—it never reached the stage. Fascinated by the theme, the poet had over the years done a considerable amount of research, and he relates these "Erläuterungen" to Lumley in a letter twice as long as the principal text, which he appended to the *Tanzpoem* in both the German and French editions. These "Curious Reports about Devil(s), Witches and the Art of Poetry" are not merely as interesting as the "Poem" itself, but the two parts, as Heine himself appears to have felt, form one literary, if not theatrical, work.

In both the 1851 preface and the "Commentaries" to his libretto, Heine surveys the Faust legend's literary evolution from its beginnings in the fifteenth-century Theophilus-plays through the *Volksbücher* to Marlowe and finally Goethe, for "in literature as in life, every son has a father, whom, to be sure, he does not always know, or whom he might even wish to disavow" (B, VI: 356). The "Father" with whom Heine must come to terms is, of course, Goethe: "Wolfgang Goethe had the entire arsenal of the verbal arts at his disposal to express his thoughts, . . . I operate only through a meager libretto, in which I indicate in all brevity how the dancers are to act and conduct themselves, and how I approximately imagine the accompanying music and decorations. And yet I have dared to compose [dichten] a *Doktor Faustus* in the form of a ballet, playing rival to the great Wolfgang Goethe . . ." And while Goethe spent an entire lifetime creating his dramatic poem, Heine was given a mere four weeks to furnish his meager libretto (B, VI: 373)!

Heine insists, moreover, that while he remained true to the old legend in letting his Faust go to hell, Goethe had sinned against its intent in saving him: "that is, in his *Faust* poem, we miss throughout the faithful adherence to the real legend . . . Indeed, the shortcomings of his poem originated in this offense . . ." Heine considers *Faust II* merely a feeble effort to complete the play: ". . . it was never completely finished, unless one were to consider that lame second part of *Faust*, which appeared forty years later, as the completion of the whole poem. In this second part, Goethe liberates the necromancer from the devil's claws; he does not send him to hell, but lets him enter heaven triumphantly, accompanied by little dancing angels, little catholic cupids . .My ballet contains the essentials of the old legend of Doktor Faust" (B, VI: 374). If Heine has not succeeded in putting down Goethe's *Faust*, he certainly put up a fight to overcome a formidable Father.

However, Heine did diverge from the old legend, for in his libretto Faust has signed over his soul to a female devil, Mephistophela, in order to gain the love of a beautiful, lascivious duchess, whose image Mephistophela had conjured up for him. The duchess, who represents sensuous pleasure,—rather than the thirst for knowledge—, is the Devil's instrument to damn Faust's soul. In the second act, Faust meets the duchess in whom he recognizes a witch, a Domina with golden shoe and the devil's mark on her skin. He makes a rendezvous with her for the witches' Sabbath, which provides the setting of the third act. Here Faust attends the witches' cult of the black ram; but after he sees the Domina dance an erotic dance with the ram, Faust turns from her in disgust, demanding of Mephistophela to behold pure beauty. She conjures up Greek antiquity and Helena. In the fourth act, Faust dances with her, ideal beauty; and they then mount a throne and are entertained by the bacchantes dancing around them. But the jealous Domina appears and, when Faust rejects her, destroys the joyous scene with thunder and lightning, whereupon Faust kills her. Then he flees with Mephistophela on their magic black horses. In the last act, we find Faust in a medieval city's fairground, performing miracle cures. He falls in love with the mayor's innocent young daughter, wins her hand, and as the wedding cortege is about to enter the church, Mephistophela appears beckoning Faust to follow her. When he refuses, she confronts him with the pact signed with his blood. Again a terrible storm appears, all the townspeople fleeing into the church. When Faust tries to enter, a huge black hand rises from the ground holding him back. Mephistophela becomes transformed into an enormous snake, who strangles Faust amidst the devilish monsters that have risen from the ground. Against the ringing of the church bells in the background, the entire hellish group sinks into the earth in-flames—of hell.

Heine had high hopes for his libretto, writing to a friend shortly after its completion: "I have written my ballet and succeeded very well . . .," and in May, in a letter to Lumley, he appears certain of its success on the stage: "You will find my ballet excite a furore beyond all our expectation and even take a place in the annals of the drama" (HSA, XXII: 193 and 250).

Heine, his dramatic ambitions still unfulfilled, had endowed his dancers with truly dramatic qualities, thus relying on pantomime at least as much as on formal ballet, which was one of the reasons the choreographers rejected it. We recall that it was, after all, the great period of formal Romantic ballet, with choreographers like Perrot (at London) and Petipa (at Paris) and ballerinas like Taglioni, Carlotta Grisi and Elssler. Heine, "romantique défroqué," had again come too early for his time. The other problem posed by his *Faust* was the content. For how could her Majesty Queen Victoria's corps de ballet perform scenes like the witches' Sabbath? Heine himself had had second thoughts about it, suggesting to Lumley that the dance of the Domina with the ram might have to be left out!

Finally, a few months after writing it, Heine refers to his *Faust*, as he had to Goethe's, as a poem. In a letter to his publisher Campe of June 20, 1847, he offers him the play as: ". . . a ballet which I wrote for my friend Lumley in London, a poem which only has the form of a ballet, but otherwise is one of my greatest and most poetic productions." Yet, three years later, he still tries to get his poem staged, writing to Laube: "So you see why I am sending you my *Faust* now and burden you with its accommodation . . .," and adding regretfully: "had I only instead of a ballet written a drama that you would have produced on your talking stage" (HSA, XXII: 257 and XXIII: 24). But even his friend Laube, director of the Vienna Burg Theater, could not get Heine's *Faust* staged. It had to wait for a hundred years to be staged, by the Danish dancer and choreographer Helen Kirsova, in Sidney, Australia.

Finally, in 1948, the choreographer Marcel Luipart created at the Munich Staatsoper an *Abraxas*, a *Faust* ballet in five acts, very loosely based on Heine's libretto, to the music of Werner Egk. *Abraxas*, staged many times since in all major German houses, has become one of Germany's best-known ballets; thus Heine's ambition to contribute a major work to the theater repertory was at last fulfilled.[40]

Heine had written one other ballet libretto, *Die Göttin Diana*,[41] a year before the *Doktor Faust*, also upon Lumley's suggestion. Though the poet at one time hoped to see his *Diana* staged also, this "pantomime" never assumed the same importance for him as his *Tanzpoem*, and he wrote it in a mere two hours, as he reports to Ferdinand Lasalle in a letter of February 27, 1846: "Right after your departure, I wrote in two morning hours my ballet—succeeded very well—, which will perhaps still be produced this year in London" (HSA, XXII: 209). Thematically related to *The Gods in Exile*, the "hasty sketch" was published in 1854 appended to that text in order, as Heine explains, to protect it from literary marauders: "I am publishing it here, not in order to further my fame, but to prevent the crows from embellishing themselves all too proudly with foreign peacock plumes. For the legend of my pantomime is already essentially contained in the third part of my *Salon*, from which sundry Maestros Barthel have already helped themselves to some good pints of ale" (B, VI: 427). "Maestro Barthel," of course, is Richard Wagner, who had developed his *Tannhäuser* libretto partly from Heine's Venusberg episode in the *Elementargeister*, and his *Flying Dutchman* from Heine's

Fliegender Holländer story in the Memoiren des Herren von Schnabelewopski.[42]

Like his *Faust ballet, Die Göttin Diana*, which Heine repeatedly calls a pantomime, celebrates the joys of the senses. In the first tableau, a German medieval knight encounters the goddess Diana and her cortege on a hunt and falls in love with her. In the second tableau, the knight's wife and courtiers vainly try to cheer their melancholy master with a ceremonious ball in the castle. Suddenly Diana and her followers appear, along with Apollo and the Muses. When the knight wants to follow Diana, the chatelaine ousts the intruders who flee to the Venusberg (Venus' mountain). In the third tableau, we find the knight wandering about in the forest, surrounded by dancing undines, sylphs and fire spirits, when the Wild Hunt—recalling its night flight in *Atta Troll*—appears. Diana dismounts from her white horse and leads her knight to the Venusberg. But "faithful Eckart" intervenes to prevent the Christian knight from entering. In the ensuing single combat of Christian and Dionysian principles personified, the knight is killed. The final tableau takes us inside the Venusberg, where Diana weeps desperately over the body of her slain beloved, who is finally, however, revived by Apollo and Bacchus. Venus crowns Diana and her knight with roses, and all ends in a glorious *solemnitas*: a Dionysian bacchanalia. Thus, contrary to the *Faust Tanzpoem*, the *Diana* pantomime celebrates the final victory of the "Hellene" over the "Nazarene" principles, and the poet's nostalgia for the return of the exiled gods.[43] The *Göttin Diana* and *Doktor Faust* scenarios represent Heine's final contribution to the theater.[44]

Pierrot fumiste, of 1882, introduces one of Laforgue's principal personas, which will reappear later in three of the *Complaintes*, the seven "Pierrots" and sixteen "Locutions des Pierrots" of *L'Imitation de Notre-Dame la Lune*, and in "La mélancolie de Pierrot" of the *Fleurs de bonne volonté*. While Heine's ballets celebrate classical and medieval myth, Laforgue's playlet features a figure which has since assumed mythic proportions in modern art, and whose literary heritage has stimulated recent scholarship.[45] Like Heine's ballets, *Pierrot fumiste* represents a dramatic sub-genre, the sketch of a farce which, after several scenes, turns into the scenario of a pantomime. Haskell M. Block has shown how *Pierrot fumiste* grew out of Laforgue's fascination with cabaret poets, circus and music hall.[46] Its immediate source, moreover, might well have been Huysman's *Pierrot sceptique*,[47] a *saynète* in the *commedia dell'arte* manner, published in 1881, and about which Laforgue inquires in a letter of the same year.[48]

The opening scene of *Pierrot fumiste*, labeled "scène unique," pictures Pierrot—"poet, very lyrical and stockbroker, 30 years old"—and Colombinette leaving the Madeleine after their wedding, as the church is already being decorated for the next service, a funeral. Pierrot is disconcerted, especially by the initials of the departed: "he notices the black hangings being put up, and the initials C.P. Suddenly he lets out a shrill, fearful cry that upsets the entire square and goes back up the boulevards." Then, when the typical church-door beggar asks him for alms by recalling his five hungry children, Pierrot takes offense at the remark as an allusion to his "notorious impotence," but eventually calms himself and gives the poor man a false coin, explaining to Colombinette: "it's a false louis, a louis that's false, and that's all he needs" ("c'est un faux louis, un louis faux, c'est tout ce qu'il lui faut").[49] Before proceeding with the wedding party, the groom stops at Mme Ventre's (Mrs. Belly's) newsstand, loudly demanding his favorite paper, *The Illustrated Pornographer*, to which he had just contributed an article. After an number of lazzi indicated in the stage directions,—for example, frequently Pierrot turns wheels—, and repeated attempts of the groom to escape from his new situation, the mortal implications of which had been symbolically presaged above, Pierrot finally settles in the coach beside Colombinette: "Coachmen! Off to Cythera! To the country of Watteau!"[50] Then the "scène unique" is followed by another, in the nuptial chamber at midnight, after Mme Colombine has tucked her "pauv'chat" daughter into bed. There Pierrot soon joins his bride lovingly, repressing his animal instincts. In the following scene, same place, at "3:30 in the morning," Pierrot admires his dainty sleeping Colombinette, again repressing his baser inclinations. And in a third scene, same place, somewhat later in the night, Pierrot decides to recite the "Ode on the Fall of Namur" to keep from giving in to the weakness of the flesh, because "Boileau was an eunuch," and therefore, "there must be unsuspected virtues in this ode."[51] A fourth scene, taking place at 8 o'clock the next morning, shows Pierrot gallantly serving breakfast in bed to his "Poupoule," who is enchanted at the delicacy of her artist husband who, as she discovers, is writing a work on *la Mosaïque*. But in the following and concluding prose section, entitled *Le Fumiste* (The Practical Joker), "Poupoupoupou's enchantment gradually wears off, the mother of the disenchanted virgin bride finally sending a physician and threats. Pierrot loses his bride in the separation suit, but "he made use of his last night as husband, wore her out with love like a bull, then in the morning, whistling, whistling as though nothing had happened, he packed his trunks and left for Cairo, . . . kissing her tearfully: I sure loved you; you would have been the happiest of women, but no one understood me. There you are now, an unremarriageable widow. And he departed light and laughing, dancing in his compartment at every station."[52] Thus Laforgue's pantomime celebrated not the joys and final victory of the senses, but the Schopenhauerian clown, who will reappear in much of the poetry to come and, under diverse legendary masks, also in the *Moralités légendaires*.

Like *Tessa*, *Pierrot fumiste* remained hidden until its posthumous publication. Not so *Le Concile féerique* (*The Enchanted Assembly*), Laforgue's only dramatic composition published during his lifetime, a little over a year before his death.[53]

Le Concile féerique is almost entirely composed of five poems of the *Fleurs de bonne volonté*, a collection Laforgue had been preparing for publication but abandoned in 1886.[54] The little play is thus much closer to dramatic poetry than to poetic drama,[55] with the original poems broken up into segments apportioned to *dramatis personae* comprising "Le Monsieur, La Dame, Le Choeur, Un Echo." The scene is a "Starry Night," and a division of the text, indicated by "Silence; starry night.—

Dawn," divides the play into two parts, if not acts. Laforgue sent it to Gustave Kahn in June of 1886, mentioning also *Des Fleurs de bonne volonté* in the accompanying letter which suggests that the composition of *Le Concile féerique* out of that group of poems was a hasty one. "I am sending you *Le Concile féerique*, give me a word about it. I am still in a sweat over it."[56] Kahn published the play the following month, in the July 12 and 19 issues of *La Vogue* and then, also under the imprint of *La Vogue*, brought out a very limited sixteen-page edition of the text. *Le Concile féerique* was staged once, in a performance at the Théâtre d'Art, in January of 1892, as part of a program also featuring Maeterlinck's *Les Aveugles* (*The Blind*).[57] Haskell M. Block has described that performance, as well as audience and critical reactions to the play, and I agree with him that "it is indeed difficult to imagine why so urbane and amusing a piece as 'Le Concile féerique' should have almost created a riot in the theatre."[58]

Le Concile féerique has no plot in the conventional sense, and the verses spoken by Le Monsieur and La Dame amount to characterization; she is "la Femme," he the male:

> * Vous n'êtes que de braves mâles,
> Je suis l'Eternel Féminin! . . .[59]

Their meditations before and after their nocturnal embrace are echoed and commented on by the Echo and Chorus, the latter speaking approximately half of the 169 lines of the play, and manifesting the Monsieur's—the male—rather than La Dame's—the female—bias. We are familiar with double- or multiple-voicing in Laforgue's poetry, as for example in the "Complainte des voix sous le figuier boudhique," or the "Complainte des formalités nuptiales" which is broken into lines spoken by "him" and "her," or the dialogue of husband and wife in the "Complainte de l'époux outragé."[60] Warren Ramsey points to the "movement toward dramatization, a

*You are only good males, I am the Eternal Feminine.

tendency, having its origin in the self-awareness and self-defense," in many of *Les Complaintes*, and concludes that "this movement was ultimately to occasion *Le Concile féerique*."[61] Dana Carton Caprio, in her thesis on the play, too, sees its fundamentally dramatic structure in a series of movements from disillusionment (self-awareness) to reaction (self-defense), apportioned to the characters which all are, however, reflections of the poet's projected narrator: "the narrator's revelation of a source of disillusion necessarily implies a prior state of illusion. In *Le Concile féerique*, three illusions repeatedly involve any one or combination of the following three concepts: God (and the universe), man (and the human condition), and woman."[62] And while "the source of disillusion is typically accompanied by portrayals of melancholy or frustration, evocation of death and destruction,"[63] the resulting despair is, in the Heinean manner, tempered by irony from the outset. Thus the ironic reversal of Goethe's "Ewig Weibliches" above; and at the play's opening, the romantic setting, projected by La Dame whose purpose it serves, is deflated by the sobering male voice of the Chorus:

> * La Dame: Oh! quelle nuit d'étoiles! quelles saturnales!
> Oh! mais des galas inconnus
> Dans les annales
> Sidérales!
> Le Choeur: Bref, un ciel absolument nu.

Another Heinean trait in *Le Concile féerique* is its exceptional liberty of sexual expression: "The Echo: Good; if your spleen tells you so, universal havoc! The Chorus: Your creatures all have a sex, and are too ordinary. Make havoc!" This mode is particularly prominent in the second part, with the total disillusionment of the lovers after the fact, a note on which the play closes:

*The Lady: Oh! what a starry night! What saturnales! Oh! but unknown galas in the sidereal annals! The Chorus: In short, an absolutely nude sky.

* La Dame: De tous nos bonheurs d'autochtones!
Le Monsieur: Tu te pâmes, moi je m'y vautre!
Le Choeur: Consolez-vous les uns les autres.[64]

The above, then, Heine's two youthful tragedies *Almansor* and *William Ratcliff*, the *Tanzpoem Der Doktor Faust* and the ballet *Die Göttin Diana* composed later in his life; Laforgue's adolescent comedy *Tessa*, his scenario for the *Pierrot fumiste* pantomime, and finally the poetic playlet *Le Concile féerique*, represent the poets' dramatic production, a meager output considering their life-long ambitions in the genre. Despite these ambitions, Heine and Laforgue remained lyric poets and brilliant prose writers, not dramatists.

Notes

[1] Lilian R. Furst, *Counterparts: The Dynamics of Franco-German Literary Relationships 1770–1895* (London: Methuen, 1977).

[2] B, I: 784ff.

[3] B, I: 797ff. In the Hoffman und Campe edition of *Heinrich Heines Sämmtliche Werke*, the two tragedies appear in one volume (IV) along with *Shakespeares Mädchen und Frauen*.

[4] *Drames et fantaisies* (avec une préface de Saint-René Taillandier) (first ed. 1864).

[5] Saint-René Taillandier, "Les Débuts d'un poète humoriste," *Revue des Deux Mondex*, XLVII (1863): 497–529.

[6] DA, VII: 174: "How pleasantly surprised I was, therefore, in the year of our Lord 1819 when, as a very young man, I attended the University of Bonn and there had the honor of seeing Herrn poet A.W. Schlegel, the poetic genius, in person. . . . Today I can still feel the holy shudder that went through my soul when I stood before the raised platform and heard him speak. . . . Herr A.W. Schlegel wore kid gloves and was dressed in the latest Parisian fashion; he was still all perfumed from high society and 'mille fleurs' water; he was daintiness and elegance itself, and when he spoke of the Lord High Chancellor of England, he added 'my friend,' and beside him stood his domestic in the most baronially Schlegelian livery and trimmed the candles burning in silver chandeliers which stood beside a glass of sugar water on the lectern before the wondrous man. . .what unheard-of things in the seminar of a German professor!"

* The Lady: Of all our aboriginal joys! The Gentleman: You faint, I wallow!
The Chorus: Console each other.

[7] Altenhofer, Norbert, ed., *Heinrich Heine. Dichter über ihre Dichtungen*, 3 vols. (Munich: Heimeran Verlag, 1971), I: 36.

[8] In the 1851 "Vorrede" to the piece, Heine recalls: "I wrote *William Ratcliff* in Berlin unter den Linden, in the three last days of January 1821 (sic) . . ." He means 1822. B, I: 341.

[9] Heinrich Mutzenbecher, *Heine und das Drama* (Hamburg: Verlag Lucas Gräfe, 1914), 17–18.

[10] B, I: 785.

[11] Taillandier, "Les Débuts d'un poète humoriste," 520.

[12] Mutzenbecher, *Heine und das Drama*, 27.

[13] Voigt, *Ritter, Henker, Harlekin*, 129. Also Hartmut Kircher, *Heinrich Heine und das Judentum* (Bonn: Bouvier Verlag, 1973), 186.

[14] Sammons, *A Modern Biography*, 69–70.

[15] Ludwig Rosenthal, *Heinrich Heine als Jude* (Frankfurt: Verlag Ullstein, 1973), 113–14.

[16] Kircher, *Heine und das Judentum*, 186 and 191–93.

[17] A letter to Moses Moser of September 1823 reflects Heine's state of mind: ". . . Just at a time, when I stood quietly to let the waves of hatred for the Jews surge up against me. . . . I feel the force of this hatred from all sides . . . Friends, with whom I have spent the greater part of my life, are turning away from me. . . . You see me . . . in my continued law studies, which shall subsequently give me my livelihood. As you can imagine, the subject of baptism comes up for discussion here. No one of my family is against it, except myself. . . . from my way of thinking, you can well figure for yourself that baptism is an indifferent act for me . . . And yet, I consider it below my dignity and dishonoring for me to let myself be baptized in order to obtain a position in Prussia." HSA, XX: 112–13.

[18] Charlene A. Lea, *Emancipation, Assimilation and Stereotype: The Image of the Jew in German and Austrian Drama (1800–1850)* (Bonn: Bouvier Verlag Herbert Grundmann, 1978), 29.

[19] Walter Kanowsky, "Heine als Benutzer der Bibliotheken in Bonn and Göttingen," in *Heine-Jahrbuch* (1973), 129–53. Kanowsky furnishes a complete listing of the books Heine consulted at Bonn and Göttingen, followed by excellent commentary which gives us insight in Heine's preparatory reading.

[20] Mounir Fendri, *Halbmond, Kreuz und Schibboleth: Heine und der Islamische Orient* (Hamburg: Hoffmann und Campe, 1980), 15–74. The author demonstrates Heine's sympathy with Islam and his knowledgeability, due to his studies for *Almansor*.

[21] Mutzenbecher, *Heine und das Drama*, 30–40, shows several parallels between that play and *William Ratcliff*.

[22] *Heinrich Heine über die französische Bühne und andere Schriften zum Theater*, ed. and Introduction by Christoph Trilse (Berlin: Henschelverlag Kunst und Gesellschaft, 1971), 11.

[23] Kanowsky, "Heine als Benutzer der Bibliotheken," 141.

[24] *Revue des sciences humaines*, 178 (1980–2): 9–129. The manuscript was acquired by the Harvard University Library in 1956, its provenance unknown.

[25] Cf. Michele Hannoosh, "The Early Laforgue: *Tessa*," *French Forum*, I (1983): 20–32.

[26] Some of the lines Tessa finds in Guido's evil book are taken verbatim from Challemel-Lacour's reminiscences of Schopenhauer's statements during his visit with the philosopher. P. Challemel-Lacour, "Un Bouddhiste contemporain en Allemagne, Arthur Schopenhauer," *Revue des Deux Mondes*, XCVII, (1870): 296–332; cf. specifically 311–12. For Laforgue's reading of Schopenhauer, cf. my "Laforgue and His Philosophers" (cf. note 25, Chapter I).

[27] *Revue des Sciences humaines*, 91: "Pour comprendre *Tessa*, il faut revenir en arrière, à Tarbes où, après sept annees [sic]d'internat, Jules voit avec joie revenir sa famille. A son entrée en seconde il devient externe, ce qui lui donne l'occasion de connaître son 'premier amour'; il s'agit d'une jeune fille blonde au ruban bleu, Marguerite, qui le dédaigne. Ce grand petit fait constitue sans doute le point de départ de *Tessa*."

28 *Dictionnaire de le langue française* by E. Littré (Paris: Librarie Hachette, 1963), 418.

[29] I am thinking here of such *proverbes dramatiques* as *One ne badine pas avec l'amour* and *Il ne faut jurer de rien*.

[30] *Pages de la Guêpe*, 100–101.

[31] Gustave Kahn, *Symbolistes et Décadents* (Paris: Librairie Léon Vanier, 1902), 27. Cf. also the chapter entirely devoted to Laforgue, 181–98.

[32] Laforgue, *Lettres* II: 146.

[33] Laforgue, *Lettres* I: 189 and 215.

[34] *Lettres* II: 10 and 16.

[35] *Lettres* II: 41 and 44.

[36] *Oeuvres completès de Jules Laforgue* (Paris: Mercure de France, 1902–3), III, *Mélanges posthumes*, 86–107.

[37] *Lettres à un Ami*, 72.

[38] Thus Eduard Wedekind reports in July of 1824: "Heine denkt einen *Faust* zu schreiben; wir sprechen sehr viel darüber. . . . Heines *Faust* wird gerade das Gegenteil vom Goetheschen werden." *Dichter über ihre Dichtungen*, I, 296. And in a letter to Moser of April 1, 1825, Heine mentions among ideas of books to write "zum Beispiel ein angefangener *Faust*." HSA, XX: 192.

[39] B, VI: 351–96. *Der Doktor Faust Ein Tanzpoem nebst kuriosen Berichten über Teufel, Hexen und Dichtkunst*. The French translation by Saint René Taillandier, "La Légende de Faust," part of which first appeared in the *Revue des Deux Mondes* in 1852, is in the French edition of Heine's works in the volume *De l'Allemagne* II: 119–79. Jószef Turóczi-Trostler in his "Heine und Faust" recalls: "In Deutschland nahm am Vorabend der Revolution die

Entfremdung von Goethe immer mehr zu. . . . In Frankreich war aber die Ausgestaltung eines neuen Goethe—und Faustkults zu erleben. Es genügt an George Sand, Berlioz, Victor Hugo, Nodier, J. S. Ampère, Edgar Quinet als an die bekanntesten Vertreter dieser Mode zu erinnern, oder an den Umstand, daß Gérard de Nerval 1840 den zweiten Teil der Tragödie übersetzte.'' ''Faust-Studien,'' *Acta Litteraria Academiae Scientarium Hungaricae*, 6 (1964), 205.

⁴⁰ For an excellent history of Heine's *Doktor Faust* ballet, cf. Max Niehaus, *Himmel Hölle und Trikot* (Munich: Nymphenburger Verlagsbuchhandlung, 1959), 49–61.

41 B, VI: 425–36, *Die Göttin Diana* Nachtrag zu den 'Göttern im Exil'. The French text, *La Déesse Diane Appendice aux Dieux en Exil* in the volume *De tout un peu*, 337–53.

⁴² For Heine's and Wagner's relations, Wagner's adaptations of Heinean material, and finally Wagner's ''Bacchanale'' ballet in the *Tannhäuser*, cf. Niehaus, *Himmel Hölle und Trikot*, 67–71. Cf. also 35–45, for the survival of Heine's version of the legend of the Willis from the *Elmentargeister* (B, III: 654), in one of the great Romantic ballets, *Giselle*, for which Gautier had been one of the librettists, as I have noted on p. 20 above. For Heine's relations with Wagner, cf. also Eberhard Hilscher, ''Heinrich Heine und Richard Wagner,'' *Neue Deutsche Literatur* 4 (12) (1956). The author traces their relationship and quotes from Wagner's infamous article on ''Das Judentum in der Musik,'' in which the composer writes about Heine: ''Keine Täuschung hielt bei ihm vor: von dem unerbittlichen Dämon des Verneinens dessen, was verneinenswert schien, ward er rastlos vorwärtsgejagt, durch alle Illusionen moderner Selbstbelügung hindurch, bis auf den Punkt, wo er nun selbst wieder sich zum Dichter log'' (111).

⁴³ Cf. Benno von Wiese, ''Mephistopheles und Faust. Zur Interpretation von Heines Tanspoem 'Der Doktor Faust','' in *Herkommen und Erneuerung: Essays für Oskar Seidlin*, eds. Gerald Gillespie und Edgar Lohner (Tübingen: Niemeyer, 1976), 226: ''Beide Tanzdichtungen [*Faust* and *Diana*] sind überdies nur vom Horizont der Heineschen Geschichtsphilosophie mit ihrem Gegensatz von christlichem Spiritualismus und heidnischem Sensualismus zu verstehen.'' Von Wiese further stresses the profound significance which dance had for Heine: ''Daß Heine . . . diese und keine andere Form für seinen *Faust* wählte, ist nur verständlich, wenn mann die universale Bedeutung kennt, die der Tanz als Signatur des menschlichen Daseins für ihn immer wieder gehabt hat'' (229).

⁴⁴ I agree with Robert E. Stiefel, who in his ''Heine's Ballet Scenarios, an Interpretation,'' *Germanic Review*, 44 (1969): 197, says: ''In Heine's works dance is easily an area of study in its own right, for it is seemingly ubiquitous. The author seems to find the dance a rhythmic expression of spiritual condition and emotional state, and to organize dance and to restrict it is to paralyze its function. The ideal dance is instinctive and uninhibited . . . The sensuality of

this concept places it outside the Christian sphere and within that of the heathen and the Satanic. . . . Dance is at its core both magical and sexual, and it is especially the latter attribute which fascinates Heine."

45 Cf. note 41 of the preceding chapter.

46 Haskell M. Block, "Laforgue and the Theatre" in *Jules Laforgue Essays on a Poet's Life and Work* (Carbondale: Southern Illinois University Press, 1979), 77–79.

47 J.-K. Huysmans, *Oeuvres complètes* (Paris: Crès & Cie., 1928), 95–133.

48 Laforgue, *Lettres* I: 67 (letter to Charles Henry of December 1881): "Avez-vous lu *la Faustin? Pierrot sceptique* de Huysmans et Hennique?"

49 *Mélanges posthumes*, 88–89.

50 *Mélanges posthumes*, 97.

51 *Mélanges posthumes*, 102.

52 *Mélanges posthumes*, 107.

53 Laforgue, *L'Imitation de Notre-Dame la Lune*, 69–80.

54 For the transposition from the original poems into the play, cf. *L'Imitation de Notre-Dame la Lune*, 224.

55 Block, "Laforgue and the Theatre," 83.

56 *Lettres à un Ami*, 190.

57 Laforgue, *L'Imitation de Notre-Dame la Lune*, 224.

58 Block, "Laforgue and the Theatre," 88–91.

59 Laforgue, *L'Imitation de Notre-Dame la Lune*, 78.

60 *Les Complaintes*, 46, 84, 122.

61 Ramsey, *Laforgue and the Ironic Inheritance*, 119.

62 Dana Carton Caprio, "Jules Laforgue's *Le Concile féerique*: A Stylistic Structural Analysis," Doctoral Dissertation Columbia University, 1973 (University Microfilm International, 73–28, 191), 167.

63 Carton Caprio, *Le Concile féerique*, 76 and 80.

64 Laforgue, *L'Imitation de Notre-Dame la Lune*, 76 and 80.

IV

Heine's Shakespeare and Laforgue's

We have noted Shakespeare's repercussions in Heine's *Almansor*, the young lovers' tragic suicide fated by their families' hostility, and the hero's hesitations and reflections before he can act. In *William Ratcliff* we found a hero driven by his father's ghost to avenge his murder, lovers whose tragic fate is divined and sung by the lucid madwoman Margarete, and a final bloody, corpse-strewn scene. Heine himself made a jesting allusion to those affinities in *Ideen Das Buch Le Grand* (*Ideas The Book of Le Grand*) of 1826: "It is generally accepted, Madame, that one proclaims a monologue before killing oneself. Most people use Hamlet's 'To be or not to be' at such occasions. It is a good passage, and I also would gladly have cited it here— but charity begins at home, and if one has, like myself, also written tragedies containing such *Lebensabiturienten* (life-departure) speeches, for example the immortal *Almansor*, then it is very natural to give the preference to one's own words, even over Shakespeare" (DA, VI: 174–5).

I remarked that Heine wrote his tragedies under the influence of his teacher A.W. Schlegel, whose lectures on the history of German language and literature he attended in Bonn in 1819. "There is no doubt," writes one of Heine's commentators, "that Schlegel spoke about Shakespeare in these lectures and aroused Heine's interest in the English dramatist," and he notes that "a careful study of all Heinean Shakespeare citations leaves the definite impression that Schlegel used *Hamlet* and *Romeo and Juliet* as model dramas for his Shakespeare interpretation and as examples with which he compared all other dramatic works.

Heine quotes most often from *Hamlet* and *Romeo and Juliet*, and his remarks about them demonstrate a deeper understanding and higher appreciation of these than of all of Shakespeare's other plays."[1] And it is, of course, *Hamlet* also that most profoundly marked Heine's disciple Laforgue.

I have pointed out Heine's changing attitude toward his great teacher, which shifted from profound admiration[2] to open hostility. Yet, despite his disillusionment with Schlegel in *Die Romantische Schule* of 1835, Heine there objectively credits his former teacher's accomplishments as translator: "If I am to speak of his literary merits, I must again first of all praise him as translator. Here he has unquestionably accomplished something extraordinary. For his translation of Shakespeare into German is masterly, unsurpassable (DA, VIII: 168). It is clearly Schlegel who revealed Shakespeare to Heine.

Even the superficial reader will recall the poet's homage to Shakespeare in two of his most famous titles, the verse epic *Atta Troll Ein Sommernachtstraum* (*Atta Troll a Midsummer Night's dream*) of 1841 and *Deutschland Ein Wintermärchen* (*German A Winter's Tale*) of 1844. And Shakespeare himself appears, along with Goethe, in *Atta Troll*'s Wild Hunt, followed by his commentator:

> * An des Mundes holdem Lächeln
> Hab ich auch erkannt den William,
> Den die Puritaner gleichfalls
> Einst verflucht; auch dieser Sünder
>
> Muß das wilde Heer begleiten
> Nachts auf einem schwarzen Rappen,

   * By the sweet smile of his mouth, I recognized William, whom the Puritans likewise once had cursed. This sinner, too, must accompany the wild host at night on a black horse. Beside him, on an ass, rode a man—And, good heavens! By his feeble prayerful mien, the pious white night-cap, his fear of soul, I recognized our old friend Franz Horn! Because he erstwhile commented on the worldling Shakespeare, the poor fellow must now ride with him after death in the turmoil of the wild hunt!

Neben ihm, auf einem Esel,
Ritt ein Mensch—Und, heil'ger Himmel!

An der matten Betermiene,
An der frommen weißen Schlafmütz,
An der Seelenangst, erkannt ich
Unsern alten Freund Franz Horn!

Weil er einst das Weltkind Shakespeare
Kommentiert, muß jetzt der Ärmste
Nach dem Tode mit ihm reiten
Im Tumult der wilden Jagd!

Thus Heine's warnings to a great poet's mediocre critics, for:

* Wenn es manchmal im Galopp geht,
Schaut der große William spöttisch
Auf den armen Kommentator,
Der im Eselstrab ihm nachfolgt,

Ganz ohnmächtig, fest sich krampend
An den Sattelknopf des Grauchens,
Doch im Tode wie im Leben,
Seinem Autor treulich folgend (B, IV: 538–39).

Ernst August Schalles lists Heine's relatively few verbatim quotations as well as his far more numerous indirect, parodied Shakespeare passages in his thesis on "Heines Verhältnis zu Shakespeare" ("Heine's Relation to Shakespeare");[3] and Siegbert Prawer has brilliantly analyzed "Heine's ways with quotations from Shakespeare" in his Oxford inaugural lecture on *Heine's Shakespeare*,[4] a most profound treatment of the subject. Not only do Heine's indirect Shakespeare quotations outnumber by far his direct ones; the poet freely adapts the original to make his own point, most frequently using the altered quotation to evoke "two worlds at once, a royal, heroic, tragic

* When they sometimes fall into a gallop, the great William looks back mockingly to the poor commentator who follows him in donkey trot, all faint, hanging tightly onto the pommel of his mount, yet in death, as he had in life, faithfully following his author.

world (that of Shakespeare), and a bourgeois, narrow, comic one. 'Ay, every inch a king', Lear says of himself; Heine has poor fat Louis-Philippe of France rise up 'in dicker Majestät, jedes Pfund ein König'—'in most portly majesty, every pound a king.' ''.⁵

Shakespeare is often linked to Goethe and Cervantes, Heine's great poetic triumvirate. Thus in his "Einleitung zum *Don Quixote*" of 1837: "Cervantes, Shakespeare and Goethe form the triumvirate of poets which in the three poetic genres, in the epic, the drama and the lyric, has accomplished the greatest achievements" (B, VI: 163). Hamlet, as I have noted, is most frequently quoted by Heine, who shares the German fascination with this Shakespearean figure, from Goethe (*Wilhelm Meister*) to Schlegel, Tieck and their descendents. In *Die Romantische Schule*, in a paragraph beginning with Cervantes, Heine continues with Goethe and then leads into a reflection on Hamlet's honesty: ". . . as Cervantes during the time of the Inquisition had to resort to humorous irony to indicate his thoughts, . . . so Goethe, too, used to express in the tone of humorous irony what he, a minister and courtier, did not dare to say openly. Goethe has never concealed the truth, but when he could not reveal it nakedly, he dressed it in humor and irony. . . . It is the only expedient left to honesty, and in its humoristic and ironic presentation this honesty is, moreover, most movingly revealed. This reminds me again of the strange Prince of Denmark. Hamlet is the most honest soul in the world. . . . In all his humorous and ironic jokes, he always lets it purposely show through that he is only dissembling. . . . Hamlet is honest through and through; only the most honest person could say: 'We are all imposters', and in acting crazy, he also does not want to deceive us, and he is mentally conscious of the fact that he is really crazy" (DA, VIII: 183–84). Heine's own identification with Hamlet, though veiled, is as obvious here as is Laforgue's.

Heine had seen Shakespeare plays in Berlin during his 1821–22 stay;⁶ and during his 1827 London visit of nearly four months, he assiduously visited the Drury Lane Theater to see Shakespeare performed by Edmund Kean, notably in the roles of Othello,

Shylock, Richard II, and Macbeth. Heine recalls the great actor's memorable performance in *Über die französische Bühne* (*About the French Stage*), a text I shall discuss at length in the following essay. Thus he writes in 1837: "Kean was not a many-sided actor; though he could play many roles, he always played himself in these roles. But in that way, he always gave us a most impressive truth, and although ten years have passed since, I can still always see him before my eyes as Shylock, as Othello, Richard, Macbeth; and in many an obscure passage of these Shakespearean plays, his acting disclosed their full significance to me" (DA, XII: 262). In the same essay Heine again links Shakespeare to Goethe, in a passage about poetic and artistic originality: "But nothing is more foolish than the reproach of plagiarism. There is no sixth commandment in art. The poet can help himself wherever he might find the material for his work, and he may even appropriate entire columns with chiseled capitals, as long as the temple he is supporting with them is splendid. This Goethe understood well, and before him Shakespeare" (DA, XII: 260–61). Although ostensibly defending Alexandre Dumas here against charges of plagiarism by pointing to what were to him the two greatest poets, Heine is obviously pleading *pro domo*.

In the correspondence, Heine refers to Shakespeare occasionally, as in this passage from an 1824 letter to his friend Moses Moser: "But I have always been comfortable in Byron's company, as with a completely equal companion. With Shakespeare I cannot be comfortable at all; I feel only too strongly that I am not his equal. He is the almighty minister, and I am a mere privy councillor, and I feel as though he could dismiss me any minute." In a letter of the following year to Friederike Robert, he again links Shakespeare and Goethe in expressing an idea we find elswhere in his texts, that the terrible must, if it is not to lose its poetic quality, be expressed "in the motley garb of the ridiculous . . . conciliatory as it were—that is why Shakespeare had the most terrible things in *Lear* said by the Fool, that is why Goethe chose the form of the puppet-play for the most dreadful, for *Faust*, that is why that even greater poet (the Archpoet,

Friederike says), namely our Lord, has added a good dose of merriment to all the horror scenes of this life (HSA, XX: 170 and 219).

Finally, Heine's readers are familiar with his profound and enduring admiration for the Bible; and in linking Shakespeare to its style, he probably pays him his highest compliment. Thus Heine writes from Helgoland in July of 1830: "I have again read in the Old Testament. What a great book! . . . Only in a single author do I find anything that recalls that direct style of the Bible. That's Shakespeare. In him, too, the word sometimes stands out in that awful nakedness that startles and shakes us; in the works of Shakespeare we sometimes behold the bare truth without the raiment of art" (DA, XI: 44).

Heine devoted only one text entirely to Shakespeare, the controversial *Shakespeares Mädchen und Frauen* of 1838,[7] commissioned by the Parisian book dealer Delloye, who wanted to publish a German edition of a group of prints of Shakespeare's heroines with the English commentary replaced by a new German one. Heine, according to a letter to Campe of July 23, 1838, accepted the generously remunerated assignment because otherwise Delloye would have addressed himself to Tieck. In the same letter, in which he asks Campe to handle the book's distribution in Germany, Heine appears not too confident about its worth, saying apologetically that the poor condition of his eyes had forced him to dictate the text, "between you and me: not a masterpiece, but nevertheless good enough for the purpose (HSA, XXI: 284). In a letter of the following month to Karl Gutzkow, Heine claims that he had recently "read the entire Shakespeare" (HSA, XXI: 292), a claim which has, however, been questioned.[8]

The French edition of the text occupies the larger part of the volume *De l'Angleterre*, the editors noting that "the volume which we are publishing today under the title *About England* should more exactly have received the following: *Shakespeare's Heroines and Fragments About England*. . . . all of Heine's work on Shakespeare offers us, moreover, not merely the most exquisite and rare intellectual pleasure of hearing one poet comment on another; it also gives us, thanks to a multitude of quick intuitions whimsically uttered here and there in these pages which Heine envisioned merely as a commentary to a series of prints, the key to the English genius itself, as well as its moral character, of which Shakespeare, the most universal of modern poets but at the same time also the most English, is the representative par excellence."⁹ This "Notice" surely must have aroused the interest of Laforgue.

Shakespeare's Mädchen und Frauen is divided into four parts; a twenty-page opening essay on the poet's reception in England and Germany and about German Shakespeare scholarship; the central section is divided into two parts, the first dealing with the heroines of the tragedies, the second with those of the comedies; the twelve-page closing essay deals with Shakespeare's fortune in France.

Heine begins his book with an amusing anecdote about the Hamburg Christian who could not get over the fact that Christ was born a Jew and "belonged to the pack of those unsnuffed long-noses, . . . whom he so thoroughly despises." Thus Heine with Shakespeare: "I feel faint when I think that in the end he is indeed an Englishman and belongs to the most repugnant people God has created in his wrath" (B, IV: 173). Heine's readers are familiar with his dislike for England—from its earlier Puritanism to its contemporary industrialized capitalism—from other texts, notably the *English Fragments* of 1828.¹⁰ Heine then discusses that Puritanism which suppressed Shakespearean drama under Cromwell, expounding his famous dichotomy between Hellene and Nazarene: "This old, irreconcilable aversion toward the theater is but one side of the hostility which has been holding sway for eighteen centuries between completely heterogeneous world views, one of which originated in the barren soil of Judea, the other in flourishing Greece." Shakespeare's genius fell victim to the Nazarenes' persecution, like the gods in exile. "Indeed, for eighteen centuries the animosity has lasted between Jerusalem and Greece, between the holy sepulcher and the cradle of art, between life in the spirit and the spirit in life"

(B, IV: 175). Clearly, Heine here passes beyond the confines of his subject, as he will throughout the book.

Heine devotes a sizeable section to Shakespeare's double role as poet and historian: "Shakespeare's mission was not merely poetry, but also history" (B, IV: 178), as he most faithfully and poetically recorded not merely the history of his own people, but also that of antiquity. Heine defends Shakespeare against charges of "formlessness," in opposition to the French school. The same fidelity to "Wahrheit" and truth which he manifests toward history, Shakespeare shows toward nature. Great poets like Shakespeare do not "hold a mirror up to nature," but they are born with nature's truest reflections imprinted on their spirit.

Then, here as elsewhere, Heine pleads against biographical criticism, those attempts to trace the poet's life from the Sonnets or other sources. Heine insists: "The poets present themselves to the world in the brilliance of their works, and especially when one sees them from afar, one is dazzled by the light. Oh let us not behold their lives close-up" (B, IV: 181)! Again, this plea is not only for Shakespeare, but for all poets, including Heine himself.

Among the poet's English critics, only Hazlitt finds grace:[11] "with the sole exception of William Hazlitt, England has not produced a single significant Shakespeare commentator," but— and here Heine shares a widespread German prejudice—"the Germans have understood Shakespeare better than the English" (B, IV: 183). Among the first in Germany to appreciate Shakespeare's genius was Lessing, whom Heine always admired. In fact, according to Heine, one could say "that Lessing's entire *Dramaturgie* was written in Shakespeare's interest." Then Heine turns to Wieland and his Shakespeare translations, followed by the third eminent German to honor the English poet, Goethe. He next treats Schlegel, for "it would be an injustice if I refused to acknowledge the merits that Mr. A.W. Schlegel has earned through his translations of Shakespeare's dramas and his lectures on same" (B, IV: 184). Then he even more grudgingly passes on to Tieck, who "has earned some merit as Shakespeare commentator" (B, IV: 186). Heine closes his survey of German Shakespeare criticism with poor Franz

Horn, whom we met in *Atta Troll*. About his five volumes of commentary, Heine says: "There is spirit in it, but such a twisted and diluted spirit that it seems even more unpleasant to us than the most mindless dullness" (B, IV: 187). After briefly commenting on famous Shakespearean actors (English, French and German), Heine concludes by introducing the "portrait gallery" that follows: "I am the gatekeeper who opens this gallery for you, and what you have heard so far was a mere vain rattling of keys" (B, IV: 190).

Heine's framing essays, and particularly his opening "eitel Schlüsselgerassel," constitute, in my opinion, the essence of his book, whose center consists, with some exceptions which I shall note, of less important material dictated by the iconography on which he was committed (and commissioned) to comment. He opens his "portrait gallery" with the heroines of the antique plays, first the Greek *Troilus and Cressida*, then the Roman tragedies *Coriolanus*, *Julius Caesar*, *Antony and Cleopatra*, and *Titus Andronicus*. Then come the English history plays (with the exception of *Richard II*), followed by the remaining tragedies, among which Heine also groups,in final position, *The Merchant of Venice*. The disproportionately meager comedy section consists of mere quotations from the plays in which some of the best-known heroines portrayed appear. Obviously, Heine is not nearly as interested in this "Bildersaal" as in Shakespeare's genius, as well as other issues for whose sake he freely departs from his ostensible subject to engage in subjective considerations.

In "Cressida," Heine contrasts Shakespeare and the Greek dramatists: "In contrast to the antique tragedians who, like the antique sculptors, merely strove for beauty and nobleness, Shakespeare first of all aimed for truth and substance, whence his mastery of characterization" (B, IV: 193). But in "Johanna d'Arc," Heine chides Shakespeare for assuming the British prejudice in representing the heroine as a witch. In commenting on the portrait of "Lady Gray," Heine credits the poet with such veracity in his representation of the English kings that he appears to have been their very chancellor, and he applies F.

Schlegel's remark about historians, which I quoted in connection with *William Ratcliff*, to Shakespeare: "What Friedrich Schlegel writes about the historian applies intrinsically fully to our poet: he is a prophet gazing into the past" (B, IV: 230). Heine always profoundly admired *Macbeth*: "*Macbeth* constitutes the transition to those poetic works in which the great Shakespeare's genius unfolds its wings most freely and boldly" (B, IV: 237). In presenting "Ophelia," Heine again identifies with Hamlet: "She was a blond, beautiful girl, and especially in her voice there was a magic which already moved my heart when I traveled to Wittenberg and went to her father to bid him farewell" (B, IV: 239), and critics have thus read Heine's own unhappy love for his cousin into the passage. Needless to recall, the poet, who closes his commentary by saying: "We know this Hamlet as we know our own face which we see so often in the mirror, and which is, however, less well known to us than one might believe" (B, IV: 241), would not have appreciated such a reading. Writing on "Cordelia," Heine admires Shakespeare's expositions, as he does elsewhere, and finds that "It is almost impossible to judge him in this tragedy in which his genius soars up to the most dizzying height" (B, IV: 242). He reads *Romeo and Juliet* as a hymn to love, "the highest and most victorious of all passions," but wonders, like Hazlitt before him, why Shakespeare first let the hero fall in love with Rosalinde: "I do not dare criticize Shakespeare in the least, and I only wish to express my amazement that he first had Romeo feel a passion for Rosalinde" (B, IV: 246). And Heine's reflections in this connection on love in general, and a second love in particular, have a distinctly Laforguean resonance: "That is a desperate feeling, when in the most ardent fervor we think of future emptiness and coldness and know from experience that these highly poetic and heroic passions come to such a miserable, prosaic end" (B, IV: 245–46)!

Treating "Desdemona," Heine for once really concentrates on the heroine: "She is a daughter of the South, tender, sensitive, patient, like those slim, luminous women with large eyes that shine forth from Sanskrit poems so lovely, so soft, so dream-like. She always reminds me of the 'Sakontala' of Kalidasa, the Indian Shakespeare" (B, IV: 248).

Heine reserves his most weighty and extensive commentary for the play which he moved from the comedies to the closing position among the tragedies, *The Merchant of Venice*. And it is his discussion of that play also which has caused the greatest controversy. In opening this presentation of "Jessica," Heine recalls one of the play's performances at the Drury Lane Theater which he had attended, and in which, at the end of the fourth act, a beautiful, pale English girl had broken out in tears over Shylock's fate, crying out "The poor man is wronged." Thus Heine justifies his notion of the play's genre: "But when I think of these tears, then I must count *The Merchant of Venice* among the tragedies." For Shakespeare here wrote a tragedy despite himself: "the poet's genius, the world spirit that rules him, stands always higher than his private will, and so it came about that in Shylock, despite his shrill grotesqueness, he expressed the justification of an unhappy sect." The play, in fact, deals with oppressor and oppressed: "Shakespeare's genius rises above the small disputes of two denominations, and his drama shows us in effect neither Jews nor Christians, but oppressors and oppressed and the latter's frantic shouts of joy when they can pay back with interest to their arrogant tormentors the insults inflicted on them" (B, IV: 251). Thus the theme of the play, a tragedy for Heine, as well as for some readers of our own day.

It is not surprising that Heine's thoughts about the Jewish experience in Europe, from the Middle Ages through the nineteenth century, which had also, I believe, inspired his own tragedy *Almansor*, should lead the poet to general reflections on the subject and far away from the portrait of Jessica. Heine finds an affinity between Jewish and Germanic morality, due to the Bible, that great "family chronicle of the Jews," and its function as "Erziehungsbuch" (educational book) of the entire Germanic world (B, IV: 257–8). Then follow some strictly historical considerations, up to contemporary Frankfurt with its fixed quota of Jewish marriages. Finally Heine sees the source of

much of contemporary hatred of the Jews in their wealth: "They forced them to become wealthy, and then hated them on account of their wealth" (B, IV: 261). The discussion continues in the portrait of "Portia," which includes the poet's dream vision of his visit to the Synagogue of Venice: "While looking for old Shylock, I carefully examined all those pale, suffering Jewish faces, and I made a discovery which unfortunately I cannot conceal. That is, I had the same day visited the insane asylum of San Carlo, and now, in the Synagogue, I noticed that in the eyes of the Jews there flickered the same fatal, half fixed, half unsteady, half cunning and half stupid gleam which I had shortly before seen in the eyes of the mentally ill at San Carlo" (B, IV: 264). Again, as in *Almansor*, the poet's words are tragically prophetic: "What martyrdom they have already suffered . . !
. . . What greater martyrdom is still in store for them! I shudder at the thought, and infinite compassion fills my heart" (B, IV: 265). In his dream, the poet never found Shylock, but heard a broken voice, crying out: "Jessica, my child!" Heine's commentary on *The Merchant of Venice* confirms what we already know: it is a poet's text that we are reading, not a literary critic's.

In the closing essay, about Shakespeare's reception in France, Heine reports on the poet's recent veneration by the avant-garde: "For ten years Shakespeare has been the object . . . of the blindest worship in France" (B, IV: 281); but do we not hear a certain ironic twist in the qualifier "blindest"? Heine credits Victor Hugo as "mediator," but not without reservations; he compliments more freely Alexandre Dumas for paving Shakespeare's way in France, then passes to Alfred de Vigny's preoccupation with the poet. But, "if it is already difficult enough for the French to understand Shakespeare's tragedies, the understanding of his comedies is almost completely denied to them" (B, IV: 285). The exception here is Musset, who has succeeded in creating fine comedies in imitation of Shakespeare. Among the critics, Heine praises Guizot, from whose *De Shakespeare et de la poésie dramatique* he quotes several pages. Finally the book closes again with a dream, in which some of the magical figures of Shakespeare's comedies bewitch the poet: " 'My friend, you would like a definition of Shakespearen comedy, would you?' I don't know whether I assented, but the lovely woman had at the same time dipped her hand into the water and splashed the tinkling sparks into my face, so that general laughter resounded, from which I awoke" (B, IV: 291). Thus the poet, not the literary critic, concludes the work.

Contrary to Heine's expectations, *Shakespeares Mädchen und Frauen* was so successful that a few years later he was unable to obtain a copy anywhere. Some critics consider it a weak work, pieced together from earlier texts, poorly balanced and, certainly, often straying far from the announced subject.[12] Yet, if we read *Shakespeares Mädchen und Frauen* not as a critique, but as the reverie of one great poet on another, it cannot fail to delight us.

Before closing this discussion of Heine's Shakespeare, we must consider one more text, a Shakespeare parody embedded in one of the "Reisebilder," in *Die Bäder von Lucca (The Baths of Lucca)* of 1829, which Heine wrote shortly before his move to Paris (B, II: 391–470).[13] This text has become famous for Heine's bitter polemic against Count August von Platen-Hallermünde, appended in the two final chapters which, however, need not concern us. In this burlesque "Italian Journey"—"There is nothing more boring on this earth than reading an Italian travel book—except perhaps the writing of same" (B, II: 426)—the narrator, "Heinrich Heine, Doktor juris," meets two old Hamburg acquaintances, the banker Christian Gumpel, who travels in Italy as "His Excellency, the Marchese Christophoro Gumpelino" to refine his taste and deepen his culture, and his valet, the former lottery agent "Herr Hirsch," who is now "Hyazinth," and whose new bright livery outshines that of Rothschild's men.

The Marchese Gumpelino is madly in love with one Lady Julia Maxfield, jealously watched over by her brother-in-law. He has also found a poetic model for his plight: Romeo. " 'O Julia'— Gumpelino sighed—'if I only were the yellow leather glove on your hand kissing your cheek! Doktor, have you ever seen the

Crelinger in 'Romeo and Juliet'?' ''[14] As Gumpelino is becoming gradually paler, if not thinner, over his unrequited love, he consents to undergo a partial cure, guaranteed by Hyazinth. When Gumpelino empties the fateful glass of "sal mirabile Glauberi," a powerful laxative, he recalls the Crelinger's famous Julia, and that of Sophie Müller:

> 'For I am the greatest enthusiast for Crelinger, but Müller, when she emptied the cup, transported me. You see'—he said, while picking up the glass, into which Hyazinth had emptied the powder, with a tragic gesture,—'you see, she held the cup like this and shuddered, so that one felt it all when she said:

> > 'Kalt rieselt matter Schauer' durch meine Adern,
> > Der fast die Lebenswärm' erstarren macht!'

> 'And she stood like this, as I am standing right now, and raised the cup to her lips, and with the words:

> > * 'Weile, Tybalt!
> > Ich komme, Romeo! Dies trink ich dir',

she emptied the cup. !

'' 'To your health, Mr. Gumpel' said Hyazinth in a solemn voice; for the marchese had emptied the glass in imitative enthusiasm and thrown himself on the sofa, exhausted from his declamation'' (B, II: 436). But at that very moment a messenger arrives from Julia Maxfield, informing Gumpel that her brother-in-law is out of town, inviting him to their love's consummation that very night! '' 'Woe is me, fool of love,' lamented Gumpelino,'' who will have a night of diarrhea, instead of love. It is too late to change the course of events, '' 'Here no living man can any longer be of help,' sighed Hyazinth'' (B, II: 437). ''When we are made to watch Gumpelino drain a laxative,'' comments Prawer,[15] ''to the accompaniment of 'Romeo, I come! This do I drink to thee' and constate its effects with the words 'O

---

* *Romeo and Juliet*, IV, 3: Juliet: I have a faint cold fear thrills through my veins, / That almost freezes up the heat of life. . . . . Stay, Tybalt, stay!

true apothecary! Thy drugs are quick'—then we may well be moved to protest at the gusto with which Heine has wrenched these lines from their original context to accommodate them in Gumpelino's world.'' But, then, parody is never kind—neither in Heine nor Laforgue.

One of the earliest Shakespearean reverberations in Laforgue occurs in a poem he wrote for *La Guêpe* in which it appeared in 1879, "Excuse macabre," dedicated "A Hamlet, prince de Danemark.''[16] The dedication is most appropriate as the persona addresses the skull of "Margaretha, ma bien-aimée" in a burlesque pastiche of Hamlet's reflections to Horatio about "poor Yorick;" and the lines ". . . moi / Qui crois qu'ici-bas tout finit au cimetière, / Un vieux crâne est le peu qui reste encor de toi! / Et, n'est-ce pas le sort de la nature entière?''* surely parody Hamlet at the graveyard: "And now how abhorred in my imagination it is! My gorge rises at it. Here hung those lips that I have kiss'd I know not how oft.'' Laforgue elaborates this Hamletic theme in another early poem, "Un Crâne qui n'avait plus sa mâchoire inférieure" ("A Skull which no longer had its lower jaw"), a sonnet whose opening quatrain reads:

> † Mon frère—où vivais-tu? dans quel siècle? Comment?
> Que vécut le cerveau qui fut dans cette boîte?
> L'infini? la folie? ou la pensée étroite
> Qui fait qu'on passe et meurt sans nul étonnement?[17]

There is yet another, untitled reflection upon a skull, published posthumously among Laforgue's "Feuilles volantes" ("Drifting leaves") by *La Revue blanche* in 1896.[18] Here the poet again celebrates the theme: "D'où viens-tu vieux crâne?''—a theme which had, in fact, assumed obsessive proportions in his artistic universe, borne out by his many sketches of skeletons with

---

* . . . me, who believe that here below everything ends in the cemetery, an old skull is all that's left of you! And is this not the lot of all of nature?

† My brother!—where did you use to live? In what century? How? What was the life of the brain housed in this box? The infinite? Madness? or narrow thought which makes one pass and die without any astonishment?

hypertrophied skulls, or just skulls, among the notes. Some of these, too, are published in *La Revue blanche*.[19] In the opening chapter, I have pointed to possible echoes of Heine's *Shakespeares Mädchen und Frauen* in "Excuse macabre."[20]

Among the early poems in *La Guêpe*, there is another one marked by Shakespeare, "Au lieu de songer à se créer une position" ("Instead of thinking about getting ahead"),[21] which bears the epigraph "O! fie, fie this world. (Hamlet)." Laforgue here evokes Hamlet's lines to his father's ghost, "O earth! . . . And shall I couple hell! O fie! Hold, my heart, / And you, my sinews, grow not instant old, / But bear me stiffly up. Remember thee!", in a poem which opens, like the play, with a father's advise to his son: "Mon cher fils, Retenez bien ce que je vous dis."* In another early poem, the sonnet "Moeurs" ("Mores"), which addresses itself to "O virtuosities in twos," "little Hamlets" are advised to return to the bosom of lawfulness: "Return, little Hamlets, into the fold of legitimacy."[22]

In Laforgue's contributions to *La Guêpe*, there is only one reference to Shakespeare, in the nineteenth "Chronique parisienne" of September 25, which opens with: "Oh horrible, horrible! (Shakespeare, *Hamlet*, translation Letourneur)," but then passes from the standard French Shakespeare translation of the period on to expounding one of Laforgue's favorite subjects in these reportages which I have discussed at length above, "les *jeunes* et le théâtre," the plight of young dramatic writers like himself. However, this installment deals not with a Shakespeare production taking the place of a contribution by "les jeunes," but that of a "Cinderella," a *féerie* to be produced at the Chatelet. Then the article closes in echoing its opening: "Horrible! horrible! . . ."[23]

These earliest Shakespearean echoes reveal already that, in essence, Laforgue's Shakespeare is *Hamlet*. Thus we will find no less than twelve *Hamlet* passages placed as epigraphs over poems of *Des Fleurs de bonne volonté*, as well as in two of the *Derniers Vers*.[24] Both posthumously published cycles bear

---

* My dear son, retain well what I have to say to you.

Hamlet epigraphs under their titles, *Des Fleurs de bonne volonté* Ophelia's "O, what a noble mind is here o'erthrown!" after her interview with "mad" Hamlet (III,i), as well as the dying Hamlet's "Had I but time—. . . O I could tell you— / But let it be. . . ." addressed to Horatio in the play's final scene (p. 81). And this last quotation certainly carries a bitter dramatic irony, as Laforgue did not have the time to say all, nor even to publish himself the poetry we are reading. The epigraphs of *Derniers Vers* consist of lines from Hamlet's letter to Ophelia, read by Polonius to the Queen in II, ii: "I have no art to reckon my groans . . . : This evermore, most dear lady / Whilst this machine is to him," the letter then signed "J.L." instead of "Hamlet," thus stressing the identification of the poet persona with that figure. Then follows in its entirety Ophelia's long speech to her father (II,i), describing Hamlet's behavior: "He took me by the wrist and held me hard," this second epigraph closing with Polonius' response: "This is the very ecstasy of love" (p. 81).

The *Hamlet* passages placed over the cycles, as well as those over the individual poems, frequently have no direct and obvious relationship to the texts they precede, but serve instead as allusive and yet pervasive devices in the poet's reader manipulation, a strategy which never lets us forget that this poetry reflects the fate of a modern Hamlet. All the quotations are taken from the first three acts, mainly II and III, and allude to Hamlet's relationship to Ophelia and that unfulfilled love whose tragic dimension is most bitterly expressed in Hamlet's irony.

Thus one of the epigraphs originally placed over "Figurez-vous peu" ("Just imagine"), the second piece of the *Fleurs de bonne volonté*, Hamlet's last words: "The rest is silence," Laforgue later crossed out, as not fitting his intention. Much more appropriate, for example, is Polonius' aside "Though this be madness, yet there is method in't" for "Maniaque" (p. 87), or Ophelia: " 't is brief, my lord.' Hamlet: 'As woman's love' " for "Aquarelle en cinq minutes" ("Aquarelle in five minutes") (p. 90). "Romance," in which the persona sends away the fiancée is preceded by Hamlet's "To a nunnery, go" (p. 91); and at times fairly lengthy dialogue passages precede the poems, like "Dimanches XVI" in which an orphan girl escapes woman's fate by drowning, and whose epigraph is "Hamlet: 'Have you a daughter?' Polonius: 'I have, my lord.' Hamlet: 'Let her not walk i' the sun, conception is a blessing; but not as your daughter might conceive' " (p. 105). Another "Dimanche" (Sunday) (XXVII) is preceded by Hamlet's lengthy dialogue with Ophelia, beginning with "Lady, shall I lie in your lap?", the poem's persona then taunting his girl even more cruelly: "Que je te les tordrais avec plaisir, / Ce coeur, ce corps"* (pp. 126–7). One other "Dimanche" poem (XXXIV) must be mentioned, for Laforgue's persona here repeats his oft-expressed complaint against "elle" urging her to abandon her false appearance and deceptive finery to become instead a true companion:

> † Là, là, je te ferai la honte!
> Et je te demanderai compte
> De ce corset cambrant tes reins,
> De ta tournure et des frisures
> Achalandant contre-nature
> Ton front et ton arrière-train.
> Je te crierai: "Nous sommes frères!"

This poem is most fittingly preceded by Hamlet's similar complaint: "I have heard of your paintings, too, well enough. God has given you one face, and you make yourself another; you jig, you amble, and you lisp . . . Go to, I'll no more on't; it hath made me mad . . . To a nunnery go" (pp. 137–38). Laforgue's persona more than once sends his financée off to the "nunnery" via "Hamlet" epigraphs, as also in "Petites Misères d'automne" and the final poem of *Dernier Vers* (pp. 149 and 215).

Laforgue's passion for *Hamlet* was crowned by his pilgrimage to Elsinore on New Year's Day, 1886, when he wrote to Kahn:

---

* How I would love to twist them for you, that heart, that body.

† There, there, I would put you to shame. And I'd ask you to account for this corset curving your haunches, your bearing and false curls causing to thrive against nature your forehead and your hind-quarters. I'd cry out to you: "We are brothers!"

"I am writing you from Elsinore, the country of Hamlet. . . . . I have spent an awful New Year's Day, glacial wind, mud, gulls . . ."[25] This site (unseen) had already served as setting for one of the poet's most famous texts, *Hamlet, ou les suites de la piété filiale*, a lengthy "legendary morality" finished in August of the year past. Laforgue has left us two literary souvenirs of his visit, the poem "Avertissement" ("Notice"), one of whose drafts had been entitled "To the French of Tomorrow, preface," a rather Hamletic meditation dealing with a father's memory and a son's inability to live and love:

> * Mon père (un dur par timidité)
> Est mort avec un profil sévère;
> . . . .
> Alors, j'ai fait d' la littérature;
> Mais le Démon de la Vérité
> Sifflotait tout l' temps à mes côtés:
> "Pauvre! as-tu fini tes écritures..."
>
> Or, pas le coeur de me marier,
> Etant, moi, au fond, trop méprisable!
> Et elles, pas assez intraitables! !
> Mais tout l' temps là à s'extasier!...
>
> C'est pourquoi je vivotte, vivotte,
> Bonne girouette aux trent' six saisons,
> Trop nombreaux pour dire oui ou non....
> —Jeunes gens! que je vous serv' d'Ilote!
> Copenhague, Elseneur.
> Ier janvier 1886.[26]

The other memento of that visit is the prose vignette "A propos de Hamlet" which appeared in *Le Symboliste* in October

---

* My father (a hard man by timidity) died with a severe profile; . . . . Then, I did some literature; but the Demon of Truth all the time whistled by my side "Poor fellow! have you done with your writing . . ." Well, not having the heart to get married, being myself, basically, too contemptible! And they, not uncompromising enough!! But always there, going into ecstasies! . . . That's why I go on keeping body and soul together as best I can, a good weather vane of thirty-six seasons, too numerous to say yes or no. . . .—Young people, let me serve as your Helot!

of 1886,[27] a miniature "Reisebild" of that rainy day at Elsinore, where the narrator met his hero:

> Far from Paris, far from the French language (whose well-being is very dear do me), far from relations, far from letters and fine arts,I established my solitary presence the first of last January at Elsinore, by the shore of that sea whose monotonous waves surely inspired Hamlet with this epitaph about Human History: "Words, words, words."

The narrator was, of course, not about to leave these shores "deserted in the rain," and "the sea, melancholy as in the worst of days," without seeing "Lord Hamlet of Shakespearean memory." Thus, toward evening, our hero calls forth his alter ego "by dint of whistling the victory motif of Wagner's *Siegfried* (but in a sad tone) into the wind" ! A Hamlet à la Delacroix (his wonderful lithographs of the Prince can be seen at the Delacroix museum, rue Furstenberg in Paris) appears—"his psychological age, thirty; . . . shaven like an actor happily endowed with a liver ailment, dressed in black, wearing a toque"—, immediately recognizing his modern brother. He wants to know how Irving played in his role, and when the narrator recalls that perform-ance in Berlin, Hamlet muses over the country of his university days: "And at Berlin, you say? Oh Germany! Oh Wittenberg where I spent my student days! Oh country of Faust, Faust who profoundly upset me!" But he would be disappointed today, for things have changed in Germany: "Today, Highness, it is no longer the same. The state which I would call *faustian* is a state very poor or too rich. The Germans of today . . . are undergoing the crisis of the newly rich. You would have a wretched time in Berlin these days, Highness." In Paris things are a bit better, for, among other things, "there is me, who take you mirthfully, Highness, à la Yorick." Hamlet asks what Ophelia is doing, "she is doing us in, Highness. Ophelia is more irresistible than ever, thanks to industrial inventions . . . She is no longer a believer and pious," and, also, she insists on getting married: ". . . would have us, in order to sign over support and fidelity to her, go through the giddy joys of organ music." The best way the narrator, who is a poet, can describe her is to quote his "La

Femme, mûre ou jeune fille" ("Woman, mature or young girl") from the *Concile féerique*, the lines which are the poem "Esthétique" from the *Fleurs de bonne volonté*. Thereupon Hamlet once again appears to be losing his mind, "twisted his arms, sneered fixedly, and began shouting: 'To arms, citizens! There is no longer any SENSE [RAISON]!' " His madness infects the poet, who begins to dance "the Criterion of Human Certainty step," which consists of describing "with his feet the figure of the square of the hypotenuse, that Gibraltar of certitude, simple and immortal figure," and which is danced until one falls and breaks one's nose. After this "best conclusion" to their interview, prince and poet part, promising vaguely to meet again.

We meet Laforgue's Hamlet one more time, in *Hamlet, or the sequels of filial piety*, which first appeared one month after the above, in the November-December issues of *La Vogue.*[28] Like Heine's *Romeo and Juliet* episode in *Die Bäder von Lucca*, Laforgue's *Hamlet* is a parody, not episodic, however, but comprising the entire forty-page text. By parody I here refer, to use Genette's terminology, to a hypertext, Laforgue's, constituting a ludic transformation of the hypotext, Shakespeare's;[29] yet, Laforgue's *Hamlet* cannot be contained in Genette's tabulations, as his ludic transformation at the same time partakes of satire, like Heine's Gumpelino-Romeo. For as Heine's text satirizes the "Bildungsphilister," Laforgue's ironic self-portrait satirizes the *ego scriptor* (to borrow a Valéryan term) of the closing nineteenth century.

In this "moralité légendaire," moreover, Hamlet is no longer the persona's fraternal alter ego as in "A propos de Hamlet," but the identification is now complete, and the persona *is* Hamlet, orphan and aspiring playwright, presented by a narrator who, after establishing the setting, effaces himself behind the protagonist's monologues.

The setting is a tower into which "Hamlet, bizarre character," has retreated since his father's "irregular decease," a "forgotten leprous sentinel" at the far end of the royal park, depository of the withered flowers of ephemeral feasts, the whole surrounded by the stagnant waters of the Sund. Fitting setting, for "this corner of the water is indeed the mirror of the unfortunate Hamlet in his outcast tower," on this "fourteenth of July, 1601, a Saturday" (p. 7). His room in the tower is decorated with "a dozen views of Jutland, impeccably naïve pictures," reflections perhaps of those views of Prussia lining the walls of the Prinzessinnenpalais in Berlin. But between the two windows, there are "two full-length portraits; the one of Hamlet, as dandy, . . . his smile attractive against a background of sulphury semi-darkness; the other, his father, in handsome new armor, the eye roguish and faun-like, his late father Horwendill, deceased in irregular circumstances and in a state of mortal sin, and whose soul may God take according to his well-known mercy." Among other objects, there is "a dung-heap of books" of course, and two small wax statues of "Gerutha, Hamlet's mother, and her present spouse, the adulterous and fratricidal usurper Fengo, both with their hearts childishly pierced by a needle, much good that will do" (p. 8).

Thus the frame for the first monologue of Hamlet, "dressed in black, the little sword at his side, wearing his noctambulist's sombrero," here committed to the Hartmannian metaphysical Unconscious, who "wraps up the happy unconscious panorama with an ad hoc gesture and . . . rambles thus: 'Ah! if I were only driven to go to all the trouble! . . . I'll gladly concede life, if I have to . . . But a hero!' " He also knows the continental rationalists, who lived after him, "Method, Method, what do you want of me? You know well that I have eaten of the fruit of Innocence! . . . me, who am bringing the new law to the son of Woman, and who am going to dethrone the Categorical Imperative installing the Climateric Imperative in its place" (pp. 9–10)! He also knows the British philosophers. Thus in his next tirade he suspects Ophelia of Hobbesian selfishness: "She may well have been adorable and most mortally sensitive; in scraping a little, you'd find the Englishwoman, saturated from birth with Hobbes' egotistical philosophy, underneath. 'Nothing is more pleasing in the possession of our goods than to think that they are superior to those of others,' said Hobbes. Ophelia would have loved me like that, like her 'property' " (p. 10).

And, to be sure, Hamlet had a great deal more of all that on his heart, "more of it than can be contained in five acts, more than our philosophy can scrutinize between heaven and earth." But then he notices the approach of the comedians who are to perform his play tonight, which reminds him of his manuscript, two slim notebooks. He had originally written it "to put on the horrible event again," but in the creative process, "I gradually forgot that it was about my assassinated father, . . . about my prostituted mother . . . For it is a good subject!" He redid the piece in iambic verse and chose a sublime epigraph "in my good Philoctetes" (p. 12); in fact, the play *is* the thing, and much more important than its occasion. He therefore feels a bit guilty, but "everything is heredity. Let's be medical." Besides, the prince wishes he were free of all those family entanglements and court intrigues and "a simple clerk in Paris, Mount Sainte-Geneviève, where a school of neo-Alexandrians is flourishing at the moment" (p. 13)! We clearly hear Laforgue, exiled at the imperial court at Berlin, longing for his Paris where Symbolists and Decadents flourished in his day.

However, Hamlet most graciously receives the two principals of the troupe, named William and Ophelia, offers them cigarettes, "here's some Dubeck and here some Bird's-eye;" but the ingenue's name is unacceptable. "What! another Ophelia in my potion! . . . Ophelia, that's not real life, that! But pure stage stories. . ." And so he will call the young actress—"Heavens, how beautiful she is! More trouble" (p. 14)—by her baptismal name, Kate, which he likes much better. Their repertory, which contains a *Doktor Faustus* and a *King of Thule*, interests Hamlet much less than his own play to be performed tonight, and whose plot he outlines to William and Ophelia-Kate. William objects that, generally, they only play "sympathetic characters," whereupon Hamlet exclaims: "Sympathetic? Bunch of fools! And by what do you think you can swear that a person is sympathetic, here below? And then, what about progress" (p. 16)? After sampling a selection of the princely poet's verse and accepting a sizeable honorarium, William and Ophelia-Kate, "the two stars, pocketing the money, exit backwards" (p. 18). The evening's program arranged, Hamlet again engages in extensive narcissistic reflections which he terminates, however, with a decision to act: "But tonight, I must act, I must objectify myself! Forward over the tombs, like Nature" (p. 20)! And in this call to action we seem to be hearing something to be taken up by another Decadent anti-hero a few years later, Gide's equally Faustian Urien who, setting out for the voyage named after him, proclaims similarly: "One must always represent."[30] On the way to the tombs, that is the cemetery, however, Hamlet briefly stops to kill a "warm canary" sleeping in his cage. "These strange destructive impulses often seized him since his Father's irregular death" (p. 21), which leads to a flashback of a recent hunting expedition during which Hamlet had turned into a sado-masochistic monster torturing and killing everything on his way, from beetles to butterflies, an orgy that culminated with the hero washing his hands in pounds of broken eyes! "Ah, that was THE DEMON OF REALITY! the mirth of ascertaining that justice is just a word, that everything is allowed—and for a very good reason, in God's name!—against narrow and silent beings" (p. 22). This pre-Nietzschean Hamlet had also read Flaubert.[31]

Continuing on his way to the cemetery, "with a straggling and correct pace," our nineteenth-century Hamlet passes "herds of proletarians" which briefly arouse his social conscience: "By God! Hamlet thinks, I know it as well as you do, if not better: the existing social order is a scandal fit to suffocate Nature" (p. 24)! It is not the crownprince, but the feudal parasite, "et moi, je ne suis qu'un parasite féodal," who momentarily rebels, if weakly, against the order of things. And in this, Laforgue's Hamlet does not reflect Heine so much as, perhaps, an imperial French reader at the Court of Prussia. He quickly soothes his conscience, moreover—"and to think that I have for a moment had my apostle's madness, like Çakia-Mouni, son of a king! O dear me, me with my good little unique existence" (p. 25)—as he approaches the grave-diggers arranging Polonius' fresh tomb. They are full of ale and most upsetting revelations.

For Hamlet learns from them that he is not the queen's son, "I say, not at all! His lordship has perhaps heard of the incomparable late fool Yorick . . . Well, Prince Hamlet is simply his brother by the mother," whereupon the incognito prince exclaims: "Hamlet, brother of a court fool!" Thus, in the transformation of Laforgue's principal persona from Pierrot to Hamlet, the new Hamlet did remain the brother of his former self. Yorick's and Hamlet's mother had been "the most diabolically beautiful gypsy that, with all due respect to you, has ever been seen" (p. 27); and we recall that the king had "l'oeil coquin et faunesque"! The other revelation is that Ophelia was found drowned near the locks; her brother had just come to order her grave. Laertes, poor fellow, is "much loved. You know that he is taking care of the problem of workers' lodgings!" Things are going from bad to worse, for, did his lordship know that "Prince Hamlet went crazy" (p. 28)? Things are, in fact, so bad in Denmark that one of the grave-diggers has already converted his savings into Norwegian securities! At this point, Hamlet seizes Yorick's skull and intones one of his most famous soliloquies, "Alas, poor Yorick!" (pp. 28–31), a masterful parody in which Albert Sonnenfeld sees "one of Laforgue's most dazzling achievements".[32]

After stagnating like the surrounding Sund, action finally begins to pick up as Hamlet, having deposited his brother's skull among the bibelots in his chamber, goes down to see how the rehearsal of his play is progressing. But there, among the trunks and sets, he finds beautiful Kate in tears. Hamlet's play has so deeply moved her, and the aspiring author presses her to explain. "Continue, continue, Ophelia." And she: "Oh, well then, while I was getting dressed, I rehearsed the monologue at the church, and suddenly my heart burst . . . If you only knew what a big heart I have! . . . Tomorrow I'm leaving everything, and going back to Calais and enter a convent in order to devote myself to the poor wounded of the Hundred Years war." This is the novice playwright's consecration, "although well brought up, he could hardly contain his artist's joy. It is his baptism as poet" (p. 38)! Ophelia-Kate must explain her minutest reactions;

and their entire lives have changed: "we will leave this night in the so lucid moonlight! I will read everything to you! we'll go live in Paris" (p. 30)!

During the performance that night, the king faints and stops the show, but Hamlet no longer cares, "and I don't care a rap about my throne either" (p. 40). He escapes with Kate from Elsinore in the general confusion, but on the way to fame and freedom, he stops at the cemetery: "Kate, wait for me a minute. It's my father's tomb, the poor man who was assassinated!" But then—driven by the Unconscious?—"he goes straight to the tomb of Ophelia, the already so mysterious and legendary Ophelia." There he encounters Laertes, who wants to spare his life, for the poor demented creature, Hamlet, "is not responsible according to the latest scientific findings." But fate and three centuries of literary tradition will it otherwise. In their brief exchange, Hamlet insults Ophelia's memory, so that "that's too much!" And Laertes, "seizing Hamlet's throat with one hand, . . . plants a real dagger into his heart with the other." Our hero falls to his knees, vomits his blood, and renders "his Hamletic soul to impassible Nature," articulating "Ah! Ah! . . . qualis . . . artifex . . . pereo" (p. 45)! Kate goes back and confesses all, gets a beating from Bibi, "(Bibi is an abbreviation of Billy, diminuative of William)." Eventually, "everything returned to order. With one Hamlet less, the race is not going to die out, you can say that again" (p. 47).

"Laforgue's best-known single work, *Hamlet*," comments Haskell Block, "reflects the intimate awareness of the theatre's ways and means. A scenario as well as a *nouvelle*, it brings together soliloquy, gesture, and dramatic dialogue in depicting the vivid interplay of the real and the make-believe. Hamlet is himself both actor and playwright, seeing life and art as performance and masquerade."[33] And Laforgue's *Hamlet* has, in fact, been adapted for the stage and performed several times,[34] as have some of the other "moralités légendaires."

Barker Fairley once said about Heine: ". . . for him in very truth all the world is a stage and life a ballet";[35] and therein lies another profound affinity between Heine and Laforgue, which for both pivots on the poet and dramatist they admired the most, Shakespeare.

Notes

[1] Walter Wadepuhl, *Heine-Studien* (Weimar: Aron Verlag, 1956), 116.

[2] Cf. for example Heine's sonnet "An A.W. v. Schlegel"of 1821, in whose closing tercet the poet says: ". . . bei deinem Gruße / Aufwachte lächelnd Deutschlands echte Muse, / Und sank in deine Arme liebestrunken." DA, I: 115. For a discussion of Heine's relationship with Schlegel, as well as that of the poet's two other sonnets to his former teacher, cf. Herbert Gutjahr, *Zwischen Affinität und Kritik, Heinrich Heine und die Romantik* (Frankfurt: Peter Lang, 1984), esp. 13–16. This entire study deals with Heine's debt to and separation from Romanticism.

[3] Ernst August Schalles, *Heines Verhältnis zu Shakespeare*, Inaugural-Dissertation, Königl. Friedrich-Wilhelm-Universität zu Berlin, 13. Februar 1904, 14–17.

[4] Siegbert Prawer, *Heine's Shakespeare*, Inaugural Lecture, University of Oxford, May 5, 1970 (Oxford: The Clarendon Press, 1970), 22ff.

[5] Prawer, *Heine's Shakespeare*, 22–23.

[6] Wadepuhl notes that as Heine here attended performances of *Romeo and Juliet*, *The Merchant of Venice*, *Richard II*, *Henry IV*, *Macbeth*, and probably also *Hamlet*, but never quotes from these plays during the period, he most likely at that time did not read but merely saw the plays. *Heine-Studien*, 117.

[7] B, IV: 171–293. Reproductions of the prints are included in this edition of the text.

[8] Wadepuhl who has examined the manuscripts of *Shakespeares Mädchen und Frauen* finds that "sie sind in Heines eigener Handschrift geschrieben und zeigen die sorgfältigen Korrekturen, die wir in seinen Manuskripten zu finden gewohnt sind. Wir haben also den schlüssigen Beweis, daß Heine weder den ganzen Shakespeare las noch sein Buch über Shakespeare diktierte" (*Heine-Studien*, 128–29). Wadepuhl's findings have, however, been questioned by Karl Josef Höltgen, "Über 'Shakespeares Mädchen und Frauen,' Heine, Shakespeare und England," *Heine-Studien*, ed. Manfred Windfuhr, Internationaler Heine-Kongress 1972 (Hamburg: Hoffmann und Campe Heinrich Heine Verlag, 1973), 465. Höltgen ascertains that what Wadepuhl had considered to be a final draft was in fact an earlier one.

[9] Henri Heine, *De l'Angelterre* (Paris: Calmann Lévy, 1881), 1 and 3. (Original ed. 1867).

[10] In this text, Heine says: "But send no poet to London! This sheer earnestness of all things, this colossal uniformity, this machine-like movement, this discouragement of joy itself, this exorbitant London stifles the imagination and mangles the heart" (B, II: 538).

[11] Höltgen has shown to what extent Heine's own text is indebted to Hazlitt's *Characters of Shakespeare's Plays* of 1817, "Über 'Shakespeares Mädchen und Frauen'," 483ff. And he concludes his brilliant essay on Heine's relationship to Shakespeare and particularly our text: "Ein wesentlicher Vorzug des Heineschen Shakespearebuches is die farbige, geistreiche, flüssige, gemeinverständliche, überwiegend unterhaltsame Darstellung, die sehr viel breitere Leserschichten anspricht als schulmäßige Literatur. . . . Heine wollte kein Buch für Fachgelehrte schreiben, und es ist besser, daß seine Leser die erhellenden Betrachtungen Schlegels und Hazlitts durch ihn erfahren als überhaupt nicht" (487–88).

[12] Thus Wadepuhl: " 'Shakespeares Mädchen und Frauen' ist eines der schwächsten Werke von Heine, und es errascht deshalb nicht, daß es Shakespeare Forschern ganz unbekannt ist und sogar die Forscher der deutschen Literatur nicht damit vertraut sind" (*Heine-Studien*, 134). I certainly agree that the text does not constitute a scholarly work or a *Forschungsbericht*! Cf. note 11 above. For some of the contemporary critical response to the work, cf. Hans Henning, "Heines Buch über Shakespeares Mädchen und Frauen," *Shakespeare Jahrbuch*, 103–117, 113 (1977), 115–16.

[13] In the French edition, *Les Bains de Lucques* occupies 119–206 of *Tableaux de Voyage* II. I recall that the *Tableaux de Voyage* was one of Heine's most popular works in France.

[14] For a discussion of Heine's use of the "Romeo and Juliet" parody in the ninth chapter of *Die Bäder von Lucca*, cf. Klaus Pabel, *Heines "Reisebilder"* (Munich: Wilhelm Fink Verlag, 1977), 193–98.

[15] Prawer, *Heine's Shakespeare*, 21.

[16] *Les Complaintes*, 168–9.

[17] *Les Complaintes*, 283.

[18] Laforgue, "Feuilles volantes," in *La Revue blanche*, X, (1896): 367–77.

[19] Jules Laforgue, "Plans de Nouvelles et Notes," in *La Revue blanche*, XI, (1896): 545.

[20] Cf. p. 17.

[21] *Les Complaintes*, 172–73.

[22] *Les Complaintes*, 313.

[23] *Pages de la Guêpe*, 140 and 142.

[24] Laforgue, *L'Imitation de Notre-Dame la Lune*, 229–303; Pascal Pia here gives a list and translations into French of these *Hamlet* quotations and epigraphs.

[25] *Lettres à un Ami*, 143.

[26] Laforgue, *L'Imitation de Notre-Dame la Lune*, 83. Line 5 mockingly alludes to Mallarmé's prose poem "Le Démon de l'analogie."

[27] Laforgue, *Moralités*, 334–38.

[28] *Moralities*, 2–47. The text is preceded by two epigraphs: "La reine de Saba à Saint Antoine;—'Ris donc, bel ermite! . . .' Gustave Flaubert," the

other: "C'est plus fort que moi." And the text in *La Vogue* had a Latin epigraph from Lucretius and one from *Hamlet*: "If thou didst hold me thy heart [sic], / Absent from felicity awhile [sic], /And in this harsh world draw thy breath in pain, / To tell my story. Hamlet."

²⁹ Genette, *Palimpsestes*, 14ff. In this connection, I should like to draw attention to Michele Hannoosh's forthcoming book on Laforguean parody, *Parody and Decadence, Laforgue's "Moralités légendaires."*

³⁰ André Gide, *Romans, récits et soties* (Paris: Gallimard, 1958), 19. I am convinced that Gide had read Laforgue's *Hamlet* at the time he composed *Le Voyage d'Urien*," that mock-Symbolist quest, whose protagonist has much in common with Laforgue's.

³¹ Peter Brooks, in a brilliant essay on Laforgue's *Hamlet*, "The Rest is Silence: Hamlet as Decadent" in *Laforgue, Essays on a Poet's Life and Work*, 93–110, was the first to see that Laforgue here "parodies the famous hunting expedition in Flaubert's *Légende de St.-Julien l'hospitalier*" (103). Eric's orgies of the killing of the birds in "Le Voyage d'Urien" (Gide, *Romans, récits et soties*, 54–5) may well have been influenced by Hamlet's rampage. The Laforguean text also recalls again Mallarmé's "Le Démon de l'analogie."

³² Albert Sonnenfeld, "Hamlet the German and Jules Laforgue," *Yale French Studies*, 33 (1964): 92–100. Sonnenfeld finds "his *Alas, poor Yorick* monologue, with its sardonic and often incoherent mixture of anachronisms, puns, aphorisms from German philosophy, parodies of Shakespeare, and ironic imagery is one of Laforgue's most dazzling achievements" (98).

³³ Block, "Laforgue and the Theatre," 91.

³⁴ For these, Laforgue, *Moralités*, XXIII. The best-known of these is surely Barault's at the Théâtre de l'Atelier in 1939.

³⁵ Barker Fairley, "Heine's Vaudeville," *University of Toronto Quarterly*, III (1934): 202.

V

The Poets on the Performing Arts

In counterparting Heine and Laforgue and their endeavors in the theater, we must also consider their commentary on theater and its related performing arts, such as music, opera, dance and the circus. For their fascination with all of these is reflected in various texts dispersed throughout their work.[1] We have already encountered some of that commentary in the poets' earliest journalism, Heine's *Briefe aus Berlin* of 1822 and Laforgue's *Chroniques parisiennes* of 1879–80.[2] The *Briefe* were overshadowed by a musical controversy, the Spontini-Weber rivalry raging in Berlin at the time, whose characteristically Heinean reportage I have discussed in the opening chapter. But they contain also other theater and opera news. In the first of his three letters, Heine relies on his "Kammermusikus": "What's new, my dear Mr. Chamber musician?" "Nothing at all," says he, but then rambles for two pages (DA, VI: 17–18) about opera, theater and theater directors, actors, dancers, and singers, authors and composers from Shakespeare to Weber and Spontini—all of it interspersed with other news, literary, political, and even academic. Franz Bopp has just given his inaugural lecture on Sanskrit at the University.

From the second letter, most of it devoted to the Spontini-Weber matter, we learn that a performance of Kleist's *The Prince of Homburg*, a play which was to become a German classic, has been called off the Berlin stage because a noblewoman felt one of her ancestors misrepresented in it (DA, VI: 31). Heine's not apolitical intention in reporting his theatrical news item is clear. Then the chamber musician, whom the author had met at the Café Royal yesterday, brings "a lot of minor news." "It goes without saying," comments Heine, "that most of the news from the musical chronicle is scandalous," before telling us what actors are playing where, that Michael Beer has written a new tragedy, and his brother Meyerbeer's new opera is being performed in Milan (DA, VI: 33). The last letter, principally devoted to the royal wedding which has the city in an uproar, does not have much on the theater—"thus this time I will write you little about drama"—except for a brief discussion of some of the currently popular actors and actresses, especially Amalie Neumann: "The enthusiasm for the Neumann is raging like the plague here . . . Truly, she is a Venus, or, as a merchant from Altona said, a 'Venussin' " (DA, VI: 44–5). She is Heine's counterpart to Laforgue's Sarah Bernhardt in the *Chroniques parisiennes*. More significant in retrospect are Heine's comments on "a musical wonder, a second Mozart," the young Felix Mendelssohn, Berlin's only musical genius, according to Heine (DA, VI: 47). Again there is news from the University, where Ludwig Tieck will soon be giving lectures on Shakespeare (DA, VI: 49).

In his *Chroniques parisiennes*, we saw Laforgue assume his master's "impressionistic technique," and the rambling, free association of ideas-topics which gives Heinean journalism its entertaining allure. So we find Laforgue's theatrical comments, like Heine's, freely intermixed with other news. Yet, the theater is a persistent theme in these reportages, with no fewer than sixteen of the twenty-six numbered pieces partly devoted to it. One of the principal themes was that of "les Jeunes," the plight of young dramatic writers like Laforgue himself. In his second chronicle, he reports on a recently founded society of *jeunes auteurs*, which will soon give its first presentation.[3] The entire third chronicle deals with Labiche, famous for his comedy *The Straw Hat of Italy*, a writer again made very popular by his recently published *oeuvres complètes*. The Odéon gave his

Voyage of M. Perrichon last week; and the play was to gloriously successful that its author might well be on his way to membership in the Académie Française.

In the fourth article, Laforgue deplores the absence of the Comédie-Française, on tour in London: "*oyez* the lamentable story. . . .the Comédie-Française will for two long months delight the barbarian sons of Albion" (pp. 104–5). Is it not "the abomination of desolation" that the unique company should abandon its Parisian public, "delicate enough to be worthy of it," to entertain "a people who puts the necessary above the superfluous and for whom a theater is above all a commercial enterprise" (p. 105)! We seem to be hearing Heine himself, who always reproached the English for their commercialism. Then Laforgue derides the British tourists in Paris, much in the Heinean vein:

> Here is, moreover, what I have seen. One evening, they were giving *Hernani*. A car stops in front of the theater in which was enthroned a hop-pole of an Englishwoman flanked by her two daughters, tender buds blooming in the shade of the maternal rosebush, and protecting their freckle-bespattered peonie faces under those delightful green gauze veils you recall. One of them gets out, approaches the billboard, comes back, and with a gesture of disappointment says: "It's in verse," . . . And the car sets out again in quest for a prose play. I blushed for the fatherland of Byron, after which I indulged in an extremely patriotic monologue about certain little giddy-brained girls who ought to have their noses blown and be sent out skipping rope (p. 106).

The June 19 chronicle announces "la belle saison" and the closing of the theaters; and "during that time the Comédie-Française is a success in London;" but during the august company's absence, "the house of Molière is being renovated" (p. 108). The entire "Chronique parisienne" of July 3 is devoted to our theme because, the theaters being closed, "this would be a good moment to draw up the balance sheet of the theatrical year" (p. 112). Alas, the number of the past season's plays that will remain in the repertory is limited indeed. Let us not speak of operettas, "the baby plays" [les pièces à biberon], continues the reporter, of which he then, however, lists a few before passing on to "our foremost theaters." The only fault of the Comédie-Française is to live a bit too much on the past, its premieres being rare; "you have to admit that two premieres of one act, that's a little meager for one year" (p. 113). Then follows a review of the year's second-rate plays, all of them totally forgotton today. But "the theaters will reopen in October," and the Comédie-Française promises plays by Sardou and Dumas. Finally Laforgue suggests the famous house open a branch theater, where half of its not very busy troupe might "interpret the attempts of the young authors who are waiting for a theater to come their way unexpectedly (pp. 114–15).

In his tenth article, Laforgue reports on Sarah Bernhardt; not her acting, but her equally famous eccentricities: "the flashy member of the Comédie-Française gets herself almost as much talked about as a man condemned to death. Her life is a fabric of eccentricities" (p. 120). The public, of course, loves these as much as her art; and currently the big question is whether she will accept the American engagement offered to her in London. "I can hardly be happy seeing our foremost tragedienne proceed to the Yankees. Who will do *Phèdre* and *Marie de Neubourg* from now on? . . . And the revival of *Le Roy s'amuse*, are we going to be deprived of it? For who will interpret the role of Blanche if Sarah Bernhardt is no longer here?" She never should have gone to England! "Ah! cursed trip to London! . . . Michelet is a hundred times right, the English are our eternal enemies and France has only one saint, Joan of Arc" (p. 121)! Are we again hearing a Heinean echo?

But happiness returns, with the twelfth article about "an epic evening! Last night the Comédie-Française gave its brilliant reopening which I have had the good fortune to attend." Not only was the newly renovated house impressive, but "what a public" (p. 124)! They were all there, from the Government (Grévy, Gambetta) to critics (Sarcey) to authors (Banville)—"I am not talking about Victor Hugo, who never goes to the theater and goes to bed with the chickens"—for the gala performance of *The Imaginary Invalid*. And "when Sarah Bernhardt—who did not leave—came forward in her turn, the house shook with applause" (p. 125)! Over a hundred years later, Laforgue's readers can only wish they had been there!

After the above, the remainder of the *Chroniques'* theater news, like the re-opening of the Odéon, the Ambigu, or even the Opera, must seem anticlimactic. Thus also two new dramas by Victor Hugo, and a new volume of plays by Alexandre Dumas, an author who had been dear to Heine, announced in the final *Chronique parisienne.*

These early reportages are already characteristic of their authors' future literary journalism, and we should thus not expect closely argued critical and theoretical discussions on theater from either. Frequently reviews devoted to one of the performing arts might jump to others, so that a text on theater might also deal with opera, dance, or music.

To my knowledge, Heine wrote only two essays on specific plays, *Tassos Tod Trauerspiel in fünf Aufzügen* (*The Death of Tasso, drama in five acts*) by Wilhelm Smets of 1821, and Michael Beer's *Struensee* of 1828.[4] The first, written shortly after he had finished his own first tragedy, smacks of a certain youthful pendantry totally absent from his other work. Thus, the young critic first enumerates the criteria by which he will judge the play under discussion: "We shall therefore judge the tragedy in question from three points of view: the dramatic, the poetic, and the ethical" (B, I: 402). Then follows a brief history of poetry from the lyric to the epic and the dramatic, suggesting that Heine might already have been Hegel's student at the time. The principal requisite of drama is lively progression and inter-action of dialogue and action. The author under discussion, a lyric poet, has not entirely succeeded in overcoming his own subjectivity; but, then, he has accomplished the transition from the lyric to the dramatic in this play, after having failed in his preceding one. Characterization is generally poor, most of the characters speaking in the same tone and language. The first exposition is poor, in the French manner: "how different that is in our great model, in Shakespeare, where the exposition already is a sufficiently motivated action" (B, I: 412).

Heine does not insist on the three unities, only that of action being essential to tragedy; but the present author has observed none. Tragic poets portray either noteworthy events or great passions, or they develop great characters. While the Greek tragedians concentrated on the first two, character development is essential to modern drama. In Shakespeare, however, we find all three united: "he may therefore be considered the founder of modern drama and remains our great and of course unequaled model" (B, I: 414). Smets has succeeded in the characterization of his protagonist, probably because Tasso, too, is a lyric poet. More importantly, Smets has accomplished the ethical end of tragedy in conferring on *Tassos Tod* the qualities of mildness and reconciliation: "Under this reconciliation of the passions we do not merely understand the *Aristotelian purgation of the passions*, but also the judicious observation of the limits of the purely human." Here, too, Shakespeare is the unsurpassed master: "No one can put more awful passions and actions on the stage than Shakespeare, and yet it never happens that our hearts and minds become thoroughly roused to indignation by him" (B, I: 420). On the whole, Heine gives *Tassos Tod* a passing grade, and to his readers some overtones of lectures recently heard from Schlegel at Bonn.

Heine wrote his essay on Michael Beer's *Struensee* in Munich in March of 1828, during his brief residence in Bavaria's capital, when he had vague hopes for an appointment at the University there. His review of Beer's new play was clearly influenced by those circumstances, as Beer was then a favorite at the Bavarian Court.[5] That Heine felt uncomfortable with his text is evident from his correspondence, as in a letter to Moser of April of that year, in which he says: "Our national poet, Michael Beer, is here and has his plays produced. In the *Morgenblatt* is a correspondence from Munich discussing his *Struensee*. And just imagine—I, I, I have written it! The gods themselves must be at their wit's end. . . "[6] Heine considers *Struensee* a model of good diction and an improvement over Beer's previous plays. Again, then, a young playwright's later attempt surpasses a preceding one, as with Heine's own two tragedies. *Struensee* had been criticized for featuring near-contemporary history, the story of that bourgeois minister's (1737–1772) struggle against his country's haughty aristocracy and his love for Queen Karoline Mathilde of Denmark. Heine disagrees: "but we are of a different opinion. The horror stories of the courts cannot be brought to the stage rapidly enough, and here one should, as formerly in Egypt, hold a mortal judgement over the kings and the great of this earth" (B, I: 435). The plot, in fact, is very much to Heine's liking. We may doubt Heine's sincerity, however, when on another page he praises the free people of Bavaria and their liberal king: "Here in Bavaria, where we find a free people and, what is even rarer, a liberal king, we are also encountering an equally magnanimous spirit, and we may, therefore, expect a rich harvest of art" (B, I: 433–34). We do not learn much about Heine's notions on drama from this review, as he speaks more about the plot, the protagonist's heroic struggle against the aristocracy, than its treatment by Beer.

Altogether different in style and characteristic of his mature manner is Heine's review of the premiere of a work by Beer's brother, Mayerbeer's *Hugenotten*, written in 1836.[7] Both the composer and his reviewer are well known by then, both members of "die schöne Welt von Paris" (Paris high society), one of whose memorable days Heine describes: "Yesterday was a noteworthy day for Paris [die schöne Welt von Paris]: the Opera gave the premiere of Meyerbeer's long-awaited *Hugue-nots*, and Rothschild gave his first great ball at his new residence." Thus, in the very first sentence of a review ostensibly about an artistic event, Heine passes on to one of another nature, one of the season's big society galas. Not merely are the two apparently dissimilar events connected temporally and socially, but the reviewer participated in both, being himself part of "le grand monde" about which he writes: "I wanted to enjoy both marvels on the same evening and have so exhausted myself that I am still as if intoxicated, . . . and can hardly write from all the bewilderment and fatigue. Any critical review is out of the question." As Heine himself tells us here, his review has nothing to do with music criticism (*Beurteilung*); for that, he resorts to the judgment of others: "And as the critics assure us, Meyerbeer is supposed to have shown even greater perfection of form in the *Huguenots* and still more ingenious execution of detail [than in his previous opera *Robert the Devil*].'' When he enthusiastically continues that Meyerbeer may well be the greatest living musical artist, he merely concurs with and supports the opinion of contemporary Meyerbeer fans. Thus also in comparing Meyerbeer's artistic sense to Goethe's—an opinion, needless to add, which would indeed appear extreme today—, Heine does not introduce a notion of his own, but that of *man*, of others: ''Yesterday, in the foyer of the Opera, Meyerbeer's artistic sense was very justly compared to Goethe's'' (B, I: 140–41). Heine is not a music critic, nor a theater critic, but a creative artist who transposes his experiences into texts loosely classified as literary journalism; and the emphasis for him, as for Laforgue, is on *literary*.

Heine had already reported on Meyerbeer's success in the fifth of a series of articles on the political life of France, written for the *Augsburger Allgemeine Zeitung* from 1831 to 1832, after he first arrived in Paris, and which he republished in 1832 in the volume *Französische Zustände*.[8] Heine begins his report of March 25, 1832, in discussing three noteworthy recent strategic moves of the *Juste-milieu* Government: France's support of the Belgian strugggle for independence, the French blockade of the port of Lisbon of 1831, and the occupation of Ancona by French troops, ordered by Casimir Périer in 1832. Then he passes on to a discussion of the political mood in Paris and the supporters of the ministry. They are, of course, the rich, who love to dance; and one of the most popular dances of the season's balls is the ''Nonnenwalzer'' (the waltz of the nuns) from *Robert le Diable*. Meyerbeer has accomplished the unheard of ''in that for an entire winter he was able to capture the fickle Parisians; everybody is still flocking to the Academy of Music (the Opera) to see *Robert le Diable*. This may, however, be due not merely to the music, but also to the political significance of the opera. For the protagonist, the son of the devil, ''as vile . . . as *Philippe Egalité*,'' and of a most virtuous mother, is torn between the two powers of good and evil: ''he hovers in the middle between two

principles, he is 'Juste-milieu'." The great Taglioni, incidentally, is dancing Robespierre in the opera. Thus Heine here
most skillfully links foreign affairs to internal ones, then passes
from politics to entertainment. He justifies his strategy by telling
his readers also that "since there was so much discussion of this
opera in the Chamber of Deputies, its mention in these pages is
in no way inappropriate" (DA, XII: 117). But asides to the
performing arts are rare in *Französische Zustände* (*French
Conditions*), whose principal interest and contractual subject is
French political life.

A contemporary article exclusively devoted to a concert
performance is "F. Hiller's Concert," published in December of
1831 in the *Morgenblatt für gebildete Stände*.[9] The reportage,
whose Heinean provenance has only recently been ascertained,
opens, however, by recalling Meyerbeer's popularity in Paris:
"Despite politics, which keeps all minds preoccupied, music is
this winter still able to claim special recognition. *Robert le
Diable* is still the object of general discussion." This leads to the
debate over German or Italian opera: "they argue over the
superiority of the German or the Italian school with a zeal
recalling the times of the Gluckists and the Piccinists" (DA, XII:
291). Only in the second paragraph do we approach the subject,
namely Hiller's concert. Heine praises him as an authentic and
gifted composer, among so many false ones trying to gain fame
in Paris. His symphony "is a music sprung from the source of so
poetic an imagination that the composer's genius announces
itself as very profound" (DA, XII: 291). Then follow several
pages, for Heine rather uncharacteristic, devoted to an analysis
of Hiller's music and its performance. As Heine did not choose
to include this article in his collected works, he may well have
felt the subject matter and its presentation somewhat alien to his
manner.

In May 1837, Heine wrote ten "Vertraute Briefe an August
Lewald *Über die französische Bühne*" ("Confidential Letters to
August Lewald *About the French Stage*") for the latter's *Allgemeine Theaterrevue*. Heine included these articles, in revised
form, in the fourth volume of his *Salon* of 1840, and a French

version appeared in 1857 in *De la France*.[10] This collection of essays, covering theater from tragedy to vaudeville, as well as opera, ballet and music, represents Heine's most concentrated treatment of the performing arts. Written in his prime, these "Letters" also constitute Heinean theater journalism in its most characteristic form.

Heine's fundamental strategy in these reportages is to compare and contrast the French stage with the German, as he explains in his first installment: "I shall write you a series of letters about the French stage and thereby also keep in mind . . . relations to the theater at home" (DA, XII: 230). This renders the reports equally interesting to both his German and his French readers, while permitting him to discuss any figure or phenomenon of either tradition. Thus in the first essay, he speaks at length about Ernst Raupach (1784–1852), a dramatic author popular at the time, but forgotten today. Heine had just read some of the comedies of "this lapdog of German theater directors" and reports: "not without effort was I able to work my way through to the last acts" (DA, XII: 230). However, with German comedy in a sad state, among the blind "the one-eyed man is king, and among our bad comedy writers Raupach is the best" (DA, XII: 231). The remaining pages of the article are devoted to an amusing episode—which would make a perfect comedy plot—in which Heine personally met "Herrn Theaterdichter Raupach," whom he had mistaken for his dentist.

In the second letter, Heine tells his readers the reason for the obvious inferiority of German comedy to the French. It is no longer true that the French are a more cheerful people than the Germans; since they have learned philosophy and tobacco smoking from their neighbors, their "faces have become longer. . . . No, they are no more cheerful than we" (DA, XII: 235). Nor does the situation have anything to do with political freedom; Heine shows "how it is rather the social conditions to which the comedy writers in France owe their supremacy" (DA, XII: 237). For the subject of comedy is domestic; and as in contemporary French family life all authority has broken down, the conflict between husband and wife, "their terrible domestic battles," have become the *matière* of comic plots. The French laugh about their comedies, but if one carries "a German heart in one's breast, then with the best French comedy one's amusement melts away" (DA, XII: 239). Heine here clearly assumes a surprisingly moralistic attitude. He informs his readers that what appears amusing on the Parisian comic stage ends in reality usually in prostitution and the hospitals of St.-Lazare. "Then the laughter chokes in my throat" (DA, XII: 239). This letter from Paris ends, moreover, on the strong note of an exile's nostalgia for his lost home: "that is the secret curse of exile, that we never feel quite at home in the atmosphere of a foreign country, that with our own ways of thinking and feeling brought from home, we always stand isolated among a people who feels altogether differently from the way we do" (DA, XII: 239). Heine's homesickness for Germany is more apparent in this essay *Über die französische Bühne* than in any of his other texts.[11]

The following installment continues the comparison of French and German mores, as the author passes from comedy to tragedy. In Germanic countries—"at home in Germany, as also in England and other Germanic countries"—only young, unmarried girls are the object of courtship, while in France mature women are "the object of love, in life as in art." Thus, the heroines of German tragedy are maidens, while in French tragedy they are married women; and German tragedy tends, therefore, to be more poetic, whereas French tragedy consists principally of action and the portrayal of passions. Heine insists that he will not praise one school at the expense of the other, each country's art and literature being conditioned by its own needs. But he then admits that "what in the theater has the most overpowering effect on most of the audience is precisely action and passion, and in these the French tragedians excel" (DA, XII: 243). However, the audience, too, differs from one country to the other, and "in the German theater mezzanine sit peaceful citizens and government employees, who want to digest their sauerkraut there quietly; and above, in the upper boxes, sit the blue-eyed daughters of the educated class, lovely blue souls

. . ." (DA, XII: 243–44). In the opening of his fourth article, Heine interpolates, as he does so frequently, a beautiful romantic dream, after which, reawakened to reality, he exclaims: "How fortunate the French are! They don't dream at all" (DA, XII: 246). Dream plays an important part in German drama, a literary phenomenon inconceivable for the French, whose entire education is "a product of materialistic philosophy" (DA, XII: 247). The fourth letter closes with a few humorous similes contrasting the romantic Germans with the materialistic French; but the theme which dominated almost the entire first half of these essays recedes in the fifth one, devoted to the hero of contemporary French drama, Napoleon.

After the political upheavals of the recent past, which have created an unfavorable terrain for French tragedy, Heine observes, Napoleon is the only hero France has left, and dramatic authors, from vaudeville to tragedy, continue to exploit the theme with success. Heine tells of his neighbor, an old grenadier of the imperial army, who went to see *The Battle of Austerlitz* at the Frankoni theater last night. He was "very pleased with the gunpowder smoke, also with the smell of the horses; he only objected that the cavalry at Austerlitz did not have such well-trained white horses" (DA, XII: 250). But the Emperor was the same: "'Ah! the Emperor,' the old man added, 'God knows how I love him'" (DA, XII: 250). Napoleon, we recall, was also one of Heine's heroes, to whom he paid tribute with a poem especially famous in France, "Die Grenadiere."[12] Yet, our moralizing correspondent questions the country's happiness during the Empire: "Was the time of the Empire in France really so wonderful and so happy . . .? I don't believe it. The fields were lying fallow, and men were being led to slaughter" (DA, XII: 251–52).

Like Laforgue in Berlin, Heine in Paris was an avid visitor of the theaters. But he did not appreciate the most famous French stage. In his sixth letter, he reports that he rarely goes to the Théâtre Français, which he finds dreary and unpleasant, because "here the ghosts of the old tragedy still linger hauntingly . . . ; here the powder of the classical wigs still fills the air with dust'' (DA, XII: 257). Heine does not reject French classical tragedy; on the contrary, he "honors Corneille and loves Racine." But their time is past, as their noble heroes can no longer play before their aristocratic audiences. "Today the bourgeoisie rules, and the heroes of Paul de Kock and Eugène Scribe" (DA, XII: 257). The remainder of this essay deals with the two great contemporary dramatists, Victor Hugo and Alexandre Dumas. Hugo has not been sufficiently recognized in France, Heine notes, while impartial German critics have better assessed his worth. He is the greatest living French poet and would occupy the first rank among the Germans. Like Grabbe and Jean-Paul, he frequently lacks harmony and taste; he has, in fact, lost most of his former friends, including the faithful Sainte-Beuve. Although Dumas is not as great a poet as Hugo, he is more successful in the theater: "He speaks to the heart with the heart and is understood and applauded" (DA, XII: 260). He is a born dramatist, and recent accusations of plagiarism are as unfounded in his case as they would be in Shakespeare's.

Dumas' play "Kean or the Disorder of Genius," celebrating one of Heine's favorite Shakespeare interpreters, introduces the theme of acting. And the seventh installment *Über die französische Bühne* is devoted to a comparison of English, French, and German actors and "the difference of declamation in the three kingdoms of the civilized world, in England, France and Germany" (DA, XII: 263). Heine had had great difficulty in becoming accustomed to British acting, "the shouting, the splitting shouting . . . I could not bear in the beginning." How elegant by contrast is the French with its "grace and smoothness which is entirely foreign to the English, indeed impossible for them" (DA, XII: 264).The French are, moreover, born comedians and thus naturally superior to their foreign colleagues. They are "the *comédiens ordinaires* of the good Lord," and all of French history sometimes appeares to Heine "like a great comedy which is, however, performed for the greater good of humanity." As to the Germans, "we are honest folk and good citizens. What nature denies us, we obtain through study" (DA, XII: 265)!

After mentioning some of the currently popular authors of the "boulevard" theaters, Heine explains this Parisian phenomenon in his eighth letter to his German readers: "the theaters of the boulevard . . . are the actual popular stages, which begin at the Porte St.-Martin" (DA, XII: 269–70). And then follows a graded list of some of these lesser stages and their typical repertories, from the Théâtre de la Porte Saint-Martin, specializing in drama and featuring authors like Hugo and Dumas, to the Ambigu-Comique, a stage of romantic drama, followed by the Frankoni theater famous for its "grand spectacle" productions in which one sees "more horse-rather than people-plays," like *The Battle of Austerlitz*! La Gaité, newly rebuilt after its recent fire, presents romantic drama and also vaudeville; but vaudeville is the specialty of the Folies Dramatiques. Finally we arrive at the "Funambules, where one of the most outstanding Pierrots, the famous Deburau, makes his white faces" (DA, XII: 270). Heine could hardly guess in 1837 the significance that this little theater was to assume later in the century, and to what extent the Deburaus, both father and son, were to capture and form the artistic imagination of poets like Laforgue.

The two final installments *Über die französische Bühne* deal with music. The Opera is a major part of parisian theatrical life, and its two great contemporary composers are Rossini and Mayerbeer. Heine, refusing to take sides in arguments about Italian versus German opera, loves them both: "Ich beschränke mich darauf sie beide zu lieben" (H, XII: 274). Whereas in Rossini melody predominates, in Meyerbeer it is harmony; and Meyerbeer's music is also "more social than individual." Thus, while Rossini triumphed during the Restoration, "Meyerbeer is the man of his time" (DA, XII: 276), that is the present. After the July Revolution, he conquered the world—we know that for Heine the world is Europe—with *Robert le Diable*; but with the *Huguenots* the composer won "his immortal citizenship in the eternal spiritual polis, in the heavenly Jerusalem of Art" (DA, XII: 279). At this period, then, Heine sings Meyerbeer's praises unreservedly.

Under the direction of "the great Veron," Heine notes, the

Paris Opera began to mount "grand spectacle" productions à la Frankoni that were financially so successful that the present director, M. Duponchel, has continued in that manner. He gives the rich bourgeoisie what they want and pay for. But the more distinguished public, "die schöne Aristokratie," frequents the Italian Opera, a "musical oasis, where the great nightingales of Art are still warbling." The season's concerts are less noteworthy, except for those of Berlioz and Liszt, who "surely are the most remarkable figures of the Parisian musical world" (DA, XII: 287). Liszt is almost too exciting a performer, "no calm piano player for quiet citizens and comfortable sleepyheads"; and although Heine loves him, his music has a disturbing effect on him. For Heine must always immediately visualize what he hears. Thus, at a recent Liszt concert, the entire Apocalypse arose before his inner eye, the four mystical animals, followed by Satan, Death, and finally Christ in golden armor riding a black horse! But the pianist of the musical elite, those who seek "the highest pleasures of the spirit," is Chopin who, not merely as performer, but also as composer, has attained the ultimate.

The letters *Über die französische Bühne* close on a nostalgic note, as Heine compares himself to the Flying Dutchman, tossed about eternally in the cold seas, far from home: "Ah! it has been a long time already that I have been living away from home, and with my fabulous homesickness I sometimes seem to myself like that Flying Dutchman and his crew . . ." (DA, XII: 290). In its original form in the *Allgemeine Theaterrevue*, this passage was longer and sadder: "Oh, how many of my loved ones have passed away, while my life's ship, far from home, is driven to and fro by the most fatal storms" (DA, XII: 503).

Heine also discussed French theater in the *Berichte über Politik, Kunst und Volksleben* which he wrote from Paris in the early 1840's for the *Augsburger Allgemeine Zeitung*.[13] He republished these "Reports" in a volume entitled *Lutetia* in 1854, and the following year the French edition, *Lutèce*, came out in Paris, preceded by a now famous preface, in which Heine sets forth his social and political views of the past and present. In this preface he also begs his beloved Paris to accept his apologies for not being able to pay her his homage more elegantly, as he is not writing in his native language, and assures her that he never intended to offend her in those articles written many years ago:

> It is painful, very painful, to see oneself forced to go to pay one's respects to an elegant goddess on the banks of the Seine in such unfitting garb, while one has the most beautiful apparel and more than one magnificently embroidered vest at home, in one's German chest.
> No, dear Lutèce, I never intended to wrong you, and if evil tongues are striving to make you believe the contrary, don't give credit to such calumnies (B, V: 220).

Most of these reportages are devoted to politics and "Volksleben," very few exclusively to "Kunst," and in his characteristic manner, Heine frequently amalgamates diverse topics in a given essay. But his report of April 30, 1840, is entirely about his friend George Sand and the premiere of her play *Cosima.* Heine here calls Sand France's greatest new writer; yet, the success of her play is not guaranteed, as all the hostile "professional theater-poets" have plotted against her: "All the author's antagonists had come together for a rendezvous in the colossal Théâtre Français which holds over two thousand persons" (B, V: 257). We recall that Heine does not like that theater; its actors were, moreover, very poor, even "the famous Dorval" playing no better, but also no worse, than usual. This discussion leads Heine to contrast the mores of French and German actresses, clearly to the advantage of the latter. In Germany, actors and actresses are respected and, therefore, respectable. In France, the old prejudices against the profession still prevail, and "since people always become bad when they are treated badly, so with few exceptions the actors live in the obsolete condition of base bohemianism." Thus, in Paris "all beautiful actresses have their price" (B, V: 259), and most of them are the kept mistresses of wealthy spendthrifts and parvenus. No one has better described this type of woman than "our friend Honoré de Balzac . . . He describes them as a scientist describes an animal species, or a pathologist an illness, without any moralizing purpose, without partiality or aversion" (B, V: 260–61). So Heine concludes his essay on George Sand with a deep bow to their much more significant common friend, Balzac, and the literary realism which he fathered.

In the report of July 29, 1840, about Guizot and foreign affairs, Heine muses about the success of the English in that domain. He believes that "their superiority consists in their lack of imagination. This lack constitutes the entire strength of the English and is the ultimate reason for their success in politics, as in all other realistic enterprises . . . They have no imagination; that is the whole secret." Their poets are "only brilliant exceptions;" as for the others, "the odor of the lotus blossom intoxicates them as little as the flame of Mount Vesuvius warms them." It is, therefore, no wonder that the Taglioni did not meet with success in London last year. In fact, for Heine "that is truly her greatest fame. Had she pleased there, he would begin to question the poetry of her feet" (B, V: 305). The English are the worst dancers, and Strauss [Johann, father] claims that not one of them can keep time. "Really," continues Heine, "there is nothing more horrible on earth than English music, except perhaps for English painting. They have neither ear, nor a sense for color . . ." (B, V: 306). Heine simply did not like the English.

"The new year," Heine reports on January 6, 1841, "began, like the old, with music and dance. At the Opera, the melodies of Donizetti fill the air while a new work by Meyerbeer, his *Prophet*, is being eagerly awaited. In the Odéon—the Italian Opera—the aging Rubini and the eternally young Grisi, "the singing flower of beauty" (B, V: 335), continue to delight their audiences and Heine. In April of that year, the Salon revealed "merely a motley impotence" (B, V: 356). It appears that the present is the era of music; in fact, one almost drowns in it, and one of its most remarkable representatives is Franz Liszt, whose concerts border on the fabulous; "besides him all pianists fade— with the exception of a single one, Chopin, the Raphael of the pianoforte" (B, V: 358). The competing concerts given by Maurice Schlesinger, director of the *Gazette musicale*, and the brothers Escudier, directors of *France musicale*, constitute a rivalry which keeps music lovers well entertained. If the German singer Johanna Löwe did not succeed in Paris, it is not her fault, for "in the voice of Mlle Löwe is German soul," and Beethoven's "Adelaide," this "arch-German *Lied*" on her program (B, V: 362), could not possibly touch French hearts; it was, in fact, ridiculed as "transrhenanische Sensiblerie" (B, V: 362). Some homesickness still?

The entire February 7, 1842 report is devoted to dance, "and here we must first speak of the Royal Academy of Music [the Opera], where that honorable *Corps de ballet* still exists which faithfully preserves the choreographic traditions." Heine does not like the ballet of the Opera any more than the venerable Théâtre Français, but he cannot help admiring its two great stars, Marie Taglioni and Carlotta Grisi. While the former is touring Russia, and Fanny Elssler America, the Grisi, in one of her most famous roles, "Giselle," "shines forth in a completely singular way from the respectable company of the rue Lepelletier [home of the old Paris opera], like an orange among potatoes. Beside the fortunate subject matter, borrowed from the works of a German author, it was mainly the Grisi who secured an unheard-of vogue for the ballet 'The Willis' [Giselle]. How delightfuly she dances! Seeing her, one forgets that the Taglioni is in Russia and the Elssler in America" (B, V: 390). Heine is also reminding his readers here that the libretto of this great Romantic ballet is indebted to the "Willis" legend of his *Elementargeister*.[14] But aside from its great stars, Heine does not appreciate classical ballet; for him "French ballet almost smells of the Gallican church," and he compares it to French classical tragedy which, as we read in his letters *Über die französische Bühne*, he finds outmoded. Both epitomize the age of Louis XIV: "in this respect, French ballet is a congenial counterpart to Racinean tragedy and the parks of Le Nôtre. Here prevails the same regulated style, the same measure of etiquette, the same courtly coldness. . ." (B, V: 392). Heine is obviously much better informed about Racinean tragedy than the great Romantic ballet whose flowering he was witnessing toward the middle of the nineteenth century in Paris. We should observe, however, how far his own ballet librettos and his conception of dance were ahead of their time, and how his *Tanzpoem Der Doktor Faust* had to wait for a hundred years to be staged.[15]

In April of that year, the great musical event was Rossini's *Stabat*, performed perfectly by the Italian Opera which Heine so loved. "The Italian Opera seemed like the vestibule of heaven; there sacred nightingales were warbling and the most fashionable tears were flowing" (B, V: 399). That little ironic twist at the end confirms what we learned in the reports *Über die französische Bühne*, that since the Opera had become a bit vulgar with too much "grand spectacle," the distinguished musical audience, including Heine, had shifted to the Italian opera. This irony further, of course, undercuts his own emotions, his heart so deeply touched by this "divine music."

In March of the following year, Heine again remarks about the boredom of the outmoded French classical tragedy—"the monotony which French classical tragedy exudes"—which even one of its most brilliant stars, Rachel [Elisa Félix], cannot relieve. It appears to Heine like a punishment for the rich; and it is hardly mitigated by the Romantic drama of Hugo! "Not only does Mademoiselle Rachel serve them every evening the mouldy dregs of the antique night-cap, but now they even have to swallow the scum of our Romantic kitchen, versified sauerkraut, Victor Hugo's *The Burgraves*" (B, V: 434). Since the essay of 1837, not only has Hugo changed, but, even more so, Heine's attitude toward him. Heine calls Hugo's play featuring a German theme "versifiziertes Sauerkraut" and finds it "indigestible." The work of the poet whom he had once considered the greatest of France, now "shows evidence neither of poetic intensity nor harmony, neither enthusiasm nor freedom of spirit, it does not contain a speck of genius, but mere stilted artificiality and motley declamation" (B, V: 434). The reigning money bourgeoisie must pay for its sins not merely by listening to classical tragedy and Hugo, but also by suffering another "Kunstgenuss (artistic pleasure) . . . namely that piano playing which one cannot escape anywhere now, which one hears in every house, at every social gathering, day and night" (B, V: 434–5). This complaint must have found a most sympathetic ear in Laforgue, in whose poetry the "complainte des pianos qu'on entend dans les quartiers aisés" was to become a major motif.[16]

In a report of the same month, Heine speaks again of currently popular pianists, only two of whom he appreciates, Thalberg and Chopin. Then follows a brief note on Richard Wagner, whom Heine had met during the latter's stay in Paris from 1839 to 1842: "What sad experiences Mr. Richard Wagner had to undergo, who finally, obeying the voice of reason and that of his stomach, has given up the dangerous project of establishing himself on the French stage and has fluttered back to the German potato country" (B, V: 443). The tension between the two famous Germans is barely disguised in this remark. The essay ends with Schubert, whose popularity in Paris is very great, especially due to his Heinean songs. These are so poorly translated into French, however, that the author was glad to discover that the music editors did not take the trouble of giving him credit; they "have no scruples about concealing the real author and substituting the name of some obscure French librettist on the title page of those songs" (B, V: 446). This dishonest practice might just have something to do with copyright law, and Heine tells us that for over twenty years he has been exploited by hundreds of German composers.

The concluding report of May 1, 1844, deals with the opera, Spontini's hatred of Meyerbeer, with Italian opera, "the eternally blooming, singing, forest into which I flee when the chills of life become unbearable" (B, V: 542). An appended "Spätere Notiz" is devoted to "the Swedish nightingale," Jenny Lind, who represents not merely her own little country, but "the entire Germanic clan—she belongs to Germany, as, according to Franz Horn, Shakespeare, too, belongs to us" (B, V: 546). Though Heine is clearly ironic here, he does feel that this singer is particularly "germanisch," which explains her fabulous success in England: "all of Great Britain celebrates singing maidenhood in Jenny Lind, sung virginity." And this "gesungene Jungfernschaft" has resolutely refused to come to Paris and turned down all offers! Is it only her sense of chastity, her

"Keuschheitssinn," that makes her refuse to come near "the modern Sodom"? Or might the Germanic singing maiden fear "the frivolous Parisian music critics, who judge not a singer's morals but the voice, and who consider a lack of formal training an artist's greatest sin" (B, V: 547)? Heine is somewhat divided between irony and admiration for this Germanic star that refuses to shine on Lutetia. The report ends on a sad note, Donizetti's terrible illness: "while his melodies fluttering with joy delight the world, he himself is sitting in a hospital near Paris, a shocking picture of insanity" (B, V: 548).

This appended essay originated in the summer of 1847 and, as Heine explains, was his last. For him, "all music has ended since then, and I could not guess, when I sketched the sorrowful picture of Donizetti that a similar and much more painful affliction was approaching me" (B, V: 545). Banned to his "Matratzengruft" (mattress-grave), Heine was soon to be cut off from the world which he so loved and shared with us, Parisian theater, opera, dance and music.[17]

Both *De la France* and *Lutèce* were extremely popular in France, the former having six, the latter eight printings during the nineteenth century.[18] We cannot be sure whether Laforgue read any of these reports about his favorite city, written by his favorite author, during his long days at the Bibliothèque Nationale in the late 1870's and early 1880's, but it is not unlikely. His own reports on Parisian theater are concentrated in his earliest journalism, the contributions to *La Guêpe* and *L'Enfer* in which, as we saw, he was reporting from the capital to his hometown readers as was the young Heine in his *Briefe aus Berlin*. After Laforgue left for Berlin, in December of 1881, he was to spend only his summer vacations in France, mostly with his family in Tarbes, until his return to Paris toward the end of 1886, less than a year before his death.

Although Laforgue regularly visited the theater, opera, concerts, and the circus in the Prussian capital, he wrote no formal reports about them. Only toward the very end of his stay in Berlin, he contracted with *L'Illustration* to write a series of articles on the city and the imperial court, which that review intended to publish upon the death of the Emperor who was then almost ninety years old. But nothing came of these plans in 1886; the old Emperor William I (1797–1888) outlived the young poet, and the articles were posthumously published in the volume *En Allemagne* under the title *Berlin, la Cour et la ville.*[19] Thus we glean most of Laforgue's reflections on the Berlin stage from his correspondence with family and friends, or from personal jottings posthumously published as "Agenda (1883)."[20]

In his first, and rather enthusiastic, letter to his sister Marie written from Coblenz on November 30, 1881, Laforgue reports that the Court will tomorrow move to Berlin, where he will see his new friend, The Empress' old physician Dr. Velten, every day, and "we will go to the Opera together."[21] In January 1882, Laforgue tells Charles Ephrussi about his two new young acquaintances, musicians who will remain his closest friends throughout his life, the Ysaie brothers, the one a violinist, the other a pianist. Through them Laforgue will receive his initiation in music. Thus with Massenet's new opera *Hérodiade*; he writes to Ephrussi: "Ah! you know that I know *Hérodiade* now. I have two friends here. The one is a violinist (he . . . will play before the Empress Friday) and his brother, the pianist. They have deciphered the entire partition. Isn't that great? I believe we will soon have Saint-Saëns here."[22] But Laforgue soon becomes homesick for Paris. A letter of the following month to Mme Mullezer, the poetess Sandra Mahali, is dated: "Sunday morning, Spleen." It is one of the poet's most famous letters, containing the passage about his five consecutive nights spent at the circus and presaging the principal persona of his poetic universe: "Do you adore the circus? I have just spent five consecutive evenings there. The clowns seem to me to have arrived at true wisdom. I should be a clown, I've missed my calling; it is irrevocable, finished. Isn't it too late for me to start now?" At the end of the letter, Laforgue notes Saint-Saën's presence: "we have Saint-Saëns here; I have spent a very strange evening with him yesterday."[23] A year later, Laforgue writes to Charles Henry from Berlin: "My life is always the same. I hear a lot of music. What else is there to do in Berlin, except to hear a lot of music?"[24]

For the next three years, from 1884 to 1886, Laforgue shares his theatrical experiences mostly with Gustave Kahn. As the language barrier separates him from the German stage, these are mainly musical. He finds the ballet of the Berlin Opera uninspiring, as he reports in a letter of February 1884: "I am very exhausted. Yesterday's balance sheet: three hours at the Opera, idiotic ballet, tights without soul."[25] And in a melancholy letter from the end of that year, Laforgue seems to be giving up writing altogether, except for notes for future use; music appears to be his only relief: "Ah! I'm bored to death here, aside from music (I have in two weeks heard the *Walküre*; four piano concertos; Liszt; the Essipoff [a pianist], and even *Carmen* and a Schumann quintet and a Brahms quartet: you know that Brahms has just published a symphony). To write, or compose, a novel, or a play, impossible here. At best, I can take notes on the streets and the museums."[26]

A year later, in February of 1885, Laforgue asks Kahn about Parisian theater from his exile in Berlin, which had become a burden: "Did you see the performance of Becque's *Parisienne*, [the play had premiered that month]. My exile weighs more and more heavily on me. Add to that that I often notice that I really don't know German correctly. In short, I only think of the pleasure of coming back to Paris." Meanwhile music became his chief diversion: "Am I drowning in music? This morning I heard concerts by Schumann, Litolf, and Liszt, piano and orchestra."[27]

Most of Laforgue's operatic fare in Berlin—besides *Carmen*, the Empress' favorite opera—is Wagner, whose fame was already enormous toward the end of the century in both France and Germany. In March 1885, Laforgue writes: "I have seen *Tristan and Isolde* three times here last year; it is even one of those Berlin pleasures which you urge me to consume." Music, and the circus when it came to town, were in fact the exile's only "voluptés berlinoises." While his interest in music was stimulated by his linguistic isolation in Germany and by the capital's generous offerings, the poet's musical taste was surely influenced by his two musician friends. In his next letter to Kahn of April 1885, he asks him about his impressions of Hans von

Bülow, one of the most famous conductors of the time, adding: "he is very cool, though with a touch of madness, but impeccable, and a consummate Beethovenian. For many 'piano-virtuosos' he is a god, for those who prefer this sort of strange and feverish flawlessness to the uncontested and genial wildness of Rubinstein." The year's "concert season is finished here with this week when we will have Clara Schumann and two or three *minores*." At the Opera, Wagner reigns: "Sunday saw *Tannhäuser* again, tonight the Rienzi." Kahn was planning a trip to Germany during the summer, and his friend informs him: "You inquire whether any Wagner operas will be performed where we will spend May, June and July. Alas! none; perhaps some fragments at the Baden casino."[28] In a letter written a month later from Baden, the Court's summer residence, Laforgue reminds Gustave Kahn that there will be no *Festspiele* at Bayreuth this year during his visit: "So you will only see Wagner operas sung by ordinary casts." With his predilection for Wagner, Laforgue was simply following the path of French poets from Baudelaire to the Symbolists. He continues to drown his spleen in music, as he notes in the same letter: "yesterday I had music up to my neck . . . This week there were music festivals at Karlsruhe . . . I spent yesterday, Saturday, there. I heard two big concerts. I found myself sitting very close to the old charlatan Liszt. We heard two piano concerts, Brahms, Borodin, Liszt's Dantesque Symphony, a number of *Lieder*, violin, etc., etc. . . . Madame Montigny-Remaury [a pianist] played Liszt, Chopin, Godard."[29]

The following November, Laforgue goes to Cologne especially to hear Bülow's orchestra and reports: "Tonight I heard Beethoven's Fourth Symphony and Berlioz' *King Lear*, conducted by himself." And a month later, back in Berlin, he is again inundated with Wagner: "We have the second part of the triology [he means the Tetralogy] here, *Siegfried*, which I heard the day after a performance of the *Walküre*." In March 1886, he writes: "I have heard the *Walküre* ten times, *Siegfried*, etc., Gluck's *Orpheus*, etc."[30] No wonder that Wagner inspired one of his most famous *Moralités légendaires*, *Lohengrin, fils de Parsival*.

Three of the essays on *Berlin, la Cour et la ville* deal with the stage. The chapter "Théâtres" is devoted entirely to the Opera and opens with a tribute to the capital's musical offerings which reflects what we know from the correspondence:

> Berlin is a musical Mecca. Just as one can get one's purely musical instruction there for seventy-five centimes an evening, the Opera offers you in one season a good number of works. The artists are prepared to play successively, aside from the classical repertory, *Lohengrin*, the *Flying Dutchman*, the *Valkyrie*, *Tannhäuser*, *Siegfried*, *Tristan and Isolde*, the *Mastersingers*, and even *Rienzi*.

From time to time, the Opera also presents symphony evenings. Operatic premieres are not considered especially important; and Laforgue was astonished to find that foreign operatic stars sing their parts in their native language while the rest of the cast sings in German. For a year, the Opera has had a new foyer where, during intermission, "everybody goes round in the same direction, while the officers stand in the center . . ."[31] One wonders whether Laforgue is being intentionally ironic here, or merely describing what he saw. At any rate, Heine would have appreciated the passage.

The following essay describes "the *Reichshallen* . . . the true Berlin music hall [café-concert]" where families gather around huge tables to drink their beer, the men smoking cigars while the women knit, and the children roam about freely. Hot and cold dishes are consumed, except in the boxes, where the more elegant ladies and gentlemen only drink beer. "The show is always divided into three parts, the intermissions are long, the orchestra plays as though one had come because of it (which is somewhat true of this public). The whole is of an unbearable length;" but the Berliners love it, "and the beer flows fast." The show before this eating and drinking audience "is composed above all of the singer, acrobats, curiosities, and ends with a pantomime." And, indiscriminately, "the enthusiasm of the audience is always the same, for all the artists."[32]

At the ballet at the Victoria Theater, the French visitor encountered a very German custom, which no Parisian audience would tolerate: "something typically German; when *Excelsior* was being performed, before each act, an actor came out declaiming explanations for the instruction of the public. You can imagine the rebellion of the audience of the Eden in Paris against anything like that." When the ballet *Amor* was put on, before an audience including the royal family, officers, and embassy personnel, Laforgue found the production far from elegant: "The show is distasteful, the tights don't fit, and they have pell-mell engaged first-comer supernumeraries. Poorly glued paper, hastily gilded sets and trinkets, and scamped costumes."

At the Comedy, Paul Heyse's "Le Droit du plus fort" ("The Right of the Strongest") is on the program, a play "that no man of letters in Paris would recommend to any director, so poor and banal are the characters." Thus, neither ballet nor comedy in Berlin measured up to the young Parisian's taste. And when he describes the capital's "théâtre populaire," the "vast garden with superb trees," where "thousands of good people enjoy the fresh air, drink, smoke and attend a three-penny show,"[33] the tone is hardly less condescending. Not even "a clown with a Berlin repertory" succeeds in amusing the poet of Pierrot.

Clearly, Heine and Laforgue were both intensely interested in the performing arts throughout their lives, both at home and abroad. However, Heine embraced French culture much more readily than Laforgue the German, and Laforgue's much greater distance from things German is evident in all that we have read. Further, in Heine we hear the voice of a mature writer, totally in possession of the tools of his craft, while Laforgue wrote all his texts as a brilliant beginner.

Notes

[1] Numerous scholarly works have been devoted to Heine and the performing arts. A thorough, but dated, commentary on Heine and the theater is Mutzenbecher, *Heine und das Drama*. On Heine and dance, cf. Niehaus, *Himmel Hölle und Trikot*. The best study on Heine and the performing arts is Trilse's Introduction to his edition *Heinrich Heine über die französische Bühne und andere Schriften zum Theater*. On Heine and music, cf. Michael Mann, *Heinrich Heines Musikkritiken* (Hamburg: Hoffmann und Campe, 1971); Jocelyne Kolb, "Heine's Amusical Muse," *Monatshefte für deutschen Unterricht*, LXXXIII, 4 (1981): 392–404; Albert Pfrimmer, "Heine et les musiciens romantiques allemands," *Europe*, (mai-juin 1956): 115–20; in the

same issue, Fréderic Robert, "Heine et les musiciens," 121–24. Heinz Becker has devoted a book-length study to Heine's relations with Meyerbeer, *Der Fall Heine-Meyerbeer* (Berlin: Walter De Gruyter, 1958). No comparable studies exist so far for Laforgue in this domain.

[2] *Pages de la Guêpe*; DA, VI- 7–53.

[3] *Pages de la Guêpe*, 102, Debauve explains that Laforgue must be speaking here of one of the Sunday afternoon "matinées des jeunes" that the Théâtre Cluny had begun to feature in May of 1878.

[4] B, I: 401–21 and 430–44. These essays are in the volume *De tout un peu* of the French edition of Heine's works, 123–60 and 175–202.

[5] For biographical details of this period of Heine's life, his brief stay in Munich before the Italian journey, cf. Sammons, *A Modern Biography*, 132–38.

[6] HSA, XX: 329. In a letter of the following month, to Wolfgang Menzel, Heine writes about his review: "So much the more I see the two great lights of the day, the Dioscuri on the starry sky of local poetry, M. Beer and M. E. Schenk. I have reported about the former's tragedy in the *Morgenblatt* and shown the world how little I envy him, how little his fame annoys me—" (331).

[7] B, V: 140–42; in the French edition, the essay entitled "La première représentation des 'Huguenots'," is in the volume *De tout un peu*, 361–66.

[8] DA, XII- 63–226. The article under discussion is on 116–28. In the French edition, these articles appear in the volume *De la France*, under the title "Lettres écrites à la *Gazette universelle d'Augsbourg* (1831–1832)." Our reportage is on 96–123.

[9] DA, XII: 291–94. Its Heinean authorship having been ascertained only in the 1950's this report is not contained in the French edition of Heine's works.

[10] DA, XII:227–90. A French translation of these "Letters" appeared in 1857, in the second edition of Heine's *De la France*, 236–323.

[11] Cf. Henri Roger Paucker, *Heinrich Heine, Mensch und Dichter zwischen Deutschland und Frankreich* (Bern, Verlag Herbert Lang & Cie A.G.: 1967), 70 and 80: "Sehr oft, wenn Heine von Deutschen und Franzosen spricht, verraten Wendungen wie 'wir Deutsche' . . . eindeutig, daß er auch in Frankreich nie aufhörte, sich als Deutscher zu fühlen." ". . . ins letzte Drittel seines Lebens fällt dann die große Anzahl jener Bemerkungen, aus denen wir vor allem seine Sehnsucht nach Deutschland und seine Klagen über das Exil herausgehört haben."

[12] DA, I:77–78. This poem, like the "Lorelei," was in numerous French school texts of German poetry, like *Textes allemands du brevet supérieur*, session de 1903, 1904, 1905; also in the *Examen du brevet supérieur*, 1907–1909; also in "L'Epreuve d'allemand au brevet supérieur (écrit-oral)" (1910–1912).

[13] B, V: 217–548. The French edition, *Lutèce*.

[14] Cf. Chapter III, note 42.

[15] Cf. Chapter III, note 40.

[16] Cf. Chapter I, note 54.

[17] For an excellent discussion of Heine on the performing arts, cf. Trilse's Introduction to *Heinrich Heine über die französische Bühne und andere Schriften zum Theater*, in which he stresses two essential aspects of Heine's theater criticism: "Heine betrachtet alle Erscheinungen des Theaters nicht für sich, sondern nur im gesellschaftlichen und kulturellen Ganzen, im Zuge seiner Zeiten- und Weltschilderungen, seiner Tagesberichterstattung und Geschichts-schreibung, seiner literarischen Publizistik und Kulturkritik. . . . Und die zweite Erkenntnis: kaum ein zweiter seines Ranges war so dem Tage verhaftet wie Heine" (14).

[18] *De la France*, originally published in 1833, was republished in 1857, 1860, 1863, 1867, and 1884; *Lutèce*, first published in 1855, had a second edition that same year, and additional ones in 1857, 1859, 1861, 1863, 1866 and 1871. The last is especially remarkable in view of the political situation in 1871.

[19] *En Allemagne*, 5–191, "Berlin, la Cour et la ville."

[20] *En Allemagne*, 216–59, "Agenda 1883."

[21] La forgue, *Lettres* I: 36.

[22] *Lettres* I: 108.

[23] *Lettres* I: 123–4.

[24] Laforgue, *Lettres* II: 11–12.

[25] *Lettres à un Ami*, 53

[26] *Lettres à un Ami*, 63

[27] *Lettres à un Ami*, 72 and 80.

[28] *Lettres à un Ami*, 84 and 103–4.

[29] *Lettres à un Ami*, 117–18.

[30] *Lettres à un Ami*, 137, 141, and 166.

[31] *En Allemagne*, 148–49.

[32] *En Allemagne*, 150–52.

[33] *En Allemagne*, 153–54.

VI

Heine's "Französische Maler"

With his reports about the *Gemäldeausstellung in Paris 1831* (Exposition of paintings in Paris 1831),[1] which constitute the essence of his art criticism, Heine followed a tradition established by Diderot in 1759,[2] the result of a celebrated Franco-German literary friendship. For one of Diderot's best friends, the German diplomat and man of letters Melchior von Grimm, had proposed to him to write about the "Salons," the official French art expositions, for his *Correspondance littéraire*.[3] Years after he had begun his famous *Salons*, Diderot wrote to his friend: "If I have any coherent notions on painting and sculpture, it is to you, my friend, that I owe them; I would have followed the crowd of the idle at the Salon; . . . It is the task which you proposed to me that fixed my eye on the canvas and made me turn around the marble."[4]

Heine's *Salon* was a self-imposd task, his first journalistic activity after his arrival in Paris in May 1831, and surely in part inspired by the memory of that great free-thinking predecessor, Diderot.[5] Opening the month Heine arrived in Paris, the Salon closed in August, thus giving him time for frequent visits and a review of its local critical reception before he began writing his own reports in September for Cotta's *Morgenblatt für gebildete Stände*, in which they appeared from October 27 to November 10 of that year.[6] In 1833, Heine wrote a "Nachtrag" (postscript) which he published together with the 1831 essays as *Französische Maler* in the first volume of his *Salon*, printed in Hamburg in 1834. A French version, entitled *Salon de 1831*, appeared, with some modifications, in 1833 in the volume *De la France*, without the "Nachtrag," which was placed as *Salon de*

1833 into the volume *Allemands et Français* years later.[7] In 1832, *Le Globe* published excerpts of Heine's *Salon* under the title *Exposition de 1831*. Heine's art criticism was thus diffused in both France and Germany almost immediately after its composition.

Heine begins his reportage in a minor key: the Salon is now closed, and its paintings had been for the most part merely accorded fleeting glances by people preoccupied with other matters, with "uneasy politics." The poet insists, moreover, that, newly arrived in the capital, he can even less than the others muster the "necessary peace of mind" required for exploring the halls of the Louvre. Thus, from the very outset, Heine politicizes his *Salon*, which sets it apart from those of Diderot and Baudelaire and the later art criticism of Laforgue. The three thousand "pretty pictures" exhibited appeared to Heine like art's "poor children, . . . begging in silent pain for a little empathy or acceptance in some corner of the heart." But they begged in vain. It was like being in an orphanage none of whose wards resembled each other, and which "moved our soul like the sight of degrading helplessness and youthful inner strife." Indeed, the only redeeming note in this dismal prelude is that of youthfulness, while the "Zerrissenheit" might well be not so much in the eye as in the heart of the beholder.

What a contrast with a gallery of Italian art, where all paintings have drawn their nourishment from "the breasts of a great common mother" and appear like one family, "at peace and at one, and speaking, if not always the same words, the same language" (DA, XII: 11). Heine here metaphorically expresses his view of art as a product of its historical moment and reflecting its "Zeitgeist."[8] Now that the Catholic Church, once the common mother of the arts, has become impoverished and helpless, every painter paints on his own and at his own risk, and for his own price, thus depending "on the whims of the rich." Add to that the misunderstood Romanticism raging among the French painters, each striving to paint "completely different than the others paint," and one can easily imagine the products. Heine, of course, in no way suggests a return to a past that can no longer nourish the present. That was the error of German Romanticism.[9]

The French have themselves judged the Salon correctly and recognized the few pearls, in this "motley sea of paintings." The pictures which they praised were by the eight artists whom Heine will present to his German readers: A. Scheffer, H. Vernet, Delacroix, Decamps, Lessore, Schnetz, Delaroche and Robert. For he will limit himself—not without a measure of irony—to merely reporting "public opinion." He will, moreover, avoid discussing "technical merits or shortcomings," as this would hardly be of interest to readers who will in all probability never see the paintings. And with his emphasis on "the subject matter and the significance of the paintings" (DA, XII: 12), Heine does not pretend to assume the role of an art critic but, on the contrary, appropriates the genere of the *Salon* for his own ends; that is, in Jeffrey Sammons' words, "he converted painting into literature."[10]

Of the seventeen paintings Scheffer exhibited at the Salon, the "conscientious reporter" discusses seven, opening his essay on the artist with two paintings inspired by German literature, *Faust dans son cabinet* and *Marguerite au rouet*, as well as closing it with another depiction of a German literary figure, *Leonore, les Morts vont vite*. The choice was not merely due to Heine's own fascination with the Faust figure, or for the sake of appealing to his German readers, but "the Faust and the Gretchen of this master have, after all, attracted the most attention in the first months of the exhibition" (DA, XII: 12). Heine now takes a negative approach in relating the claims of Scheffer's hostile critics: "his enemies accuse him of merely painting with snuff and green soap;" and he agrees that those "brownish shadows frequently appear affected and miss the intended Rembrandtesque light effects." Zepf's documentation reveals that the French critics had, indeed, pointed to the dull colors,[11] Heine thus, as he had promised, following "public opinion." But then he shows his readers what *he* sees, and what we are contemplating are not the pictures of an exhibition, but those presented by his text. Thus with Gretchen. Heine begins with a rather precise description of the Scheffer painting: the subject's pose, the expression on her face, her clothing, the objects surrounding her and their illumination. But then he continues: "She is, to be sure, Wolfgang Goethe's Gretchen, but she has read the entire Friedrich Schiller, and she is much more sentimental than naïve and much more heavily idealistic than lightly graceful. . . . At the same time she has something so trustworthy, so solid, so real, like a pure louisdor which one still has in one's pocket." The ideal virtues of the maiden evoked are ironically undercut with that "solid" piece of gold buried safely in one's pocket. "In a word," continues the poet, "she is a German girl, and when one looks deep into her melancholy violet eyes, one thinks of Germany, of fragrant linden trees, of Hölty's poems, of the solid Roland statue in front of city hall, of the co-rector and his rosy niece, . . . of cheap tobacco and good friends, grandmother's graveyard stories . . . Truly, Scheffer's Gretchen cannot be described" (DA, XII: 14). And Heine is, of course, not describing any painting, but instead painting a Gretchen of his own, a symbolic figure for the Germany he has left behind. He is thus holding up the mirror to his German readers. *Ut pictura poesis*—and our poet is an ironist.

Heine proceeds in the same manner in discussing "Le Prince de Talleyrand," whose name he never mentions. Scheffer's "vague, false, dead and characterless colors" are perfectly appropriate for the portrait of a face famous for never revealing its true thoughts. Heine again departs from the painter's portrait to paint his own: "He is the man who has sworn fourteen false oaths, and whose talents for lying have been utilized by successive French governments whenever some deadly perfidy was to be perpetrated, so that he recalls that ancient poisoner Locusta who, like a criminal legacy, lived in the house of Augustus and silently served one Caesar after another with her diplomatic potions" (DA, XII: 14).[12] But Heine brings us back from ancient Rome to contemporary European history and politics, remarking that he could not help being chilled by the thought of what poisonous combinations that man was presently preparing in

London. The poet chose to omit this last remark from the French version of his text.

One further example from the Scheffer essay, the discussion of the *Portrait équestre de Henri IV* and the *Portrait équestre du Roi*, will serve to illustrate Heine's strategy. He has quickly done with the first; since Henry IV lived before Heine, the poet cannot say "to what extent he is hit off." But "the other, the king of the barricades, the king by the grace of the sovereign people, is my contemporary, and I can judge whether his portrait resembles him or not." Yet, before giving us his customary description of the life-size painting, Heine instead recalls the day he saw the King in person, his own equestrian portrait thus preceding the painter's: "I saw him in too heightened a state of mind perhaps, namely on the feast day of the most recent celebrations of the Revolution, as he rode through the streets of Paris, amidst the jubilant citizens' guard and the newly decorated heroes of the July Revolution . . ." A most detailed and lengthy description follows, showing the King high on his horse, "half like a forced conquering hero, half like a voluntary prisoner who was supposed to adorn a triumph," continuing right down to the details of his face. "His fleshy cheeks glowed forth from the forest shades of his long sideburns, and his sweetly greeting eyes gleamed with pleasure and embarrassment" (DA, XII: 15). Thus Scheffer's painting serves Heine as a mere occasion for presenting his countrymen with his own profoundly ambiguous portrait of the new French King. Is he the victim of his own victory—"gezwungener Triumphator"—or a voluntary actor of his historical role—"freiwilliger Gefangener"? The King's glance expressed both confident affirmation—"pleasure, *Lust*"—and also discomfort—"Verlegenheit." But most of all, Heine painted the triumphant and jubilant July Revolution in Paris for his readers across the border, while in the Scheffer painting, we see only King Louis-Philippe on his horse. The King's features, favorite subject of contemporary caricaturists, also receive the poet's ironic stroke; not the famous pear, but: "eine Tann' im tiefen Tal, / . . . unten breit und oben schmal'' (a firtree deep in the valley, . . . broad below and narrow on top).[13]

Before turning to his last Scheffer painting, *Leonore*, Heine devotes a rare page to a strictly aesthetic matter, concerning the art of portraiture. He divides portraitists into two categories. The first have ''the wonderful talent'' of painting the model's essential traits, so that even those who have never seen the original will grasp his or her essential character. Holbein, Titian, and Van Dyck represent that type of artist. The other kind of portrait painters, common among the English and the French, aim for facile recognition by those who know the model. But this aside to art criticism per se appears to me merely Heine's polite bow to the genre.

Of the fourteen paintings exhibited by Horace Vernet, Heine discusses *Judith et Holoferne*, *Le Pape Léon III porté dans la basilique de Saint-Pierre à Rome*, *Arrestation du prince de Condé, du prince de Conti et du duc de Longueville* and *Camille Desmoulins au jardin du Palais-Royal*. Heine is most interested in the first, which shows the Biblical heroine rising from her bed of shame (and fame) and ''about to kill Holofernes,'' her left hand pushing up her right sleeve, ''for with the right hand she has just drawn the scimitar against the sleeping Holofernes.'' She is all action and constitutes thus a contrasting figure to Scheffer's contemplative Gretchen. She is also, moreover, much more French than Biblical, as contemporary French critics were quick to note: ''. . . it is easy to grasp the difference existing between the Hebraic Judith and the French Judith as we conceive her in 1830.''[14] Heine's detailed description, the most extensive of his *Salon*, accentuates the heroine's contrasting traits with a string of oxymorons. She is ''all divinely pure and yet stained by the world;'' her head is ''marvelously graceful and charming in an awful way,'' framed by black curls ''frightfully gracious.'' Wolfdietrich Rasch has pointed to the obvious kinship of this Judith with Heine's Herodias in *Atta Troll*.[15]

Holofernes, the ''ugly pagan,'' his bared upper body and head reclining on the couch to the right of Judith, ''actually appears nevertheless a bon enfant, sleeping so goodnaturedly in the after-bliss of his rapture." Heine's verbal equivocations—"he was just now lying in the lap of happiness, or perhaps happiness was lying in his lap"—strike a strong note of irony as he now envies the villain for passing from gratification to annihilation "without an interlude of pain or sickness;" . . . "death sends him through his most beautiful angel into the white night of eternal destruction. What an enviable end" (DA, XII: 17)! But the poetic overcharge of the very passage is surely intended to reflect Heine's fundamental dichotomy of Nazarene and Hellene, which informs this as well as all his other texts of the period.[16] Thus his concluding, almost blasphemous identification with the hedonistic enemy of the Nazarene-Jews: "when I am to die one day, you gods, let me die like Holofernes!" (DA, XII: 17), is both ironic and at the same time an expression of his credo in this-worldly Saint-Simonianism.[17]

Heine's brief treatment of the representative of that other faith, the Pope, manages to make its ironic point within the frame of the painting itself "which represents the present Pope.[18] With the golden triple crown upon his head, wearing a gold-embroidered white robe, sitting in a golden armchair, the servant of the servants of God is carried around Saint Peter's church." The ornate costume, the thrice-appliquéd gold of the tiara, of the vestments and of the chair, stand in ironic contrast to the formal title of their wearer: "servus servorum Dei." The Pope's feeble physical appearance, too, contrasts with his ornate costume and surroundings. Heine insists: "the hazy insignificance of the principal figure and the significant prominence of the secondary figures [his sturdy carriers] is an error of the painting" (DA, XII: 18). Here he points, of course, not merely to "an error of the painting," but once again to the discrepancy between the vain appearance of papal power and the sober reality of its fading, its "insignificance," in today's world.[19]

In his discussion of "one of Horace Vernet's less remarkable pictures," Heine accomplishes a most remarkable feat. For, after devoting a mere four lines to the painting portraying Desmoulins giving his historic speech in the garden of the Palais

Royal, he passes on to his own, much lengthier, reflections about this actor of the French Revolution, whom he addresses in the second person: "Poor Camille! your courage was no higher than this bench [from which he harangues the people] . . . Poor Camille! Poor fellow! that was the merry adolescence ("die lustigen Flegeljahre") of liberty, when you mounted the bench in order to smash the windows of despotism and pulled your lantern jokes; the jokes turned very cheerless later . . ."[20] But then, after a brief description of the costumes of the time as depicted in the painting, Heine's glance comes to rest on one of its secondary figures: "Robespierre himself is also seen in the picture, conspicuous in his painstaking dress and his spruce bearing" (DA, XII: 18–19). "Indeed," he continues, launching into his own historical reminiscences, "his outer appearance was always trim and polished, like the blade of a guillotine; but his inner self, his heart, too, was unselfish, incorruptible and consistent like the blade of a guillotine." Heine thus uses the Vernet painting of Desmoulins to paint his own idealistic portrayal of the man who had condemned Desmoulins to death. Robespierre was, moreover, for Heine's German readers certainly a villain, rather than a hero, of history.[21] Heine likens Robespierre to Brutus, that fanatic purist of Roman republicanism, and suggests that he must have wept when he had to condemn his old school- and childhood-friend, Desmoulins, to death: "while Camille's blood was flowing on the Grève, Maximilian's tears were perhaps flowing in his solitary chamber" (DA, XII: 19).

This celebration of the hero of the French Revolution builds up perfectly to the following essay, devoted to Delacroix and his most famous painting, *Le 28 Juillet (La Liberté guidant le peuple)*. It is the only painting of the artist's seventeen contributions discussed by Heine. He notes that he always found a great throng of people in front of it and considers it thus the most popular picture of the Salon. What Heine failed completely to note is its artistic significance. Unlike Baudelaire, Heine did not recognize Delacroix's importance. In fact, he makes excuses for the painting's quality, redeemed for him by the subject: "the sacredness of the subject permits no severe criticism of the colors . . . despite possible artistic deficiencies, a great thought animates the picture (DA, XII: 20). Then ensues a detailed description of the central figure, Liberty allegorized, bared to the waist, wearing the revolutionary Phrygian cap, with gun in one hand and tricolor in the other, accompanied by her followers, walking over the dead and dying toward victory. Heine notes her "beautiful, impetuous body" and the "bold profile" of her face, but also an "impudent" pain in the traits of "this strange mixture of phryne, fishwife and goddess of liberty."[22] Daughter of the people, she embodies not merely "that fierce strength of a people" of the July Revolution, but suggests "those peripatetic female philosophers . . . those speed-walkers of love, or speed-lovers who roam the boulevards at night." And her followers' provenance appears no less dubious to the beholder. But the essence of the revolution was that its moving idea "has ennobled these common people, this debauched mass, and has sanctified them and reawakened the defunct dignity of their souls." Heine rises to an almost hymnal tone: "Holy days of July! how beautiful was the sun and how great the people of Paris! The gods in heaven who watched the great battle rejoiced in admiration" (DA, XII: 20). For once, Heine did not need to substitute his own *pictura* for the picture, the poet and the painter's vision coinciding.

After a passing mention of the much less glorious Brussels uprising which took place a month after the July Revolution, Heine turns once more to the painting. He finds its colors broken ("eingeschlagen"), but "this very absence of varnish and gleam, with the gun-smoke and dust enveloping the figures . . . the sun-dried hues which seem to thirst for water, all this gives the picture a veracity, character, and originality in which one senses the true nature of the July days."

Exactly half-way through his discussion, Heine now turns from the painting to its spectators, among whom "a little Carlist girl" asks her papa who "that dirty woman with the red hat" is. She is told that this is the goddess of liberty who "to be sure, has nothing to do with the purity of lilies" [emblem of the monarchy]. And when the little lady remarks that "she does not even have a shirt on," papa explains that "a true goddess of liberty, dear child, usually does not wear a shirt and is, therefore, resentful against all people who wear white linen" (DA, XII: 21). Thus Heine here again hints—paradoxically and ironically through the despicable and unreformed aristocrat—at the somber underside of the Revolution.[23] When the marquis suggests to the plainclothed priest beside him that it would take only a minor event to spark off another revolution, his eminence in disguise whispers: "so much the better, Marquis! let there be many horrors . . . The Revolution will then swallow up its own instigators, especially the vain bankers who are, thank God, ruined already." Whereupon the marquis reveals "the Secret of the July Revolution," namely that the resentful rich bourgeoisie was behind it all, distributing money, dismissing the factory workers and paying the tavern keepers to let the wine flow freely . . . "et du reste, c'était le soleil" (and for the rest, it was the sun)![24] What has become of the wonderful enthusiasm of painter and poet over the glorious people's revolution? Heine the analyst—and incurable ironist—seems to be peering under the colorful surface of a revolution which had betrayed the people. "But I forget," he says in closing the key essay of his *Salon*, "that I am only the reporter of an exhibition" (DA, XII: 21–22). Heine omitted this entire second half of his Delacroix chapter from the French version.

Breaking off his political reflections, the "reporter" now turns to an artist "whose pictures seemed like a colorful echo of the voice of my own heart, or, rather, whose hues with their elective affinities resounded wondrously in my heart. Decamps is the name of the painter who exerted such magic on me" (DA, XII, 22). The Decamps essay is the only one of the eight of Heine's 1831 *Salon* primarily concerned with aesthetics. From the texts discussed so far, we have seen that when Heine chooses to deal with painting per se, he speaks about color, manifesting his "painterly" orientation, which also informs this essay. Of Decamps' five pictures exhibited, Heine discusses the *Patrouille turque*, showing the "Hadji-Bey, chief of the police of Smyrna making his round," the painting's other title. Again, Heine first gives a rather detailed, and not altogether innocent, description. The police chief "sits high on his horse, sponge-bellied, in all the majesty of his insolence, with an insultingly arrogant, ignorantly pitch-dark face, shielded by a white turban; in his hands he holds the scepter of absolute bastinadedom, and beside him, on foot, run nine faithful executors of his will *quand même*, hasty creatures with short, skinny legs and almost bestial faces, cat-like, goatish, apish, one of them indeed constituting a mosaic of a dog's muzzle, pig eyes, asses' ears, a calf's grin and the fright of a rabbit" (DA, XII: 23). Heine thoroughly enjoys this ludicrous representation of absolutism. But he returns to the colors, noting the striking contrast of the animated group's dark figures against the background of the white chalk of the houses and the bright yellow clay of the ground. The whole gives the effect of "a Chinese shadow-play."

Heine defends Decamps against hostile critics who criticized the painting for unnaturalness bordering on caricature. But before taking up his defense of the painting, he launches out against art critics in general: "France, too, has its regular art critics, who find fault with every new work according to preconceived rules." He mentions one of them by name, Auguste Jal,[25] who, writing for the *Figaro*, claimed, with ironic humility, that he was "nur ein Mensch" and with "his poor intellect" unable to grasp Decamps' presumed greatness. "The poor rascal," Heine retorts, "he does not realize how he has passed sentence on himself! For in judging works of art, the first voice appertains really never to the poor intellect, any more than it has ever played the first role in their creation. The idea of the work of art soars from the spirit (Gemüt), and it seeks the help needed for its realization from the imagination (Phantasie). The imagination then showers it with all its flowers, almost overwhelms the idea . . . The intellect merely keeps order and is, as it were, the police in the domain of art" (DA, XII: 24). Heine here points, of course, to the creative process in any and all of its forms. And he reflects both his German masters, while inspiring a young French poet, Baudelaire who, even if he did not profoundly read and understand Heine, also elevated the imagination, indeed years later crowned it "La Reine des facultés" in his own Salon of 1859.[26]

Heine's emphasis on the "Gemüt" reflects A. W. Schlegel who, in his *Vorlesgungen über schöne Literatur und Kunst* (Lectures on Literature and Art), discussing "Painting," insists on its importance: "Everything is unquestionably based on the nature of our feelings, and the painter . . . will characterize his picture appropriately in every way and attune its inner disposition (Gemüt), already before it has become acquainted with its object, in a certain way."[27] Thus also Hegel, who in the chapter on "Painting" of his "Lectures on Aesthetics" stresses the primary role of the artist's spirit (Gemüt) in the creative process and its reflection in the work of art: " . . . however, what constitutes the essence of the content in such works of art is not the subject itself, but the liveliness and soul of the subjective conception and execution, the inner disposition (Gemüt) of the artist which is mirrored in his work and not a mere copy of external objects, but at the same time his inner self."[28] This anti-naturalistic stance will again be assumed by Heine, as we shall see later in our discussion.

Schlegel is again echoed in Heine's subsequent rebuttal of "those philosophers of art who, devoid of any poetry of their own, determined out of the existing norms a norm for all future works, and thus separated genres and contrived definitions and rules." They ought instead of asking "what should the artist do?" ask "what does the artist want, or even, have to accomplish?" Instead of applying their vain abstractions drawn from existing works, they ought to know "that every original artist and especially every new artistic genius must be judged according to his own, inherent aesthetics."[29] Thus, the only valid question is whether the artist "possesses the means to realize his idea." These being color and form for the painter, they are, however, "merely symbols of the idea, symbols which arise from the artist's spirit (Gemüt) when it is moved by the holy world spirit (Weltgeist)"(DA, XII: 24–25). This passage, too, clearly recalls Hegel, and it must also have interested Baudelaire. Oliver Boeck explains that Heine's Hegelian *Weltgeist*, however, was not inherited by Baudelaire, and that the two poets' conceptions of the symbol diverged profoundly.[30]

For Heine it is, moreover, "most praiseworthy when the symbols with which the artist expresses his idea, aside from their inner significance, also delight the senses in and for themselves (an und für sich), like the flowers of a *Selam* which, aside from their secret significance, bloom delightfully gathered into a beautiful bouquet." At this point, the poet, interpolates a lovely oriental tale, of a princess who by morning had forgotten the meaning of the bouquet gathered for her beloved the night before. But when he received her flowery greeting, the *Selam*, he was beside himself with joy, for he understood its meaning at once. Heine introduces this charming story to ask whether the artist is entirely free in his choice of secret flowers [symbols], "or does he choose and combine only what he must?" He then affirms the latter, believing that the artist is compelled by a "mystic constraint" (einer mystischen Unfreiheit) in the creative process (DA, XII: 25). And like the princess, he sometimes does not understand the secret significance of his beautiful creation.

Thus, Heine has no use for "the well-meant advice to young artists" to imitate "die Natur und wieder die liebe Natur." The poet is, as we have noted above, an anti-naturalist, and he now explains his stance in a paragraph which has become famous through its adoption and adaptation by Baudelaire: "In art, I am a supernaturalist. I believe that the artist cannot find all his models in nature, but that the most significant models are revealed to him in his soul, as it were, as an innate symbolism of innate ideas." Heine then proceeds to refute Karl F. Rumohr who, in his *Italienische Forschungen* (essays on Italian art) (1827), had maintained that the painter should seek all his characters (Typen) in nature. When Sainte-Beuve reviewed Heine's *De la France* for *Le National* in 1833, he also devoted one paragraph to the poet's *Salon* and quoted the above passage.[31] Whether Baudelaire's interest in Heine's *Salon* was aroused by the Sainte-Beuve article is not certain; it is certain, however, that he read the source text himself, for in his long and enthusiastic chapter on Delacroix in his *Salon de 1846*, he quotes Heine's entire paragraph, including the Rumohr refutation: "Here are some lines by M. Henri Heine which explain Delacroix's method rather well, a method which is, as with all vigorously constituted men, the result of his temperament: 'In art, I am a supernaturalist . . .'"[32] That Heine's "Supernaturalismus" and Baudelaire's "Surnaturalisme" are not the same, and how they differ, has been well explained by Boeck.[33] That Baudelaire applies to Delacroix what Heine had expressed in his Decamps essay, too, points to the famous misunderstanding. And that Laforgue read the *Salons* of both his favorite French and his favorite German poet appears to me, as I have suggested in discussing Laforgue's early literary journalism, most likely.

Finally, Heine returns from his general aesthetic reflections to Decamps' painting and those critics who had found fault with its "unnaturalness." The painting is not a caricature, because of "the harmony of the work, that delightful music of colors, the magic hues.[34] Caricaturists are rarely good colorists" (DA, XII: 26). They lack the necessary inner harmony. Heine recalls seeing Hogarth's originals at the National Gallery in London, which had seemed to him "mere multicolored blotches crying out against each other, a riot of strident colors."[35]

But even this essay closes on a political note. Heine nearly forgot to mention the two female figures in the painting, two women beholding the ludicrous scene in the street from behind a window above. As their faces are not veiled after the Moslem fashion, he assumes them to be Greek. Their quiet beauty stands in "charming contrast" to those other faces; and their very dignity makes us feel "so much more truly transplanted into the fatherland of absolutism."[36] "Only an artist who is also the citizen of a free state," Heine feels, "could paint this picture in good humor." And for his German readers, he adds one last touch omitted from the French version: "Any other but a French artist would have applied his colors in a more forceful and bitter manner, he would have mixed in some Berlin blue, or at least some green bile, and thus missed the undertone of persiflage" (DA, XII: 26–27).

Heine devotes a mere page to Lessore, a painter attractive in his "wonderful veracity and a luxury of unpretentiousness and simplicity" (DA, XII: 27). Of his eight paintings exhibited, Heine describes *Le Frère malade* (*The Sick Brother*), which reminds him of Murillo's beggars. The picture's treatment is best characterized with Shakespeare's phrase: "the modesty of nature" (DA, XII: 27); and its moral message is to remind its beholders of the poor outside, suffering from hunger and cold. Heine likes Schnetz much less, despite his renown. And thus he quickly passes on to L. Robert, one of his favorites.

Heine can already hear "the German guild masters" ask whether this painter is a "Historienmaler" or a "Genremaler." And feeling that he cannot evade the question, he engages in a lengthy, today rather uninteresting, discussion of the distinction between history and genre painting and its evolution. Among the genre painters, he compliments the Dutch, like Jan Steen,[37] Van Dou, van der Werff and others, for conveying wonderfully the spirit of their time, their Zeitgeist. When we look at their pictures, "we look into the windows of the sixteenth century,[38] as it were, and observe the pursuits of their time and their customs" (DA, XII: 29). Heine is amused by the heterogenous ostentation of the latter, "Mynheer with the Burgundian velvet coat and multicolored knight's beret, smoking an earthen pipe; Mifrow wearing heavy iridescent dresses with Venetian satin trains, Brussels lace borders, African ostrich plumes, Russian furs . . ." (DA, XII: 29). How different from today! Our painters' predilection for historical subjects might be due, in part, to their need for more picturesque costumes than those of modern life.[39]

After this digression, Heine introduces Robert, giving a brief history of his career before approaching the paintings, all of them presenting scenes from Italian life. They were inspired by Robert's long stay in Italy, " . . . and the painter's eloquent colors reveal its most secret charms to us; an old magic overcomes us again, and the country that once subjugated us by

its arms and later by its words, now subdues us by its beauty"
(DA, XII: 31). Heine shared the German "Drang nach Süden"
(attraction of the South), which did not die with Romanticism.
He passes quickly over Robert's *Les Piferari à Rome,*
whose colors do not please him. The *Scène d'enterrement à
Rome* interests him merely for its subject, the funeral procession
of a youth who leaves behind a grieving family. In this painting,
"life appears drab, ugly and sad, death, however, infinitely
beautiful, indeed lovely and almost smiling." But the painter
who so beautifully transfigured death knew how to represent life
even more magnificently, namely in "his great masterpiece, *The
Reapers (Arrivée des moissonneurs dans les marais Pontins).*"
For Heine, who always had a reproduction of the painting in his
Paris apartments in later years, it is "an apotheosis of life; in
beholding it, one forgets that there is a realm of shades, and one
doubts that it could be more splendid and brighter anywhere else
but on this earth" (DA, XII: 32). In fact, for Heine the painting
constituted a *pictura* of the Saint-Simonian world view which we
have already encountered in his ironic treatment of *Judith and
Holofernes.* But now the tone is not ironic, as Heine even quotes
one of the articles of that creed: "'The earth is heaven, and
mankind sacred (heilig durchgöttert),' that is the great revelation
shining forth with blissful colors from this picture."

Heine gives a detailed description of "this painted gospel," a
family of reapers, accompanied by their joyous helpers, returning in the evening sun with their ox-drawn cart and the day's
harvest. And in the text, the painting becomes, in fact, a "holy
picture," depicting "the holy family" [my quotation marks] of
the new faith. This becomes particularly apparent in the textual
sublimation of the young woman holding her child: " . . .
somewhat higher on the cart, almost exalted, stands the man's
beautiful young wife, a child in her arms, a rose with a bud"
(DA, XII: 32–33). The rose and bud metaphor clearly alludes to
the Madonna and the Christ-child, an allusion accentuated later in
the essay, when Heine points to Raphael's influence on Robert.

The poet's fundamental anti-naturalism also informs this report, and not merely its *matière*, but its very form, as once again

critical commentary becomes itself transformed into a highly overcharged poetic text: "but the painter did not, in the simplistic-honest fashion of some of his colleagues, merely faithfully copy . . . Robert first received into his spirit (Gemüt) the figures with which nature furnished him and, like the souls which in purgatory lose not their individuality but merely their earthly dross before rising to heaven in bliss, so those figures were cleansed and purified in the flaming depths of the artist's spirit, so that they might rise transfigured into the heaven of art, where eternal life and beauty also reign, where Venus and Mary never lose their worshippers, where Romeo and Juliet never die, where Helen remains eternally young and Hekuba becomes, at least, no older." The juxtaposition of Venus and Mary and their worshippers reflects the poet's Hellene-Nazarene dichotomy and his homage to the art of both, as well as to that of the past and the present.

Again, for Heine the magic of the picture lies in its colors, and "in the coloration of Robert's painting one recognizes the study of Raphael. The architectural beauty of the group, too, reminds of him. Even individual figures, especially the mother with the child, resemble the figures of Raphael's paintings" (DA, XII: 33).[40] However, Heine is careful "not to draw a parallel between Robert and the greatest painter of the Catholic era." Thus, he insists that their affinity is material rather than spiritual. For, whereas Raphael was formed by "a religion which expresses the struggle between spirit and matter, or heaven and earth, and which aims at the repression of matter, . . . Robert is French, and like most of his countrymen subscribes unconsciously to a still veiled doctrine, which does not want to recognize a struggle of spirit and matter, nor forbid mankind the positive earthly joys, . . . but which wants to render man happy already on this earth." This is Heine's most outspoken profession of Saint-Simonianism, by which he was most deeply affected during his first years in Paris, when he wrote our text. Robert's reapers are not merely free of sin; they do not know it. And while in Catholic paintings "merely the head, the seat of the mind, was surrounded by a halo, symbolizing spiritualization, in Robert's picture we see matter, too, spiritualized, as the entire human figure, body as well as head, is bathed in heavenly light, as by a halo" (DA, XII: 33–34).

This essay, too, closes with a poignant message to Heine's German readers, this time, however, not effaced from the French version: "Catholicism in modern France is not merely extinguished, but it does not even have a reactionary influence on art as in our Protestant Germany where, through the poetry which dwells on the past, it has assumed a new importance" (DA, XII: 34). The exiled poet had already explained to his readers across the border that the *Charte* (of 1830), which declared Catholicism to be the religion of the majority of the French people, was merely a gallant gesture toward Notre-Dame "who, with equal politeness, wears on her head the three colors of liberty" (DA, XII: 34).

The final and longest essay of Heine's *Salon* is devoted to the leader of the historical school, Delaroche, who "does not have a predilection for the past itself, but for the demonstration of its spirit, for writing history with colors" (DA, XII: 35). Over half of the text on four of Delaroche's paintings consists of Heine's philosophico-political reflections occasioned by them. As each of the paintings depicts a tragic moment, with the death of the historical figures imminent in three, and having just occurred in the other, Heine's textual strategy is to accentuate this fundamental life-death dichotomy by structuring his discussion antithetically. Thus, two of the paintings refer to French, two to English history. The former two are small, the two latter life-size. And while the two former "are richly peopled," the other two feature only two major figures each.

The first picture, *Le Cardinal Richelieu conduisant au supplice Cinq-Mars et Thou* (*Cardinal Richelieu taking Cinq-Mars and Thou to their Execution*), shows two boats, one behind the other, traveling up the Rhone to Lyon. In the first is Richelieu, himself ill and close to death; in the second are the two leaders of the conspiracy against the Cardinal-minister, about to be beheaded in Lyon.[41] Heine notes the radiant colors which contrast with the somber fate they depict and throw into relief the tragic antithesis underlying the scene, in which a dying old man leads two youths to their death. Again, the *poet* repaints the scene for his readers: "The magnificent rays of the sun are a mere farewell; it is evening, and the sun must itself go down; it will merely throw one more blood-red streak of color over the earth, and then all is night."

In the other painting from French history, "*Le Cardinal Mazarin mourant*" (*The Dying Cardinal Mazarin*), the Minister lies dying in a huge and stately bed, surrounded by courtiers and their ladies and servants, all engaged in frivolous pursuits. Heine assumes a light and almost bantering tone as he minutely describes the colorful fashions, the hairdress, even the card game most likely being played by one of the groups. Thus, he accentuates the contrast between the vain and luxurious hubbub of courtly life and an old man's agony.[42] He shows up a frivolous and idle aristocracy which, even in the face of death, pursues its *fêtes galantes*. Proceeding antithetically, he points to the contrast of inside and outside, or what the painting shows and what it hides. "All the ladies are pretty in the picture, all pretty court masks: on the faces smiling love, and perhaps gray melancholy in the heart; the lips innocent like flowers, and behind them an evil little tongue, like a clever serpent" (DA, XII: 35–36). Mazarin will be dead within the hour, "for the wing beat of the angel of night already touches his forehead—at this moment the lady playing cards turns to show him her hand and seems to be asking him whether she should trump with her Coeur" (DA, XII: 36). Here the syntactic break accentuates the shocking contrast.

Les Enfants d'Eduard depicts the two Princes life-size,[43] sitting on an old-fashioned bed, waiting for their execution. "The young King, still half boy and already half a young man, is an exceedingly moving figure." And then Heine wrenches us suddenly from past into contemporary history. In the eyes of the unfortunate Prince, he recognizes those of a beloved friend, who had also died young, a victim of history. Ludwig Mycielski, whose guest Heine had been during his trip to Poland in 1822, had died in February of 1831, during the recent Polish uprising against the Tsar: "alas! the dear friend is now dead, shot near

Praga . . ." (DA, XII: 37).[44] Thus Heine links past and present history, and history to his own life. That tragic Polish struggle for independence will erupt later on in the essay, when the fall of Warsaw will nearly break it off.

However, "still more grievous are the feelings aroused by Delaroche's other painting . . . a scene from that terrible tragedy that has also been translated into French and cost so many tears . . ." This is how Heine introduces *Cromwell ouvrant le cercueil de Charles Ier* (*Cromwell Opening the Casket of Charles I*), thus again linking past to more recent, and English to French history. For the regicides of 1649 and 1793 are both scenes of that *theatrum mundi* which, animated by a Hegelian *Weltgeist*, assigns their roles to the actors of the moment. Cromwell and Charles Stuart are "perhaps not heroes themselves, but simply actors, to whom their roles were prescribed by the director of the world."[45] They were cast to represent "the two hostile principles . . . the two great thoughts" of monarchy and democracy, an antithesis which Heine stresses throughout.

Cromwell is "in the fullness of life," the King is "a corpse in a coffin" (DA, XII: 38). The victim, however, is dignified by death itself, "transfigured by his martyrdom, sanctified by the majesty of his misfortune, with the costly purple on his neck, the kiss of melpomene on his white lips, forming the most forceful contrast to the raw, robustly alive Puritan figure." Not merely does Heine's complex and ambiguous attitude toward revolution, which we have already encountered in connection with Delacroix's *Liberté*, inform his interpretation of both the historical painting and the events evoked by it; but Heine, the Hellene, must perforce mourn the victory of Puritanism and the Nazarenes.[46] From this perspective, monarchy "was once the consolation and flower of humanity." And we know that for Heine, since the Puritan revolution, "England's life has been pale and gray . . ., and poetry, terrified, fled the land which it had formerly embellished with its brightest colors" (DA, XII: 39).

Heine remarks that Delaroche had intentionally invited the historical comparison between Charles I and Louis XVI and, as its corollary, that of Cromwell and Napoleon. Yet, what a difference between the royal victims, Charles losing his crown with his head, while Louis had already renounced his during his lifetime! While Charles Stuart had believed in his kingship and "fought for it like a knight, slender and fearless," Louis, "the poor Bourbon had already abdicated in donning the Jacobinical cap . . . a good, not very slim, family man." Thus for Heine, Chateaubriand's famous designation of the French regicide as "un plagiat infâme d'un crime étranger" (DA, XII: 39) is mere ultraroyalist rhetoric.[47]

In a passage omitted from the French version, Heine deplores the royalists' appropriation of the royal misfortune, for the king belonged to the entire people, and thus the sorrow, too, belongs to all. Further, "we call the somber origin of those sorrows by no means a plagiarism, much less a crime, and least of all infamous. Would we not elevate man at once too high and degrade him too low, if we were to attribute to him such gigantic strength and also such an outrage, as to have shed that blood arbitrarily" (DA, XII: 40)? No, men merely play, like their kings, the roles assigned to them by history, asserts Hegel's student. And Heine proceeds to demonstrate how little their own free will had guided most of those who had voted for Louis' death, and how even the staunchest republicans were numbed by the event.

As for Cromwell and Napoleon, it is unfair to compare them. For while Napoleon was not guilty of shedding royal blood, Cromwell, on the other hand, "never sank so low as to let himself be annointed emperor by a priest." Both are tarnished, "in the life of the one, it is a spot of blood, in that of the other, one of oil" (DA, XII: 41).

These reflections are suddenly interrupted, literally, the poet asserts, from the outside: "at this moment I hear a wild turmoil out there, louder and more deafening than ever . . . a furious throng of people, frantic and cursing with grief, the people of Paris pushing through the narrow streets, and screaming: 'Warsaw has fallen! . . . Down with the ministers! War on Russia! Death to the Prussians!' "[48] And it becomes hard for the reporter to remain at his desk, calmly writing his "poor report-age on art." Yet, if he went out into the street, he might be recognized as a Prussian, "get his head smashed, and with it all his artistic ideas." Not merely does the political reality of the day interfere with the writing and transform the text, but it transmutes even the pictures already described. In a strange reversal, reality exerts a dream-like charm on the narrator: "in such clamor, all thoughts and pictures become confused and shifted. Delacroix's goddess of Liberty confronts me with an entirely changed face, almost with fear in her wild eyes. The picture of Vernet's Pope is changing miraculously. Christ's feeble old governor suddenly looks young and healthy and rises smilingly from his chair." And in that black coffin "lies not a king, but murdered Poland, and before it stands no longer Cromwell, but the Tsar of Russia" (DA, XII: 45). Later on in the text, that oneiric vision returns and turns into sinister meta-phors: "the goddess of Liberty turns pale, our friends lie crushed, the Roman archpriest (Grosspfaffe) rises smiling vi-ciously, and the victorious aristocracy stands triumphantly at the coffin of the people" (DA, XII: 45).

In view of so much misery, it would take "an almost Goethean egotism" to pursue artistic pleasures with serenity. Yesterday, Heine continues, he kept on writing his report all the same, after he had gone out for a while, "on the boulevards, where I saw a deadly pale man collapse from hunger and misery. But when suddenly an entire people falls down on the boulevards of Europe—then it is impossible to continue writing calmly" (DA, XII: 46).

The tension between life and art, which marks the stress lines of Heine's entire *Salon*, mounts to the breaking point at its conclusion. Unless art be re-formed and reborn of and with the new age, it will not survive the socio-political (r)evolution. Thus Heine repeats his prophesy, already vaguely alluded to above, "of the end of the *Kunstperiode* which began at Goethe's cradle and will end at his grave."[49] That Goethean "art period" had made an absolute of art and elevated it sublimely above and beyond life which must, on the contrary, sustain it. The divorce has impoverished both and rendered art sterile. Heine debunks Romantic "classicism," because he believes that the art of each age must grow out of its historical moment and mirror its *Zeitgeist* (cf. p. 166 above). When he says that "contemporary art must perish because its principle is still . . . rooted in the decrepit *ancien régime*," he means, of course, not merely the visual arts. We recall his comments on Romantic classical ballet, for example, which he found as outmoded as French classical drama.

Art today, "like all withered remnants of the past, stands in the most disagreeable contradiction to the present;" and it is "this contradiction, and not the movement of time itself which is so harmful to art; on the contrary, the movement of time (Zeitbewegung) ought to be salutary to art." This, however, can only come about when, as in the past, the artist himself is firmly grounded in his time. In this argument *pro domo*, Heine evokes the great masters of the past, poets and painters, whose works "were the dreaming reflection of their time, and they themselves men of one piece . . . who stood in harmony with their surrounding world." For example, "Aeschylus wrote the *Persians* with the same truth with which he fought them at Marathon, and Dante wrote his *Comedy* not as a stock commissioned poet, but as a fleeing Guelf, deploring not the loss of his talent, but that of liberty" (DA, XXI: 47). This is the poet's most explicit plea for not merely a renewal in art, but for that *littérature engagée* demonstrated by the very text which pleads for it. Heine's position will not be assumed by Laforgue, as we shall see shortly. For while Laforgue, like Baudelaire, became a consummate critic in his texts on art, Heine, as I have stressed, appropriated the genre for his own ends, one of which was to invoke that renewal of the arts demonstrated by his own text. But even a Börne failed to understand the significance of Heine's *Salon*.[50]

Heine sounds like Hegel when he asks: "are we approaching the somber end of art"?[51] But the Salon "has through many a painting rejected this fear of death and revealed a better promise." The text ends on a confident note: "the new times will also bring forth a new art that will be in enthusiastic harmony with them;" it will not "borrow its symbols from a faded past;" it will even "bring forth a new technique, different from the present." In conclusion, Heine predicts that France "will breathe forth" a new art "from the depths of her heart and new life;" and his "Gemäldeausstellung" closes with a lovely image, a simile comparing "that light and inconstant people" to a butterfly. "But the butterfly is also an emblem of the immortality of the soul and its eternal rejuvenescence" (DA, XII: 48).

* * *

Heine opens his "Nachtrag" (*Salon de 1833*) with a retrospective glance: "When I came to Paris in the summer of 1831, nothing astonished me more than the exposition of paintings that had just opened; and although the most important political and religious revolutions claimed by attention, I could not refrain from first writing about the great revolution which had taken place here in the domain of art, and whose most significant manifestation was in evidence in that Salon." From the perspective of 1833—and its Salon which disappointed him—Heine now considers that renewal in art not merely promised, but already accomplished, by the Salon of 1831. "Painting in France," he writes in 1833, "has followed the social movement and finally become rejuvenated with the people itself."

But this regeneration in painting did not come about as directly as in the sister arts of music and poetry, "which had already begun their transformation before the Revolution" (DA, XII: 51). In support of this view, Heine now interpolates a lengthy passage about the history of eighteenth-century painting by Louis de Maynard.[52] Thus he did well to label his essay a "postscript" to his 1831 *Salon*, as he continues to sidestep the exposition of 1833. The French critic featured by Heine, who had also written about the 1833 Salon, points out that in the eighteenth century art had lagged behind, having produced its Crébillons, but no Voltaires or Diderots. The revolution in painting did not come about until after the Revolution, with

Jacques-Louis David's new manner. Heine recalls that David's fame had also spread to Germany during the Empire, as had that of some of his pupils, like Gérard, Gros, Girodet and Guérin. Much less known across the border is Géricault, who represents a new school of painting, a school, Heine reminds his readers, of which he had informed them in his *Salon* of 1831: "In describing the best pictures of the Salon of 1831, I at the same time furnished the real characteristics of the new masters. That Salon was, according to the general judgment, the most extraordinary ever produced in France, and it remains memorable in the annals of art." He adds enthusiastically: "The paintings which I found worthy of description will live for centuries, and my words are perhaps a useful contribution to the history of painting." I do not believe that Heine is being intentionally ironic here. His opinion about the 1831 paintings had shifted somewhat over the two years; especially, as he himself explains, the depressing mediocrity of the 1833 Salon convinced him of the excellence of the earlier one. And a few years later, Heine, too, recognized that the importance of his *Gemäldeausstellung in Paris 1831* lies not so much in its "useful contribution to the history of painting" as in his unprecedented manner of handling the genre.

The "Nachtrag," like the text to which it is the sequel, is not nearly so much a discussion of a series of paintings as sociopolitical reflections which it occasions. Its longest passage on painting as such as is a borrowed one, the interpolation from the Maynard article, which deals, moreover, not with contemporary art, but with that of the past century.

Heine, who will not divorce art from politics, likens the new exposition at the Louvre to "an echo in colors of this year's Chamber;" and "while the 1831 Salon was inspired by the July sun, in the Salon of 1833 there merely trickled the turbid rain of June," the former alluding to the July Revolution, the latter to the defeat of the Republican uprising in June of 1831. The two heroes of the former Salon, Delaroche and Robert, were not represented this year; and other painters who had distinguished themselves two years ago showed no exceptional works in 1833. Heine liked only painting, by Tony Johannot, who had exhibited three pictures. But as Heine does not give any description, it is not clear to which of the three he is referring. The artist who aroused his greatest interest this year is Jean-Auguste Ingres, who exhibited his *Dame romaine* and the now famous *Monsieur Bertin l'aîné*. Heine describes neither and immediately passes on, apparently completely unaware of the artistic significance of these paintings, especially the latter. Again, a political reflection intervenes, when he says that "like Louis-Philippe in politics, so M. Ingres was king in the realm of art this year, the former reigning in the Tuileries, the latter in the Louvre. The character of M. Ingres, too, is *Juste-milieu*, namely a *Juste-milieu* between Mieris and Michelangelo" (DA, XII: 54).

While painting was disappointing, sculpture, on the other hand, showed great promise in this year's Salon.[53] Heine was expecially impressed by Etex's group of *Caïn et sa race maudite par Dieu*. And with a brief discussion of French sculpture, less than half-way through the text, Heine ends his commentary on the Salon of 1833.

Instead, he now turns to the King, remarking that the artists complain about his miserliness; he had been more protective of the arts as Duke of Orléans. Louis-Philippe's real passion is building, and never had there been as much of it going on in Paris as presently. Heine's commentary shows us beautifully how the modernization of the capital was already beginning under the July Monarchy, some years before Napoleon III and Baron Haussmann. But this discussion, too, leads to politics: the King's request for the construction of fortifications outside of Paris.

In the summer of 1833, the question of the *forts détachés* animated both the Chamber and the press, and Heine gives an amusing, needless to say ironic, account of the pros and cons: "Everyone felt that Louis-Philippe only wanted to fortify himself against Paris . . . Most of the *boutiquiers* are of the opinion that Louis-Philippe is a splendid king, worth some sacrifices . . . by no means, however, is he worth . . . in the event of future uprisings in Paris, placing oneself with wife and child, and all the *boutiques*, into the danger of being shot to the

ground from fourteen fortifications" (DA, XII: 59). Those fortifications would, moreover, hurt tourism considerably, rather
than protect Paris from foreign aggression.

Heine terminates his essay with a profession of faith in
constitutional monarchy. If the European princes would only
understand that Napoleon and Louis-Philippe were godsends!
For twice, first with the one, then with the other, God has saved
institutions in Europe, "because God is intelligent and realizes
that the republican form of government is very inappropriate and
undesirable for old Europe. And I, too," Heine adds, "am of
this opinion. But we [God and Heine] might not be able to
accomplish anything against the obtuseness of the princes and
demagogues. Against stupidity even we gods fight in vain" (DA,
XII: 61).[54]

* * *

Heine's other comments on French painting are scattered
throughout the articles he wrote in the 1840's from Paris for the
Augsburger Allgemeine Zeitung, later published in *Lutetia*,
whose reports on theatre I have discussed in a previous chapter.
Thus on April 20, 1841, he reports his disappointment with that
year's Salon, which manifested a "many-colored impotence."
Now Heine feels that "after the happy impetus in painting and
sculpture, and even architecture, soon after the July Revolution, . . . followed the most lamentable falling-off" (B, V: 356).

In December of that year, Heine takes his readers on a holiday
window-shopping tour leading to an art dealer's display of a new
engraving, *The Fishermen of Chioggia* by Robert, his favorite
painter in 1831. But *The Reapers* was infinitely superior to the
more recent painting which appears, to Heine, already overshadowed by the suicidal ideas of the artist, who had killed
himself in 1835. For "just as the first picture appeases and
delights us, so the latter fills us with shocking indignation: in the
former, Robert had painted man's happiness; in the latter, he
painted the misery of a people" (B, V: 377). Heine wonders
whether Robert's suicide might not have been due "to that most

terrifying of feelings, when an artist discovers the disproportion between his creative desire and his ability; this consciousness of the lack of artistic power, which is already half a death" (B, V: 378).

In the following article, Heine again discusses engravings of paintings by an artist of the 1831 Salon. The portrait of Napoleon by Delaroche was eclectically composed, like his other pictures, and "the essential feature . . . the eclectic procedure, which conveys a certain truth, but does not give rise to any deeper fundamental idea" (B, V: 383), marks all his work. Heine recalls some of the artist's better-known paintings and finds his *Cromwell*, of which he had given a detailed description in 1831, "the most effective." In 1841, he no longer considers Delaroche a great historical painter, but "the court painter of all beheaded majesties," accentuating thus his sensationalism, rather than his art.

The last Salon Heine comments on is that of 1843, which disappoints him even more than the 1841 event. On May 7, he writes: "This year the exposition arouses unusual interest, but I am unable to arrive at a half-way reasonable judgment about the highly-praised excellence of this Salon." It lacks unity, and with its "multi-colored madness" and "anarchy in golden frames" (B, V: 480), it fails to reflect the spirit of the age, the Zeitgeist. We have already encountered this notion, which Heine also calls "die zeitliche Signatur," in the 1831 Salon, where he had found it sorely lacking and nostalgically recalled medieval and Renaissance art. While a Watteau or a Boucher reflect "the gracious, powdered pastorals, . . . the playful vacuousness" of their age, and while the paintings of David and his pupils are a "mere colorful echo of the period of republican virtues," how will "the signature of our time manifest itself to posterity, in days to come, in the paintings of today's artists?" Perhaps the reigning spirit of the bourgeoisie and industrialism has already imprinted its mark on today's art. A glance at this year's holy pictures, especially, seems to support this view. There is, for example, in the great hall "a *Flagellation* whose principal figure, with its doleful mien, resembles the director of a failed insurance company, about to render an accounting to his stockholders."

The faces in the historical paintings featuring pagan and medieval subjects, too, "recall the shop, stock market transactions, mercantilism, and Philistinism" (B, V: 480–81). There is, however, one "most noteworthy" holy picture in the Salon, by Vernet, "the only great master" represented.[55] Heine is fascinated with his *Judah and Tamar*, to which he devotes the remaining pages of his article. He assures his readers that the Old Testament subject[56]—Judah approaching his beautiful daughter-in-law sitting by the roadside and handing over to her his staff and ring as tokens so that he might lie with her—though it might appear somewhat compromising today, was not at all immoral in Biblical times. No more so than that of Judith rising from the bed of Holofernes, prepared to cut off his head. As for Judah, "it was a hot day in Mesopotamia, and the poor patriarch was thirsting for refreshment." His act was surely providential, for "without that great thirst, Tamar would not have conceived a child; this child, however, became the ancestor of David who reigned as king over Judah and Israel, and thus was also the forefather of that still greater king with the crown of thorns, whom the whole world venerates today, Jesus of Nazareth" (B, V: 482–83). Obviously, Heine enjoys the story as much as Vernet's lovely Tamar. "Her foot, leg, knee, etc., are of a perfection bordering on poetry. The bosom flows forth from her scanty dress blooming, fragrant and tempting, like the forbidden fruit in the Garden of Eden." Again, as in 1831, Vernet's depiction of a Biblical pair occasions a Heinean celebration of this-wordly Hellenism.

But in his *Berichte über Politik, Kunst und Volksleben* of the 1840's, Lutetia's politics and social life interest Heine more than her art, most likely because that art, for him, no longer reflected the social and political life of its time.[57]

Notes

[1] DA, XII: 9–62.
[2] Diderot wrote nine *Salons*: 1759, 1761, 1763, 1765, 1767, 1769, 1771, 1775, 1781.
[3] Since 1725, the *Académie Royale de Peinture et Sculpture* had organized expositions in the Louvre for the Court. During the eighteenth century, these

official expositions became public. In Diderot's time, they were held every two years; during Heine's years in Paris, they were annual, with the exception of 1832, the year of the cholera in Paris, which Heine describes so masterfully in *Französische Zustände*, DA, XII: 129ff.

⁴ Diderot, *Oeuvres esthétiques* (Paris: Editions Garnier, 1959), 439.

⁵ In *Shakespeares Mädchen und Frauen*, Heine compares Hazlitt to Diderot: "The only commentator Shakespeare's, whom I have designated an exception, and who is also in every respect to be considered exceptional, is the late Hazlitt, a mind as brilliant as profound, a mixture of Diderot and Börne, with an ardent enthusiasm for the revolution along with a fervent sense for art, always brimming over with verve and spirit" (B, IV: 183).

⁶ For a listing of the various installments and their publication dates, cf. Zepf, *Heinrich Heines Gemäldeausstellung zum Salon 1831*, 227.

⁷ Heine, *De la France*, 324–83. Allemands *et Français* (Paris: Calmann-Lévy, 1881), 223–48; (orig. ed. 1868).

⁸ Thus, twelve years later, commenting on the Salon of 1843, in *Lutetia*, Heine writes: "I torture myself in vain, trying to order this chaos in my mind and to discover the idea of the times in it . . . by which these paintings reveal themselves as products of our present times. For all works of one and the same period have such a character, the painted sign of the Zeitgeist" (B, V: 480).

⁹ Cf. "Die Romantische Schule," DA, VIII: 170ff., especially in Heine's remarks about A. W. Schlegel, like the following: "Herr Schlegel adequately understands the spirit of the past, especially of the Middle Ages, and he therefore succeeds in identifying this spirit in the artistic monuments of the past and in demonstrating their beauty from that point of view. But every thing that is the present he fails to comprehend."

¹⁰ Sammons, *A Modern Biography*, 172.

¹¹ Zepf, *Gemäldeausstellung*, 77: "*Journal des artistes*, 5 juin, 1831: 'Système de glacis et de tons sales qui en font des oeuvres incompréhensibles pour le vulgaire des specateurs.' *L'Artiste*, 1831, Iᵉʳ semestre, p. 215: 'Dans toutes les productions de M. Scheffer on remarque un abus étudié de teints bitumeuses, une imitation affectée d'effets rembranesque'."

¹² Talleyrand had served the Revolutionary government, the Directorate, then Napoleon, and after the Emperor's fall the Restoration. He also served Louis-Philippe; in 1831, the King sent him to London to work on the resolution of the Belgian question.

¹³ This is somewhat surprising, as Heine repeatedly disapproved of the famous "poire" of the political cartoonists. Cf. for example, DA, XII: 81: "It is certainly blameworthy to make the King's features the object of most of the jokes, and that he is displayed as target of ridicule in all caricature shops." Heine omitted not merely his caricature, but also his own magnificent equestrian portrait of Louis-Philippe in the French *De la France* version of his text.

[14] Zepf, *Gemäldeausstellung*, 196.

[15] Wolfdietrich Rasch, "Die Pariser Kunstkritik Heinrich Heines" in *Beiträge zum Stilpluralismus* (Munich: Prestel-Verlag, 1977), 238.

[16] Thus also Gerhard Söhn in his informative article about the background for Heine's *Salon*, "In der Tradition der literarischen Kunstbetrachtung Heinrich Heines 'Französische Maler'," *Heine-Jahrbuch*, 9–34 (1978), who notes "Für Heine waren mehr oder weniger alle Menschen entweder Nazarener oder Hellenen, Menschen mit asketischen, bildfeindlichen, vergeistigungssüchtigen Trieben oder Menschen von lebensheiterem, entfaltungsstolzem und realistischem Wesen. Es erscheint nur zu natürlich, daß auch die Kunstanschauung Heines auf dieser Polarisierung basierte." And, as we have noted above, "seine Betrachtungen über die bildende Kunst sind damit durchgängig auch weniger kunstimminente Kritiken als Reflexionen über Bildthemen" (p. 16).

[17] For Heine's interest in, and connection with, the Saint-Simonians after his arrival in Paris, thus the time during which he wrote this *Salon*, cf. Sammons, *A Modern Biography*, 159–68, "Saint-Simonianism."

[18] The Vernet painting does not portray the "jetzige (present) Papst," but his predecessor.

[19] Heine again recalls this painting many years later in *Geständnisse*, where he ironically portrays himself in the papal role—which recalls that his mother at one point had wanted to make a prelate out of her son Heinrich—, creating an image modeled after our painting: "I likewise would have let myself be carried triumphantly, with suitable peace of mind, through the pillared halls of the great basilica, and only in the shakiest case would I have clung a little tighter to the armrests of the golden chair carried on the shoulders of six sturdy chamberlains in scarlet, while bald-headed Capuchins walk beside with burning candles, and liveried lackeys hold huge peacock plumes with which they fan the head of the prince of the Church—as it is indeed lovely to behold in Horace Vernet's painting of the procession" (DA, XV: 54–5).

[20] Heine alludes to Jean-Paul Richter's famous novel *Flegeljahre*. The "Laternenwitze" alludes to Desmoulins' 1789 pamphlet "Discours de la lanterne aux Parisiens."

[21] The fact that Heine addresses himself expressly to his German readers is borne out by the fact that the entire discussion of the Desmoulins painting was omitted in the French version of the Vernet essay.

[22] French commentators, too, had had mixed reactions to this Liberté: "Des caricatures où la liberté s'élance sous les traits d'une poissarde, suivie de trois ou quatre déguenillés qui ressemblent à des voleurs arrêtant une diligence." "La liberté n'est rien moins qu'une vierge; elle a l'air de toute autre chose, et au lieu de descendre du ciel, on pourrait croire qu'elle sort de chez le marchand de vin" (Zepf, *Gemäldeausstellung*, p. 90).

[23] Cf. for example Heine's famous passage from the French "Préface" to

Lutetia: "The nightingales, those useless singers, will be chased away, and, alas!, my 'Book of Songs' will serve the grocer for cornets into which he will pour coffee or tobacco . . . I am seized by an indescribable sadness when I think of the ruin with which the victorious proletariat threatens my verses, which will perish with all that old Romantic world. And yet, I frankly admit that this same communism, so hostile to all my interests and inclinations, exerts upon my soul a charm against which I am defenseless" (B, V: 224). Although written many years later (1855) and referring specifically to communism, the text expresses the ambiguity toward revolution evident in the 1831 *Salon*.

24 Margaret Rose in her "The Politicization of Art Criticism: Heine's 1831 Portrayal of Delacroix's *Liberté* and its Aftermath," *Monatshefte für deutschen Unterricht* LXXIII (1981): 405–14, comments: "It may seem to be an irony that in the upside-down world of Revolution, the aristocrat is shown not so much as having given up his old views, but as having translated them into their opposites to oppose those of the Revolution. But the dialectics of progress are here shown, implicitly at least, to be rather dangerously perverse. . . . the revelation of 'counterrevolutionaries' amongst his audience leads Heine to depict these forces as having masked themselves; as the now liberated *Venus vulgaris* had once been masked by them" (p. 409).

25 Heine omitted the name in the French version.

26 Baudelaire, *Curiosités esthétiques, L'Art Romantique* (Paris: Editions Garnier, 1961), 320–30, the chapters "La Reine des facultés" and "Le Gouvernement de l'Imagination" of the *Salon de 1859*. I do not intend to suggest that Heine influenced or seriously marked Baudelaire's aesthetics. But, as we shall see, Baudelaire had clearly read Heine's *Salon de 1831* at the time he wrote his own 1846 *Salon*, and, perhaps, as I have suggested in the first chapter, even at the time he wrote his *Salon* of 1845.

27 August Wilhelm Schlegel, *Die Kunstlehre* (Stuttgart: Kohlhammer, 1963), 172. These lectures were not published in a critical edition until 1848, but Heine, of course, had heard some of them from the master himself. Thus, we recall also Heine's verse preface to *Almansor*: "Romantisch ist der Stoff, die Form ist plastisch, / Das Ganze aber kam aus dem Gemüte." In this connection I should also like to add that Heine's image of the paintings exhibited at the Salon of 1831 as "poor children" of an orphanage might possibly reflect Schlegel's similar designation in his "Ueber die berlinische Kunstausstellung von 1802," in whose opening he says: "Eine Ausstellung führt, wie ich glaube, diesen Namen davon, daß sie gemacht wird, damit Ausstellungen darüber gemacht werden können. Vielleicht hat man diese Benennung deswegen einer Aussetzung vorgezogen, weil die letzte an das Schicksal ausgesetzter Kinder erinnern möchte, welches in der That nicht selten ausgestellten Kunstwerken zu Theil wird" (August Wilhelm Schlegel, *Sämtliche Werke*, IX, 158 (Hildesheim: Georg Olms Verlag, 1971).

28 G.W.F. Hegel, *Werke in zwanzig Bänden* (Frankfurt: Suhrkamp Verlag,

1970), XV, *Vorlesungen über die Ästhetik III*, 26. Heine, however, did not hear Hegel's lectures on aesthetics.

29 Cf. Schlegel, *Kunstlehre*, 199: "Was von den Gruppen und Kontrasten, gilt von der Komposition überhaupt. Die allgemeinen Regeln führen dabei nicht weit: der Geist des Künstlers muß jedesmal das Schickliche und Angemessene ausfinden und die Regeln dafür nicht von außen hinzubringen, sondern sie aus seiner bestimmten Aufgabe von innen heraus entwickeln."

30 Boeck, *Heine-Parallelelen*, 115–22.

31 Sainte-Beuve *Oeuvres* (Paris: Gallimard, 1956), I, 555, "Premiers Lundis." He concludes: "Voilà de la critique certainement éloquente, et je crois, très judicieuse." This Sainte-Beuve article contains another interesting remark about Heine: "Pour tout dire, M. Heine sera davantage encore à notre niveau de Français quand il aura un peu moins d'esprit" (552). Daniel A. deGraaf, in "Quelques Rencontres avec Henri Heine dans la littérature française," *Les Langues modernes*, VII, (1956): 140–44, points to Sainte-Beuve's negative attitude toward Heine and recalls: "La première fois, c'est au dîner de Magny, le 23 février 1863, où se réunissent Charles Edmond, Sainte-Beuve, Tourgeniev, les frères Goncourt et autres convives lettrés. C'est le romancier russe qui met le nom de Heine sur le tapis pour chanter ses louanges. Seul Sainte-Beuve ne fait pas chorus avec les autres, au contraire il s'écrie 'c'était un misérable coquin . . .' Un an plus tard Sainte-Beuve revient à la charge . . . 'Vraiment, se récrie vivement Sainte-Beuve, je m'étonne de vous entendre parler de cet homme-là [Heine]. Un misérable qui prenait tout ce qu'il savait de vous, pour le mettre dans les gazettes . . ., qui a déchiré tous ses amis" (46).

32 Baudelaire, *Curiosités esthétiques*, 117–18.

33 Boeck, *Heine-Parallelen*, 116–19, "'Supernaturalismus' und 'Surnatural-isme'."

34 Werner Hofmann in "Heine und die Malerei der Zukunft," *Heine-Jahrbuch* (1981), points to a striking similarity between Heine's discussion of color in the Decamps essay and Hegel. Hegel also speaks of "die Duftigkeit, *Magie* in der Wirkung des Kolorits. Diese Zauberei des Farbenscheins . . ." "Heine stellt seine farbensensualistische Ästhetik in den Dienst neuer Inhalte. Indem er die Malerei zur Verkünderin von Freiheit und Lebenslust macht, weist er ihr eine erweckende Aufgabe und mithin bestimmte positive Aussagen zu: sie soll den künftigen Garten Eden Feiern . . ." (p. 80). But Hofmann notes that Heine's optimism again and again conflicts with his basic scepticism.

35 A. W. Schlegel shared Heine's dislike of caricature and particularly of Hogarth: "Ein weit schlimmerer Abweg ist es, wenn der Maler moralisieren will und, statt uns zu belustigen, die Häßlichkeit und Ausartung zur Warnung und zum Abscheu aufstellt . . . Hogarth war es, der diese durchaus falsche und wertlose Gattung vollendete, und dabei an allen Teilen der Malerei ein Erzstümmler war" (*Kunstlehre*, p. 203).

[36] The beautiful Greek women recall, of course, the recent Greek struggle for independence.

[37] Heine loved Jan Steen and devoted enthusiastic passages to him in *Aus den Memoiren des Herren von Schnabelewopski*, B, I: 540–42.

[38] He means the seventeenth century.

[39] We are still before the days when painters began celebrating it, like Constantin Guys, whom Baudelaire hailed as "le peintre de la vie moderne" (*Curiosités esthétiques*, p. 458–66). In contrast to Heine, we shall see Laforgue welcome the celebration of modern dress in art.

[40] Robert's kinship with the Italian painter had already been noted by French critics. Thus in the *Journal des artistes*, June 23, 1831: "Une jeune femme, debout dans le char et tenant son enfant dans ses bras, a toute la naïveté et presque toute la beauté d'une Madone de Raphaël" (Zepf, *Gemäldeausstellung*, p. 110).

[41] Cinq-Mars and Thou were beheaded on September 12, 1642; Richelieu died shortly after, on December 4.

[42] Mazarin died in 1661, almost sixty years old.

[43] They are Edward V and his brother Richard, whom Richard III had murdered in 1483.

[44] The Polish reminiscence is omitted in the French version.

[45] We recall Heine's remark in *Über die französische Bühne*, that all French history appeared to him "like a great comedy, . . . performed for the greater good of humanity."

[46] Cf. *Shakespeares Mädchen und Frauen*, p. 113 above.

[47] Chateaubriand pronounced these words in a public speech of June 1828.

[48] Warsaw fell to the Russians in September 1831, which meant the defeat of the Polish uprising of 1830–31. Gerhard Weiss in "Heinrich Heines 'Französiche Maler' (1831)," *Heine-Jahrbuch*, 78–100 (1980), shows evidence that Heine, at the moment when the fall of Warsaw was proclaimed in Paris, was in Boulogne, working on his text. This, of course, shows us again how the poet poeticized the genre!

[49] Thus in Heine's review of Menzel's *Die Deutsche Literatur* of 1828: "The idea of Art surely is at once the focus of the entire literary period which begins with the appearance of Goethe and has only now reached its end; it is certainly the essential focus of Goethe himself, the great representative of this period" (B, I: 445).

[50] Thus Heine notes in the fourth book of *Ludwig Börne eine Denkschrift*, years later: " . . . Börne had been annoyed that immediately upon my arrival in Paris I found nothing better to do than write a long report about that year's art exhibition for German papers. I shall leave it undecided for the moment whether the interest in art which drove me to such a task was so completely incompatible with the revolutionary interests of the day" (DA, XI: 92).

[51] Had Hegel not predicted that with the end of Romantic art, art itself would

die? Thus he says in the Introduction to the "Lectures on Aesthetics": "so ist es einmal der Fall, daß die Kunst nicht mehr jenige Befriedigung der geistigen Bedürfnisse gewährt, welche frühere Zeiten und Völker in ihr gesucht und nur in ihr gefunden haben. . . . Die schönen Tage der griechischen Kunst wie die goldene Zeit des späteren Mittelalters sind vorüber. . . . Unsere Gegenwart ist ihrem allgemeinen Zustande nach der Kunst nicht günstig. . . . In allen diesen Beziehungen ist und bleibt die Kunst nach der Seite ihrer höchsten Bestimmungen für uns ein Vergangenes" (Hegel, *Werke*, XIII, 24–25, *Vorlesungen über die Ästhetik* I). In the next chapter, we shall see Renan share this view.

[52] The passage is from Louis de Maynard's article "Des peintres avant David" in *L'Europe littéraire*, 10, No. 2 (1833).

[53] In general, Heine here follows French critical judgment. In one of his articles in *L'Europe littéraire*, Maynard had said: "Sans prétendre que l'art soit en décadence, il nous a paru que l'exposition de cette année était maigre et chétive. . . . La sculpture, cette année, est riche et vraiment digne d'attention," cited in HSA, VII, 84.

[54] Thus the exuberant young reporter concludes his text on the Paris of 1833 with a quotation from Schiller's *Die Jungfrau von Orleans*: "Mit der Dummheit kämpfen Götter selbst vergebens," not without including himself among the gods!

[55] I mentioned in the opening chapter that Baudelaire discussed in his *Salons* works by four painters Heine had written about in his *Salon de 1831*, namely Decamps, Delacroix, Schnetz and Vernet. But far from considering Horace Vernet "a great master," as Heine still did in 1843, Baudelaire condemned him severely in his *Salon de 1846*. For an interesting, but indeed extreme pro-Communist discussion of Baudelaire's chapter "De M. Horace Vernet" of his 1846 *Salon*, cf. Dolf Oehler, *Pariser Bilder I (1830–1848) Antibourgeoise Ästhetik bei Baudelaire, Daumier und Heine* (Frankfurt: Suhrkamp Verlag, 1979), the chapter "Ästhetischer Nationalismus. Der Verriß Horace Vernets," 100–118. The title of Oehler's study is somewhat misleading as it deals principally with Baudelaire's art criticism which is read to reveal Baudelaire as a "hermetic Socialist," a view which I cannot share. The Heinean texts quoted are likewise read for a secret pro-Communist message, but serve merely as comparison to Baudelaire's.

[56] *Genesis*, XXXVIII, 15ff.

[57] In October 1985, the German Department of Dartmouth College presented a colloquium on "Heinrich Heine Pictures from Paris," with contributions by Professors Jocelyne Kolb, David Ward and Susanne Zantop of Dartmouth, and Professors Peter Uwe Hohendahl and Sander Gilman of Cornell, and Professor Andreas Sandor of Howard University.

VII

Laforgue on French and German Art and Aesthetic Theories

In examining the traces of Heine in Laforgue's contributions to *La Guêpe* and *L'Enfer*, I have noted the poet's early interest in art and his ambition to become an art critic. In that chapter, I discussed Laforgue's earliest attempt in the genre, the witty and Heinean, brief and unconventional "Salon de 1879," which he published in *La Guêpe*.[1] Laforgue's fascination with painters and painting, as well as his plans to devote himself to writing about them, is also recorded in Gustave Kahn's reminiscences of his young friend in 1880: "He informed me that he wanted to devote himself to the history of art . . . His joy, moreover, was to live by the eye. He was a friend of the Louvre and of the Cabinet des estampes, a devotee of picture and image."[2]

I have already mentioned Laforgue's second Salon piece in connection with his "Salon de 1879," the very similar "Le Public des dimanches au Salon," of the May 21, 1881 issue of *La Vie Moderne*.[3] This short text, too, is a humorous reportage about the viewers, "le public," rather than the paintings they have come to see at the Salon. On the admission-free Sunday, the visitors—students, "polytechniciens, saint-cyriens," "clumsy bourgeois in their Sunday's best," as well as "some tanned peasants, in the capital for a short stay"—present a very Heinean array of art appreciators. And Laforgue stresses his intention to caricature by a refrain echoing through the brief text: "Behind me, someone bursts out laughing. It is the shade of Henri Monnier. . . . Let's listen to the Sunday public in front of the canvasses. Just then the shade of Henri Monnier bursts out laughing again;'' to the final line of the piece: "Oh shade of Henri Monnier, burst out laughing! Again! Louder!'' This repeated invocation of the creator of Joseph Prudhomme makes clear that so far Laforgue prefers to approach the Salon obliquely, taking refuge in the ironic mode.[4]

Art criticism, however, was already one of Laforgue's most serious cocerns. Thus during the academic year 1880/81, and perhaps even the previous year, he visited the lectures of the most famous professor of the field, Taine, at the Ecole des Beaux-Arts, as the young Heine had visited those of Schlegel at Bonn. Laforgue first mentions Taine in his November (1879) reportage in *La Guêpe*;[5] and in January of 1881, he writes to Kahn: "Yesterday Taine (whose course I am attending regularly, despite the Ingres fresco one has before one's eyes) Taine was astounding on Angelico. You like and understand Angelico, do you not?''[6] And like Heine, who had first greatly admired his celebrated teacher and later rejected him,[7] Laforgue both admired and disagreed with Taine. In fact, his notes testify to an ongoing dialogue with the master's theories.

In the most outstanding essay on Laforgue's aesthetics to date, Michele Hannoosh recalls that "Taine was at the height of his fame around 1880," and that "he had such position and influence during those years that any new aesthetic theory would have to come to terms with his.''[8] Taine published the essence of his courses of those years in *La Philosophie de l'art* (Paris: 1865) and *De l'Idéal dans l'art* (1868), and a sigificant group of Laforgue's posthumously published fragments on aesthetics appears like reading notes to the latter.[9] For not merely was Taine's notion of the Ideal in art in contradiction to Laforgue's aesthetic opinions, but it contradicted his own positivist principles as set forth in his *Philosophy of Art*. Thus Laforgue brings not merely his Hartmannian philosophy to the confrontation, but Taine's own.

Laforgue certainly agreed with the author of *La Philosophie de l'art* when he said that "in order to understand a work of art, an artist, a group of artists, one must picture for oneself precisely the general spirit and the mores of the times to which they belonged." And he also surely agreed with the positivist methodology: "the modern method which I try to follow, and which is beginning to be introduced in all the moral sciences, consists of considering the works of man, and particularly works of art, like facts and products whose characteristics must be marked and whose causes must be investigated; nothing more.[10] The entire second half of Laforgue's essay on "L'Art moderne en Allemagne" will, in fact, be based on these Tainean precepts; and in his "impressionnisme" fragments, the poet says: "Every human being is according to his point in time, his racial environment and social condition, the moment of his individual evolution, a certain keyboard on which the external world plays in a certain manner," thus reaffirming Taine's famous "race, milieu, temps" principle almost verbatim. But then Laforgue's passage significantly continues: "my keyboard is perpetually changing, and there is not another identical to mine. All keyboards are legitimate.[11] And this notion of the legitimacy and worth of all artistic products—"one must mark the characteristics and investigate the causes; nothing more"—contradicts *De l'Idéal dans l'art*, where Taine applies a scale of values to works of art, based on "the degree of importance of the character," "the degree of beneficence in the character," and "the converging degree of effects," thus clearly repudiating his own positivist stance.[12]

Laforgue took issue in his "Notes d' esthétique" not merely with Taine, but also with another reigning thinker's notions on art, Renan's second "Dialogue philosophique," on "Probabilities." In this text, Renan predicts a glorious future for science, and the coming rule of a new intellectual aristocracy of scientists, to the detriment of other forms of human endeavor. He foresees the end of art: "Science thus is the great agent of divine consciousness. . . . Art will suffer from it. Surely, even great art will disappear. The time will come when art will be a thing of the past . . . Greek sculpture, architecture, and poetry are there already . . . The reign of sculpture is over the day men cease going seminude, and when the beauty of the body's forms becomes secondary; the epic disappears with the age of individual heroism. . . .''[13] The passage also reveals a Tainean bias for "le grand art," the "ideal" and unsurpassed art of Greece. Laforgue retorts: '"The reign of statuary is finished—says M. Renan with that Olympian dilettantism which makes him judge everything with a charming phrase . . . —from the day they stop going seminude.' No, our artists are no closer to exhausting the combinations of tones and lines than Wagner his harmonic combinations." And as for the ideal of the classical nude, Laforgue objects: "'is the nude all of sculpture? And if that were the case, is the nude of a shop-girl deformed by her work, or the frail nude of a Donatello, not just as interesting as that of Diana the Huntress?" This leads to the role of modern dress in art, a point on which Laforgue repeatedly refutes Taine, who assigns the lowest rank to works of art depicting it.[14] The student of Baudelaire disagrees: "and is not modern dress rich with promise in art and sculpture? And the busts of the Ceasars of the decadence (see Taine), " the note continues, "are they not as interesting as the heads of the Niobedes?"[15] Laforgue here also rejects Taine's statement that "from the epoch of Commodus and of Diocletian you see sculpture profoundly deteriorated; imperial and consular busts lose their serenity and their nobility; surliness, agitation and languor, bloated cheeks and elongated necks, individual convulsiveness and the wear and tear of the occupation replace harmonious health and energetic activity."[16] Health was one of Taine's principal criteria for beneficence: "let us now consider the physical man with the arts which portray him, and seek what are for him beneficent characters. The first of all, without doubt, is perfect health, even exuberant health."[17] Laforgue counters this argument with a Hartmannian principle: "Learn that the Unconscious does not know sickness."[18]

From these few notes it is apparent that Laforgue is debunking the French establishment in the name of his new German creed, von Hartmann's *Philosophy of the Unconscious*. I have elsewhere noted the obvious, that Laforgue's poetry is saturated with von Hartmann's thought;[19] this is even more profoundly true of his aesthetics. We know that Laforgue was already familiar with the author in 1880, as he writes of "distracting [himself] at times by reading von Hartmann" in a letter to Kahn of December of that year. We know that in the following year, he was planning to write a novel about "a charming disciple of Schopenhauer" who dreams of writing "an epic about the three stages of von Hartmann's Illusion." And still in 1884, Laforgue writes this confiteor to Kahn: "faith . . . mine, as you know, is the philosophy of the Unconscious, it is everything and is accountable for everything."[20] Clearly, von Hartmann's doctrine of the Absolute, the metaphysical Unconscious, had assumed religious proportions for Laforgue.

Almost all of the poet's commentators have warned their (and the poet's) implied reader not to confuse von Hartmann's *Unbewusste* with Freud's. And yet, Freud's psychological Subconscious forms an essential part of von Hartmann's Absolute, which intends to reconcile and fuse Hegel's Idea and Schopenhauer's Will, as well as German Idealism with the reigning scientism of the nineteeth century. As Darnois points out, "the term unconscious encompasses the entire primordial foundation of all reality, which is a multitude of the most divergent things. Consequently, the diversity of these different elements in their comprehensive unity" makes up von Hartmann's Unconscious. He continues: "Thus von Hartmann proposes the following distinction in the notion of the unconscious: Relative Unconscious and Absolute Unconscious," the latter then divided into a "Psychological and a Physiological," and also a "Metaphysical Unconscious."[21] What made the doctrine so attractive to Laforgue was no doubt the fact that von Hartmann developed his notions from the contemporary physical sciences in order to make a stand against Materialism: " . . . only a philosophy which takes full account of all the results of the natural sciences, and accepts without reservation the perfectly legitimate point of departure of Materialism, only such a philosophy can hope to make a stand against Materialism."[22] And this statement comes from a discussion of the "Metaphysic of the Unconscious"! The Absolute, Metaphysical Unconscious, bringing forth Consciousness to reconcile Will and Idea, matter and spirit, so that their union may evolve toward ultimate deliverance from suffering into a nirvana-like annihilation, might just as well be called God. And von Hartmann himself says: "I shall continue as a rule to employ the expression, 'The Unconscious,' although the previous discussion has shown that I should have more right to use the word 'God' than Spinoza and many others."[23]

Thus, in discussing the "fureur génésique de l'art," Laforgue stresses the physiological with the term "genetic," but then he immediately points to the transcendental power which is the origin of all art and science, "the transcendental force which compels Beethoven to sing, Delacroix to seek colors, Baudelaire to search for his language, Hugo to be enormous, Darwin to ascertain natural selection . . ., the same force which forces the spider to make his net . . ."[24] This "force transcendante" is the Hartmannian Unconscious.

A following group of notes, entitled "l'Inconscient en art," is directed specifically against Renan and his thesis of the "Second Philosophical Dialogue" that "art, this spontaneous product of the first ages of man, will, like the rest of the category of instinct fall into the category of reflection." Laforgue retorts that Renan does not understand the word instinct, or art: "in art, there will always be, as there has always been, instinct and reflection, inspiring and prophetic unconsciousness and consciousness or science . . . In science, as in all human endeavors toward the Ideal, there is instinct and reflection. The Unconscious and knowledge."[25] This is precisely what von Hartmann says in his chapter on "The Unconscious in the Aesthetic Judgment and in Artistic Production," in which he equates the mediocre in art with conscious combination, while great art is inspired by "the divine frenzy, the vivifying breath of the Unconscious."[26]

"M. Renan," Laforgue continues, "sees around him the death of poetry and art, because no contemporary artist or poet appears to him to bear the mark of genius;" thus he sees science submerge art. But he does not understand that genius is "as much a reflex in the artist as in the scientist, the good old word inspiration [applies to] the artist as well as to the chemist; it is the immortal Unconscious: in the artist, in the metaphysician, the mystic, the Russian nihilist (enlightened apostle Turgenev) . . . Instinct is in everything and everywhere; it is Instinct which, through our thousands of aspiring hearts, guides the universe.''[27]

In the following two fragments, on "Le Vêtement" and "Variété de l'Idéal," Laforgue mentions Manet, Monet and Degas; and we must recall here one of the most significant developments of his short life: his meeting Charles Ephrussi through Paul Bourget in 1881. Ephrussi, a brilliant young member (merely eleven years older than the poet) of the cosmopolitan elite of art connoisseurs, distantly related to the Rothschilds, friend and familiar of the courts of Europe, became Laforgue's patron saint, decisively influencing both his material and intellectual life. Ephrussi, later also to become the patron of the young Marcel Proust, who immortalized him in Swann,[28] engaged Laforgue in July of 1881 as part-time secretary to assist him with the analytical index of his book on Dürer's sketches. The generous early patron of the Impressionists, featured by Renoir as the gentleman with the top hat in his famous *Déjeuner des canotiers* (*The Boating Party*), opened to Laforgue a new world, that of the latest contemporary art. As David Arkell says, "Ephrussi was the man who educated and groomed Laforgue for all that was to follow."[29] One of the most important things that was to follow was Laforgue's appointment later that year as French reader to the Empress Augusta at the Prussian Court, upon Ephrussi's recommendation.

In "Le Vêtement," Laforgue again counters Taine's notion that in art "fashionable dress has a very secondary significance," merely being "an outside and a decor." "So what," retorts Laforgue, "it is an *outside*, and this outside is as significant to me, a painter, as your inside is to you, psychologist . . . a bar of Manet interests me, a human heart with an artistic eye, as much as any feast by Veronese, or any other work more concerned with the human body and its 'stable character'."[30]

Under the heading of "Variété de l'Idéal," Laforgue first

objects to Taine's notion that "at the apex of nature are sovereign forces which master all others; at the apex of art are masterpieces which surpass all others; both heights are on a level, and the sovereign forces of nature are declared through the masterpieces of art."[31] "But no!" counters Laforgue, "what becomes of your ideal before the marvels of Chinese and Japanese art, Persian rugs? Do the sovereign forces of nature command us to prefer a stable landscape by Poussin . . . to an impression which lasted ten minutes in the eternal time of Claude Monet?" Furthermore, Taine's principle that "the work which exhibits a beneficent character is superior to the work which exhibits a malevolent character,"[32] applies moral standards to art which both the positivist and the disciple of Heine, Baudelaire, and Gautier must reject.[33] For the modern artist—as Degas has amply demonstrated—"the wings of the Opera are more artistic than all the phalansteries dreamed of by Fourier. Morality has nothing to do with pure art, no more than with pure love." Thus, for the pure artist, an old, decadent civilization is no less interesting then the age of Pericles. Laforgue opposes the entire exclusively classical school from Winckelmann to Taine, with his ideal of the ephermeral in art, as celebrated by the Impressionists: "For me, an ephemeral creature, the ephemeral is more interesting than an absolute hero, the same way as I, a man wearing clothing, am more interested in a creature in ephemeral garb than in a nude sculptural model."[34] Laforgue insists repeatedly in these notes that "hypertrophied individuals and civilizations are more interesting than equilibrated ones." For the important thing is "not to be mediocre. One must be new. Yes, the degree of beneficence is a moral criterion, not one of art, the artist being a solitary creature, a hypertrophied one, from Shakespeare to Michelangelo."[35]

If civilization throws us into confusion (nous détraque), destroys our equilibrium and works against nature, so be it, says Laforgue. For "that does not concern us. The Unconscious animates all as it wishes, so let us not interfere, but embellish our arts upon its stages. Everything interests me, for I piously bow to the Unconscious, the soulless pagan body, the disembodied medieval soul, and today's breakdown of both body and soul, as well as the Japanese puppet without body or soul,"[36] affirms the poet of Pierrot. Laforgue strikes a Nietzschean note in concluding this group of fragments: "the Beautiful ideal [he includes literature, philosophical systems, morals, painting, sculpture] and the hierarchy of genres, all that is a legend of mediocre minds and perpetuated by the authority of the mediocre. Mediocre minds have always been the authorities, for every State, being in its own interests conservative, has always given authority to the mediocre spirits, to the conservatives."[37]

A group of highly perceptive, if very subjective, "Réflexions sur l'art égyptien" reveals Laforgue's breadth of appreciation and interest, in contrast with "the poor nineteenth-century pedants" who "defend these works against the reproach of the hieratic," praising their "life and realism." No, says Laforgue, "they had indeed other preoccupations than realism and art for art! They had seen death! all their life, their royalty, their childhood, their birth, their civilization turns around this frightful pit. Oh dilettante schoolmasters who only work for a Chair at the Institute and not for the human creature's personal resurrection, or even that of Egypt's art!" It is precisely the narrow aesthetic provincialism of the classical school that prevents it, according to Laforgue, from comprehending both non-European and non-classical, i.e. modern art: "Exclusiveness-Taine: All that is in a world too narrow, it is classical antiquity and classical Europe. The entire Orient is neglected (it is true, it is not as well known, and not as practical as the classical world)."[38]

Laforgue assumed his duties at the Prussian Court late in November of 1881, and throughout his years in Germany his continued interest in art and aesthetics is manifest in his correspondence with his friends, especially with Ephrussi, who gave him letters of introduction to Berlin art connoisseurs, like the Bernsteins. At that time, Ephrussi was not yet editor of the prestigious *Gazette des Beaux-Arts*, but he was already very influential in the review, and later helped the aspiring young art critic to publish five articles in it from 1882 to 1886, beginning with a review article about "*Albrecht Dürer et ses Dessins* par

M. Ch. Ephrussi," the book which he had himself helped bring
to completion. And most recently another, very brief piece,
discussing the "Peintures décoratives de M. Henry Daras à
Saint-François-de-Sales," which appeared in the *Gazette*'s supplement, *Chroniques des arts et de la curiosité*, on November
12, 1881, just before Laforgue's departure for Germany, has
come to light.[39]

In one of his first letters from Berlin to Ephrussi, Laforgue
nostalgically recalls his friend's apartments, richly decorated
with Impressionist paintings; he asks whether the Dürer book
has come out yet and muses: "every line of your beautiful book
would recall so many memories to me! Above all, the hours we
spent working alone in your room, with the bright yellow
armchair.—And the Impressionists!" He recalls specifically two
Pissarros, "solidly constructed by little patient touches;"
Sisley's view of the Seine "with telegraph poles and a spring
sky;" Monet's blossoming apple trees; Renoir's wild little
Bohemian girl; Berthe Morisot's "young seated woman, with
her child, a black dog and a butterfly net in a deep fresh forest
meadow." "Another Morisot, a nurse with her child, blue
yellow, pink, sun.—And then again a Renoir, the Parisian
woman with her red lips and blue jersey . . . And Mary Cassat's
reddish-blond dancer in yellow green, red armchairs, bare
shoulders. And the nervous dancers of Degas, and Degas'
Duranty—and Manet's *Polichinelle* with Banville's verse."[40]
The very precision of his enumeration from memory indicates
the impact of those paintings on Laforgue, as well as his
gratitude to Ephrussi for revealing them to him. Later in the
same letter, he mentions that he has not yet visited the museum
in Berlin, a task he will fulfill very soon. In fact, Laforgue will
later travel to Germany's art capitals, Dresden and Munich, to
visit and comment on their collections.

Later the same month, on December 12, 1881, Laforgue writes
to Charles Henry: "I very often go to the museum. We have two
museums, like the Louvre and the Luxembourg.—small edition.—Some Rembrandts, two black and elegant Titians, some
Van Dycks less fine than ours, some Rubens, but no display

comparable to ours. But a collection of Primitives! Above all some Van Eycks! I bring back notes every time; I already have quite a few about the Louvre." Commenting about the new Berlin museum, Laforgue remarks: "I believe so far that the Germans are not artists in the complex sense that we are. . . . Those people do not merit suspecting our Impressionists." Again his nostalgia for Paris is apparent: "What an artistic city, the city which has given us Degas, Forain, Monets, Manets, etc. Ah! the atmosphere of Paris!"[41]

On the last day of that month and eventful year, Laforgue writes to Ephrussi that he is at work on the review of his Dürer book: "there are five chronicles to write about your book,—One about you, your silhouette, your young glory (of a Benedictine dandy?), your work, your collections; very Parisian. Another, about three kinds of art criticism, taking as models, for example, your method, that of the Watteau of the Goncourts, that of M. Taine."[42] Art criticism was clearly as much on Laforgue's mind as his poetry, when he began his exile in Berlin.

Almost a year later, in November of 1882, Laforgue writes to Ephrussi from Baden, where the Court sojourned every year, that he has just reviewed his notes from the exposition in Munich, which he had visited a few months previously, but that he is somewhat afraid of doing the article. On the other hand, upon his approaching return to Berlin, he will visit the big exposition of contemporary German art there, about which he will write, hoping "to be able to rise to the occasion." And the following year, his "Salon de Berlin" was, in fact, published in the *Gazette des Beaux-Arts*. Later in the same letter, Laforgue writes: "I feel, moreover, capable of writing a serious and compact volume about contemporary German art. With an Introduction which will make up one fourth of the volume and which will be all about psychology and aesthetics."[43] This text is most likely the posthumously published "L'Art moderne en Allemagne."[44]

We do not know when Laforgue actually wrote this important text; from a letter of December 1883, again to Ephrussi, it is evident that he kept reading steadily to arrive at an aesthetic theory of his own:

> Did I tell you that these last twenty days, shut up and cloistered in this chateau of Coblenz, I thought and worked unceasingly? I reread diverse aesthetics, Hegel, Schelling, Saisset, Leveque, Taine—in a state unknown to me since when I was eighteen, in the Bibliothèque Nationale. I collected myself, and in one night, from ten o'clock at night until four in the morning, like Jesus in the Garden of Olives, Saint John at Patmos, the Buddha under the fig tree at Gaza, I wrote in ten pages the metaphysical principles of the new Aesthetics, an aesthetics in agreement with von Hartmann's Unconscious, Darwin's transformism, the work of von Helmholtz . . . Have I finally arrived at the truth about this eternal question of the Beautiful?—We shall see. In any case, it is very new, touches on the most recent problems of human thought and does not conflict with modern physiological optics, nor with the most advanced work in psychology, and it explains spontaneous genius, a question about which Taine remains silent. We will see . . . At least I will have dreamed of being the definitive John Ruskin.[45]

Thus, Laforgue brings to bear on his aesthetics not merely von Hartmann's thought, but other sources to which *The Philosophy of the Unconscious*, and most likely also his friendship with Charles Henry, had led him.[46]

Laforgue places his "L'Art moderne en Allemagne"[47] under the epigraph "L'artiste s'agite; l'Inconscient le mène" ("The artist acts; he is led by the Unconscious"), echoed in such poems as "La Lune est stérile";

> * L'Art est tout, du droit divin de l'Inconscient;
>
> . . . . .
>
> Je m'agite aussi! mais l'Inconscient me mène;
> or, il sait ce qu'il fait, je n'ai rien à y voir."

And the essay's first part, "LePrincipe esthétique," constitutes in fact, Laforgue's most explicit profession of faith in the Hartmannian doctrine. The second section, "Sa Fonction en

---

* Art is everything, by the divine right of the Unconscious: . . . . I also stir about! but the Unconscious leads me. Well, it knows what it is doing, I have nothing to do with it. (It's no business of mine)

Allemagne,'' is less its application than a witty and perceptive comparison of French and German art and aesthetics.

Like von Hartmann in his chapter on "The Unconscious in the Aesthetic Judgment and in Artistic Production," Laforgue begins his essay by commenting on the two opposed systems informing the history of aesthetics, the idealist and the determinist, "the one which classifies and judges schools and works of art in the name of an ideal . . . and the other, which, naturalistic and deterministic, merely claims to sort and order the documents to permit itself to ascertain, at the very most, the laws of the whole.'' To the latter group belongs Taine, if we leave aside his *Ideal in Art*; the former is represented by Hegel and, above all, Schelling and Schiller. While the determinists or positivists demonstrate the *how* of human genius and its works, but are unable to explain their *why*, nor their essence, the idealists, on the other hand, "if by the intervention of the transcendental they can explain genius and inspiration,'' so far "they have only adored Ideals which are procrustean beds in the history of human art.'' Von Hartmann had begun his chapter on aesthetics similarly: "with regard to the perception of the Beautiful there have been current from early times two extreme opinions . . . One party, taking its rise from Plato, rely on this, that in Art the human mind *transcends* the beauty revealed in Nature . . .The other party point out that . . . aesthetic science has in its progress more and more demonstrated the psychogenesis of the aesthetic judgment from given psychological and physiological conditions, so that we may confidently expect a complete illumination of this province and its purification from all *a priori* and supernatural conceptions. I hold that each side is partly right, partly wrong.''[49] Thus Laforgue, like his master, sets out to demonstrate the shortcomings of both idealists and empiricists, and to resolve their conflicting views through the doctrine of Unconscious.

The determinists must "accept indifferently'' all works of art; they fail to see "that the simple law of natural selection, which signifies choice in itself and a unique divine tendency, . . . an Ideal which animates and orders and dominates all things,'' causes some works to survive, while others perish. Basing himself on Schelling's principle of the identity of thought with its object,[50] Laforgue continues: "let us posit first against the positivists . . . that since the human mind is the result of organic evolution on earth, placed in the universe, thought is identical with its object, as necessarily as the fact that nothing can exist outside of the whole, and that metaphysical knowledge implies a transcendental reality." Above and beyond the world of changing phenomena evolves "an Ideal, the Law." But the classical idealists fail to recognize that they have always placed themselves in a false position, namely "outside a merely ephemeral and limited stage of indefinite evolution." However, "an aesthetic formula, vast and fecund like the Law, open to the past as to the surprises of the future, as well as to the incoherence of the present, while remaining dogmatic enough to serve as touchstone to any work, could only come from an Ideal placed in an indefinite becoming and in a category—the unconscious, as we shall see—which the subject can conceive only from the limits of his perspective, an ephemeral stage of an indefinite evolution."

While my individual sense of the beautiful might change from moment to moment, "from the ensemble of these feelings, at the end of my evolution, my feeling of the beautiful may be abstracted;" likewise, also, while my own sense of the beautiful may not be superior to that of any of my contemporaries, "our entire era will be summed up in a certain formula of aesthetic sensibility." Contemporary aesthetics, moreover, is no more authoritative than that of past or future generations, "but their history, up to this known point in time, reveals a certain human soul which . . . remains invisibly imperishable, and ready for the renovating crises of tomorrow." Thus, the aesthetic sense is ever-changing like life itself, expressing "like human thought and the succession of its works, the evolution of the universal soul, of the unique Law."

Finally Laforgue spells out explicitly that new domain "which has just opened to science virgin forests of life, the occult region of being, the unconscious," revealed "in the mystic, universal principle of von Hartmann's *Philosophy of the Unconscious,* omnipresent and infallible," the only divinity not created in man's image. The Unconscious evolves according to its law, "objectifying itself in exploring worlds toward consciousness from eternity."

But what, then, is the function of art and of aesthetics in this divine plan? How do they serve the Ideal—"in what way do a given genre, such and such a work, more or less approximate divine ends, or more or less contribute to the evolution toward pure Consciousness?" The role of the "arts définis sensuels" in pursuit of "la conscience pure" is significant. "While the arts have a mere secondary role, they are marvelously necessary," however, in this divine teleology; for "their mission is to develop indefinitely the respective organs they exploit," thus contributing to the progressive refinement of the entire organism. And for the visual arts, it will of course be "the extreme development of the organ exploited, THE EYE." According to Laforgue, like all forms of life, each organ is in evolution. Thus the eye has only gradually learned to distinguish the more and more rapid and shorter and shorter light waves, from red to violet, continuing its evolution toward ultraviolet, and it "forges ahead reveling in the discoveries to which it is getting accustomed little by little [here he is clearly thinking of Impressionism] despite the conservatives of the palladium and 'the integrity of art'."[51]

The new "Ideal," as concerns the visual arts, then, advocates no general objective except "du nouveau, du nouveau et indéfiniment du nouveau," from Hellenism to Byzantinism, the Renaissance, Rococo, Romanticism, Realism, Preraphaelitism, Japonism, Impressionism, Nihilism, "briefly, uniquely that which the instinct of the ages has always exalted in proclaiming geniuses . . . only those who have revealed something new and who have, thus, marked a stage in the artistic evolution of humanity." The Ideal condemns only what true artists have always condemned: schools, conventional codes of taste, like the morally beautiful, the physically beautiful, harmony, style, and "all that which constitutes a doctrine, hieratic or academic, outside of which there is no salvation." The Ideal, moreover, "does not recognize what others call decadence and disconcerts those who with MM. Taine and Renan proclaim architecture, sculpture and poetry dead, announcing the approaching unique reign of pure science." Laforgue here incorporates some of the notes which we have already examined; and he concludes the first part of the essay by insisting again that the principle of the new Ideal is "the anarchy of life itself—laissez faire, laissez passer; l'Inconscient souffle où il veut, le génie 'saura reconnaître les siens'." "The Spirit bloweth where it listeth," and "God will recognize his own," namely the spirit of the new Ideal, "l'infaillible Loi" of the new divinity, "l'Inconscient."

In the second part of the essay, taking the Tainean "race, milieu, moment" approach, Laforgue tells us why contemporary German art remains far behind the French. The "pure Germany" is, according to him, "above all the blessed land of what we have called the immediate preoccupations of the Law, mysticism, religion, science, social dreams and of the only art which is intimately related to these, music." And the epithet which has always flattered the Germans, *Naturkind*, does indeed apply to this "pure Germany," which "is in every respect, in fact, the immediate child of Nature, and of that unconscious suspected by all the thinkers, her true sons, and revealed there." Goethe is her only Hellene: "the only one of her pagan and conscious geniuses, Goethe, the first who, feeling himself beautiful and well in that close and awkward race, proclaimed the right of pleasure outside the bosom of the family and of protestantism, and who always confessed, moreover, that music remained a world absolutely closed to him."

Laforgue evokes the cliché of romantic Germany, uncontaminated by a civilization of centuries of logic and reason, "true land of the Vedas of the North, with its pantheistic forest—as the desert is monotheistic, according to Renan—the sacred forest of Wagner's national theories; where the great melodic voice of the forest is composed of symphonies of thousands of voices," a country "peopled by a fantastic mythology, fleeting like the dream of an autumn or a Christmas night, by the ghosts of the Brocken, and the Willis of Novalis" (he forgets here that they were Heine's). It is a country "tyrannized by the climate which requires that the creature gorge himself, drink and smoke slowly, which dulls his nerves in the lymph and leaves him prostrate, lost, with his never-changing washed-out blue eyes, in digestive nirvanas, in chaste and frigid hallucinations . . . ruminating in a rich and incomprehensible language interminable cosmogonic, pantheistic, unconscious dreams, salads of naturing nature and naturated nature, voluptuous confusions about the self and the non-self, absorbing itself finally into a sort of protestant Brahma." Thus Laforgue's witty and unjust view of German art and philosophy—a caricature, in fact, of which Heine would have been proud.

Hence the Germans have not brought forth great landscape painters; for "how could the pure German abstract himself from that nature, which has enchanted every minute and every atom of his being, in order to examine it apart from himself, as though subject and object were two distinct worlds, in order to interpret it . . . and recast it according to the canons of order and taste, in short, make of it a work of art?" The Hellene, on the contrary, "and consequently the French, oldest sons of the Graeco-Roman world," the sophisticated world of the diplomat, mathematician and legist, "cut down their druidic forests in an orderly fashion, according to Malherbe, until Romanticism arrived from the North." The Hellene, Laforgue continues in a Heinean vein, "dilettant, subtle, rhetorical, euphuistic, polished, brilliant, sober, comedian, liar, was born unswathed of unconscious life, in an elitist aristocracy served by a people of slaves, in his city outside of which everything is barbarian, in the presence of a proud and refined nature, spontaneously tamable in its clear and dry atmosphere . . . under a tempered sun which is Apollo Chief of the Muses, who conquered the old Chaos with his beautiful arrows, etc." The Hellene, and the French his sons, "dualistic and penetrated by this monstrous anti-natural conviction of the free will of the thinking reed in the face of that *fatum*, under whose illiterate blows one falls at least nobly draped like the Niobedes, exercised the gymnastics of their reason in a language of honey, like the rhythm of their naked bodies, not overwhelmed and blunted by the struggle, nor by the climate or imperious food . . ." These blessed creatures, then, contrary to their heavy-souled German neighbors, "are all disposed to interpret graphically a simple nature of which they are the beautiful and reasonable gods, to let it pass through their human norm, choosing, pruning and synthesizing." In short, "if the Latin belongs to those whom, according to a German proverb, the tree prevents from seeing the forest, the German will admit that the forest has always prevented him from seeing the tree." And to know the forest "and arrive at giving pictorially its living symphony, as our landscape painters have done, it was necessary to begin by abstracting the tree from the rest, to study it and render it sparingly." For a long time, "the Latin has not seen the forest, tyrannized as he was by the ideal of the tree according to Cicero and Boileau, Poussin and Le Nôtre, by the tree measuring the forest, as the human body is measured by its seven heads . . ." But then, at the turn of the century, he "was visited by the light come from the North." At first, he was submerged and "floundered with his clockmaker god and his universe ordered by his dear final causes under this powerful stream of pantheistic becoming," until "his human heart and masterful eye finally became fecundated by it so that today he masterfully enchants the present in those arts of which he remains the feverish avant-garde." Here, again, Laforgue clearly has the French Impressionists in mind.

I have quoted so extensively from this text, for it reveals Heine's influence. We recall here one of his Leitmotifs, frequently treated in the ironic mode, the distinction between Hellene and Nazarene. As frequently with his master, Laforgue's art criticism becomes brilliantly poeticized at the expense of factual precision, a price the poet's readers are only too happy to pay.

In the remainder of the text, Laforgue wonders what will become of this "pure Germany" under the growing domination of Prussia, herself grown up "in poverty and the patient administrative, academic and military obduracy, among her sad monotheistic sands of Brandenburg." Will the two Germanies continue side by side, or will they become neutralized, and what kind of future will grow out of this "invisible conflict for the visual arts in this 'Middle-Empire' of Europe?" At any rate, German genius turns spontaneously toward science, philosophy and music, and approaches the visual arts "only when led astray by circumstances and the illusions of its indolent sensibility." And the talents that do go thus astray remain "philosophical and literary." But if they are "possessed by the demon of virtuosity, they stammer in painful and poignant incoherencies, without bringing forth the hundredth part of what torments them, and die of suppressed masterpieces, cursing Latin ingenuity and cleverness."

The new, emerging Germany, which under the influence of Berlin strives for European political and economic preeminence, also looks toward preeminence in art, creating museums and academies and pouring funds into them. But, "for art to blossom in Prussian Germany, money must first of all infiltrate everywhere, spread general well-being and superabundance, create wealth and fatten the atmosphere, so that armies of collectors may rise to overcome Gothic pedantry, sharpen the nerves and those placid young faces, and sophisticate, above all, woman, her appearance as well as her heart. Before the science of the pleasure of the eye may become genuine in the Germanic race, before it may blossom like its literature in 1770, in a new *Sturm und Drang* to give the world a personally visual interpretation of life, as it did for music, much water will flow under the bridge of the Spree—decorated with its pseudo-Greek statues—which connects *Under den Linden* with the *Museen Insel.*"

By far the best-known and most frequently discussed of Laforgue's texts on aesthetics is his essay on Impressionism, occasioned by an Impressionist exhibition in the small Gurlitt gallery in Berlin in October 1883. Laforgue reports to Ephrussi about his visit to the exhibition with Carl Bernstein, professor of law at the University of Berlin, one of the first German Impressionist collectors, and a cousin of Ephrussi.[52] Originally intended for a German review, the German version, in Bernstein's translation, of Laforgue's "explication physiologique esthétique de la formule impressionniste'' has so far not turned up, and we have only the French text (*Mélanges posthumes*, 113–45).[53] It represents an application of "le principe esthétique" set forth in the first part of "L'Art moderne en Allemagne."

Laforgue organizes his analysis under various headings, the first of which is "The Physiological Origin of Impressionism: The Prejudice of Traditional Line (du dessin)." Since the eye is to painting what the ear is to music, the Impressionist "is a modernist painter who, endowed with an uncommon sensitivity of the eye, and forgetting the paintings amassed through the centuries in our museums, forgetting traditional art school education (line, perspective, color), by virtue of living and seeing frankly and primitively in the luminous spectacles of the open air, that is outside the studio . . . has succeeded in recreating his natural eye and seeing naturally and painting naïvely as he sees." Again refuting such notions as "Absolute Beauty" and "Absolute Human Taste," Laforgue points to the three "invincible illusions by which the technicians of painting have always lived: design, perspective and studio lighting." For these three conventions the Impressionist substitutes "three evolutions which constitute the Impressionist formula: form obtained not by line, but uniquely by color vibrations and contrasts; theoretical perspective is replaced by the natural perspective of vibrations and contrasts of colors; and studio lighting is replaced by the open air." This means that the painting is executed "in front of the subject . . . in the shortest possible time, in view of the rapid changes of the light on the objects." Thus, "these three procedures of the dead language of art . . . are replaced by the unique resources of the play of light, of Life itself."

In the letter about his night of intense work and revelations, from which I have quoted above (p. 212), Laforgue wrote that he had arrived at "an aesthetics in agreement with von Hartmann's Unconscious, Darwin's transformism, and the work of von Helmholtz." And it is the work of the last that also inspired much of our text. Thus, when Laforgue continues that line is a prejudice stemming from the fact that "primitively the eye, being able to register only white light with its indecomposable shadows, and consequently unaided by the resources of discerning colorations, resorted to tactile experience," so that subsequently through habitual association of the senses of sight and touch, the sense of form gradually moved from the fingers to the eye, leading to our habit of rendering "la réalité vivante sans plan" by line and perspective, he recalls von Helmholtz's essay on "Recent Progress in the Theory of Vision" of 1868, thus the most recent findings of one of the most eminent German scientists. In this text, von Helmholtz says that "we are continually controlling and correcting the notions of spatial location derived from the eye by the help of the sense of touch and we always accept the impression of touch as decisive."[54] Likewise, when Laforgue says that "essentially the eye should only know luminous vibrations, as the acoustic nerve only knows sonorous vibrations," he again recalls von Helmholtz and his frequent comparisons of eye and ear.[55] Laforgue finds the eye as "organ of luminous vibrations considerably retarded relative to that of the ear," because the ear "generally analyzes harmonies easily," whereas "the eye sees light only synthetically and roughly and has merely vague powers of decomposing it in the spectacles of nature, despite its three fibrils of Young's theory of vision, about the three retinal processes which produce the sensations of red, green and violet," a theory analyzed by von Helmholtz.[56]

In contrasting "The Academic Eye and the Impressionist Eye: Polyphony of Colors," Laforgue again insists that "where the academic eye only sees the external outline of objects," the Impressionist "sees the real and living lines without geometrical forms, but made up of thousands of irregular strokes which, at a distance, establish life." Thus, whereas the traditional painter "sees things placed in their regular respective planes according to a skeleton reducible to pure theoretic design," namely traditional perspective, the Impressionist painter sees and renders perspective "by a thousand hardly perceptible tones and brush strokes, by the varieties of atmospheric states and their ever-moving, and not stable, planes." Here Laforgue clearly recalls von Helmholtz's notion of "aerial perspective," that is "the artistic representation of the haziness of the atmosphere to indicate depth."[57]

The "Impressionist eye is the most advanced eye in human evolution," and we recall that, according to Laforgue, the function of art is to further the evolution of the organ it exploits. In "this little exposition at the Gurlitt Gallery," the Impressionist formula "is above all evident in Monet and Pissarro . . . where everything is obtained by a thousand tiny dancing strokes in every direction . . . No longer any isolated melody, the whole being a symphony which is living and changing life, like Wagner's 'voices of the forest,' all in vital competition and struggling to become the great voice of the forest, as the Unconscious, the law of the world, is the great melodic voice resulting from the symphony of the consciousness of races and individuals."

Under "False Education of the Eyes," Laforgue reminds us that we do not see the colors of the palette in themselves, "but according to the illusions corresponding to the education we have received from the *pictures* of the tradition and, above all, we see them in the light offered by the palette itself." He suggests that we compare "the light intensity of Turner's most dazzling sun with the flame of the weakest candle." The discussion here leans on von Helmholtz's analysis of the "Variations in Brightness" from his fascinating essay on "The Relation of Optics to Painting."[58] Laforgue resolves the problem of the discrepancy of natural and painted light intensities in "the proportional language of painting," or, as von Helmholtz had expressed it, "the painter gives his colors the same *ratio* of brightness as those which actually exist."

In discussing the "Mobility of Landscape and Mobility of the Painter's Impressions," Laforgue observes that no image, no color, is ever stable. Thus, for example, "I see a certain violet, I lower my eyes toward my palette to mix it, and my eye is involuntarily drawn by the white of my cuff: my eye has changed, and my violet suffers, etc." This derives from von Helmholtz's analysis of "contrast phenomena, . . . where the color or the brightness of a surface appears changed by the proximity of some other light or color."[59] Therefore, continues Laforgue, "no work is ever the equivalent of fugitive reality, but the record of a certain optic sensibility without equal which will never be the same for that individual again, under the stimulation of a landscape at a given moment of its luminous life, which will never be identical to that moment again." Both subject and object, then, are ever-changing, but "the flashes of identity between subject and object constitute genius." Laforgue calls "any attempt to codify these flashes *une plaisanterie d'école.*" He, moreover, recalls Schelling here, for whom genius consisted of the identity of the conscious and the unconscious [subject and object], possible only in art.[60] Laforgue's art criticism is steeped in German thought.

In refusing once again the "Double Illusion of Absolute Beauty and Absolute Man," Laforgue resorts to the image of "Innumerable Human Keyboards," and, while adopting the positivist stance of Taine, rejects the latter's self-contradictory idealism in the passage about the "clavier sur lequel le monde extérieur joue d'une certaine façon" which I have quoted at the beginning of this chapter. The world thus being "a perpetually changing symphony" which plays on the keyboard of our senses, Laforgue refers to Fechner's law about the measurement of perceptions, "the law of Feschner [sic], the perception of differences decreasing in inverse ratio to the intensities," which Théodule Ribot, one of Laforgue's principal sources for Schopenhauer, discussed at length in his book on *La Psychologie allemande contemporaine.*[61] The remainder of the notions discussed in Laforgue's essay on Impressionism are those which I have already presented. A brief paragraph on the "Definition of Open-Air Painting" would have us distinguish the Impressionists from the Barbizon School; for the Impressionists, the "open-air concept governs their entire work;" it means "the painting of beings or things in their atmosphere, landscapes as well as interiors."

Laforgue defends the Impressionists against charges of "Exaggerations;" their work merely appears exaggerated to our eyes whose evolution has been retarded by the "host of mediocre painters" and their "sad and unchanging recipes of academic coloring.'' Thus, the "Program for Future Painters" should do away with their sway; modern artists demand "that the State leave art alone, that the School of Rome (the Villa Medici) be sold, the Institute closed, that there be no more medals or awards, and that artists be allowed to live in the anarchy which is life, meaning that everyone be left to his own resources, rather than being annihilated or hindered by the academic training which lives of the past.'' As an afterthought, Laforgue adds a paragraph about innovations in the framing of paintings, remarking that in their exhibitions the Independents "have substituted a variety of intelligent and refined frames for the perpetual old gilt frames of academic convention.'' But he regretfully closes his discussion in noting that "while this fashion has had repercussions in the official salons, it has only produced bourgeois novelities of various kinds there.''

Thus Laforgue's brilliant avant-garde appreciation of the most recent development in French painting—a school of painting unattainable in his opinion, as we have seen, by contemporary German artists—is saturated with German thought. I have quoted at such length from Laforgue's new aesthetics—stimulated by the Impressionists—to demonstrate that it was nourished not merely by von Hartmann, but other German philosophers as well and, above all, by that new school of physiological psychology across the Rhine.

I have noted above that Laforgue published five articles in the *Gazette des Beaux-Arts* during his stay in Germany, due to the good offices of Ephrussi, who later became its editor. These pieces, aside from his two youthful and humorous "Salons" of *La Guêpe* and *La Vie moderne* and the piece on Daras' paintings in the Church of Saint-François-de-Sales of 1881, constitute Laforgue's only "finished" pieces on art.[62] In his first *Gazette des Beaux-Arts* piece, the review article of Ephrussi's Dürer book, Laforgue sings his benefactor's praises.

The second contribution, the "Salon de Berlin" of 1883 is Laforgue's first "Salon" proper. Its writing caused him considerable difficulty, as is evident from the frequent remarks about it in his correspondence. One of his few new friends in Berlin was the artist Max Klinger, to whom he writes in June: "Yes, I am doing the Salon of Berlin after a fashion. I speak of you at length as the most personal artist, but not without reproach . . . What a sordid occupation, that of the art critic, isn't it? This profession has been dishonored by so many ignorant people, and the artists are so often right to scorn us. For my part, you cannot imagine with how much conscientiousness I apply myself to it. Not in reading books and exploring the old Museums"—Laforgue, of course, did both very diligently—"but in trying to see clearly in Nature. . . . If I were not persuaded that I have an artistic eye"—hardly any art critic had it more than he—" and that I am hostile to all artistic prejudices, and sincere and desirous of instructing a discerning public, I would not write this (i.e. a "Salon"), believe me.⁶³ However, Ephrussi must have returned Laforgue's first version for corrections, the poet writing to him in July: "Thank you so much for your letter. I have received my Salon. *Alas, poor*! I have just redone it according to your advice. I can see that you are a veteran and that I am still only a novice." Shortly after, Laforgue writes to Charles Henry, first about the Germans and art: "I have spent two years acquiring the conviction that this is the most actively anti-artistic of people known," then adding, not without some bitterness, "Ah! if I had only written my Berlin Salon for a less timorous outfit than the *Gazette*: but finally I did soothe my nerves in it a little."⁶⁴

Laforgue begins his "Salon" by explaining to his French readers that Berlin is not Germany's art capital, as Paris is that of France, and that, despite its great age, Berlin's Royal Academy of Art is still a rather unsettled institution. Its expositions do not take place every year, and they have so far no permanent locale. This 56th Salon, moreover, lacks that festive air which always characterizes the Parisian event. The official catalogue, with only 950 entries, is thin "and meagerly illustrated" (p. 170); and there are only two prizes, the large and the small medals.

In sculpture, the only remarkable artist represented is Reinhold Begas, who had obtained a gold medal in Paris in 1867. Among the painters, the two outstanding artists are the aging, Swiss-born Böcklin, and the young aquafortist Max Klinger.

They demonstrate the "characteristic trait of the race, their originality being all literary and not optical." Böcklin, with his mystical visions, might be compared to Gustave Moreau, "but whose fertile and acute artistic knowledge and profound mysticism of discreet effect he lacks" (p. 172). Aside from Böcklin's new paintings, the other "curiosity" of the Salon are Klinger's ten etchings; his work in engraving "is already significant and could serve as occasion for a curious chapter about the plastic aptitudes of this race instinctively drawn to painting in order to say something, rather than to simply paint. M. Klinger appears like a poet gone astray, of a universal imagination, an eccentric and pessimistic sensibility, whom circumstances have put into a studio." His "ruling faculty is a literary imagination, hardly confined to the power of vision" (p. 173). This observation recalls Laforgue's reflections on German painting in "L'Art moderne en Allemagne."

Religious painting is hardly represented in the Salon, and Laforgue finds it noteworthy that this country which has produced history's greatest mystics has not had a single "visionnaire sensuel." Jacob Böhme, "the greatest of them all, was a good family father and perfect citizen." Historical painting, too, is "rather without lustre" (p. 175), and there are few military paintings because the official state painters, Anton von Werner, Franz Adam, Bleibtreu, and Kolitz, who do not lack talent, did not send any pictures. Laforgue shows little enthusiasm for the portraitists, Lembach, Knaus, Richter, and Gussow; and he notes that there are "no nudes; the French school still remains the most victoriously faithful to this eternal theme." Passing on to landscape painting, "at the *National-Galerie*, as at the Salon and elsewhere, our incurable vanity would have too good a hand in playing certain comparisons. If we can respond to the great reproach with which our neighbors have never ceased to characterize us, in art as in everything else—consummate skill replacing profound faith, conviction, love of the truth, spontaneity, while attributing to themselves these qualities by divine right,—it is by this unique school of great poets of the True, which goes from Troyon to Daubigny, and is in the process of being renewed in an increasingly profound and refined adoration of our land. Though sometimes quoted in some reviews, the names which are our pride are absolutely unknown in Germany." They have never heard of Rousseau, Millet, Courbet, Corot, let alone Monet and Sisley. "No, Germany has not produced a single great landscape painter and, what is even sadder, German museums and exhibitions manifest a tepidity, a desertion of their own nature, which makes one exclaim with Courbet: 'those people! they must have been born nowhere'"(pp. 177–78).These reflections characterize the entire *Salon*, which is, in fact, a comparison of French and German art, to the detriment of the latter.

Only one of Germany's great artists finds unreserved grace, Adolpf Menzel, to whom Laforgue will devote a separate article the following year. He also mentions Skarbina, "one of those eternal born virtuosos" (p. 180), the Croatian painter who had also become his friend in Berlin and to whom we are indebted for two of the finest portraits of the poet. Laforgue concludes that German artists, while they may cultivate the hand, simply do not have "the Genius of the eye. Their eye is essentially frank and cold, transparent and not given to working out what it absorbs, neither sensual nor curious, in short, not artistic. Having as yet not digested the present in art, the German school will still have to overexert itself for a long time to come, before it can give us an art of the future, or even merely the surprises which the English school has been manifesting for thirty years." We recall, "much water will flow under the bridge of the Spree . . ." It is, nevertheless, "an article of faith here, confirmed, moreover, by the most impartial German observers abroad, that Germany is not inferior to any nation in art, whereas we [the French] have for a dozen years or so been undergoing an intellectual and moral decadence" (p. 181). Laforgue's orientation and appreciations— in his characteristic mode—are certainly unequivocal; and one might perhaps be grateful to Ephrussi for having insisted on some revisions.

Laforgue's article about the 1884 Adolf Menzel exhibition, celebrating the 50th anniversary of that eminent artist's admission to the *Künstler-Verein*, too, underwent some editorial changes. Laforgue announces his contribution to Ephrussi in June: "I am sending you three pages which have cost me much time, visits and infinite recopying, about the Menzel exposition. Give it five minutes of reading, won't you, when you have nothing else to do." A few weeks later, he writes to Charles Henry, asking him not to read the article: "it is not mine. You cannot imagine the French, the psychology, the spirit and even the affirmations which the gentleman attributes to me," referring not to Ephrussi, but the editor of the Gazette at the time, "le nommé Gonse, le directeur," who had asked Laforgue's permission to rearrange the piece a little, as he had found it "trop raffiné" for his subscribers.[65] Laforgue, as we have seen above, is enthusiastic about Menzel's work, represented by several reproductions in the article. He appreciated especially "that sting of caricature which is the basis of Menzel's genius," finding that "German art has produced nothing that flawless and incisive" (p. 78). We recall here his homage to Henri Monnier in one of his earliest articles, as well as his own caricatures in *La Guêpe*; thus, Laforgue also much appreciated Charles Keene, the creator of Master Punch.[66] Laforgue discusses some of the numerous woodcuts of Menzel's *Works of Frederick*, sketches for the *Coronation at Königsberg*, as well as "a handful of curious commissioned fantasies," and several studies for *The Market of Verona*. Some of those wonderful sketches are also reproduced in the article. Laforgue appreciated most of all "a series of pastel sketches . . . of swaggering gaitered bourgeois à la Gavarni, or with their oversized Henri Monnier-like sleeves, filling out their characteristic garments" (p. 79). One of the exhibition's special surprises were Menzel's aquarelles of animals for a *Children's Album*; Laforgue finds "the particular character of all these animals recorded with a profound intuition without equal. Menzel, with his humorist's flair, with the sheer naive intensity of drawing from life," [in the Botanical Garden] "has understood and rendered the passive, resigned soul of the animals" (p. 82). For Laforgue, he is "the greatest German painter," the only one, moreover, who might be able "to tear the

German artists away from the insipidities of the *Gemüt* and throw them into the study of fortifying realities" (p. 84).

Two years later, in 1886, Laforgue reported on the Centennial Exposition of The Royal Academy of Art in Berlin, again opening his discussion by explaining the history of the institution. Thus, although the first Salon of Berlin took place one hundred years ago, this is merely the 58th Salon. As a centennial gift, a permanent locale has now been furnished, and in honor of its centenary, the exposition is international. But as Chancellor Bismarck detests anything international, the organizers were free to invite whom they wished, as long as the event did not *officially* become international. In the resulting confusion, all European countries, with the exception of France, came to be represented. In the retrospective section, Berlin must try to hold its own in the presence of the Schools of Dresden, Düsseldorf, and Weimar, while Munich is not represented. Menzel is again alone oustanding in this retrospective Berlin collection. In the contemporary exposition, Laforgue is struck by the numerous entries of amateurs; clearly, "the artistic world here is not, as in Paris, a separate world with its traditional independence;" and he notes other characteristics, "a number of minor facts which accentuate the difference between these two worlds in Paris and Berlin." Thus, underlying this "Salon," too, is a comparison of the French and German art worlds.

The English section is impressive with Burne-Jones, Watts, Millais, and Whistler; the Belgian with Verhas, Verwée, Courtens, and Verstroete. The Austrians, "still German in their coarse aesthetic," reveal, however, a warmer, more alert art. As for the Germans, Skarbina, who had won awards in a black and white exposition in Paris recently, student of Menzel and professor of anatomy at the Royal Academy, has sent a *Fishmarket at Blankenberghe*, which represents a beginning in painting with light colors. Again, Laforgue is struck by Böcklin, whose *Play of the Waves, Elysian Fields*, and *Prometheus* he had noted in the Salon of 1883. Presently, three new paintings fascinate Laforgue, the *Island of the Dead, Heroic Landscape*, and *Spring Evening*, each of which he describes in detail. "The public is used to the audacities of Böcklin's works, always new—always in their unchanging scale of splendidly glazed tones. One remains stupefied before this oneiric unity, the blinding fantastic, this impeccable natural in the supernatural. But this time, the strange artist has reserved the surprise of a polychrome sculpture for us; it is called *The King of the Frogs*. One must give up describing this work full of horror; . . . it is of a seriousness which freezes the smile" (p. 344).[67] It is not surprising that this work should fascinate Laforgue, who was so intensely interested in polychrome sculpture and had devoted an article to this new art form in the *Gazette* the same year. After Böcklin, whom he seems to admire even more now than he had three years ago, Laforgue merely enumerates some of the better-known names—Gussow, Werner, Achenbach, Meyerheim, Gentz, Defregger—noting nothing of distinction. Among the sculptors, Reinhold Begas is again outstanding, "the first, and truly Germany's only sculptor, a master" (p. 344).

Laforgue concludes his "Salon" by reminding his readers "that the German School still remains an improvised school, hastily grafted by the national vanity of a very intellectual and sensitive race. The German is an artist so far only by the head and the ear, excelling only in poetry and music, the two abstract arts.[68] Individuals like Menzel (Böcklin was born in Basel) will for a long time to come be exceptions in Germany. Paris remains, by the consent even of German art criticism, the true modern Florence" (p. 345).

Laforgue's brief chapter devoted to "The School of Fine Arts, Exposition of Students' and Artists' Works" in *Berlin, la Cour et la ville* says nothing to contradict the above. Again, Menzel is singled out from that ungifted people: "aside from the extraordinary genius called Adolf Menzel, this art comes after the French, Belgian, Dutch, Italian and, Spanish art." And "if Berlin should become even a little artistic, it will owe it to a great extent to M. Gurlitt."[69]

As I have noted, Laforgue was deeply interested in polychrome sculpture, probably stimulated by Henri Cros' and Charles Henry's book on the subject,[70] which he mentions in a letter to Kahn.[71] And we know that a small painted wax statue by Cros was one of his cherished possessions in 1884. That January, he wrote to Kahn from Berlin: "I am as exiled as you are. I have only one friend here, a wax statue by Cros."[72] Laforgue had tried to arouse interest for these pieces in Berlin, but seems not to have had much success. Thus, he was naturally interested in the endeavors of a German art professor on behalf of polychrome sculpture. In November of 1884, he announces an article for the *Gazette* about Treu's work to Ephrussi: "May I send you an article . . . about the famous brochure by M. Treu: *Shall we paint*, etc."[73] This interest resulted in a "Correspondance de Berlin" review article about the Exposition of Polychrome Sculpture at the *National-Galerie*, which the *Gazette* published in 1886. Laforgue gives credit to Professor Treu's perseverance in bringing about the event. Treu, the director of antiquities at Dresden, had published a treatise entitled *Should We Paint Our Statues?*, which had become rather popular. And Laforgue here again notes a typically German trait: "As it has been decidedly the tradition in Germany, notably for a century, so it is here also the 'professor' who has given the impulse and prepared the way. The German artist is always given to seeking the tutelage of the book. . . . Where, in France, is the theoretician to preach about polychrome sculpture" (p. 166)? The only reason, moreover, that this new approach to sculpture could become popular in Germany is because Treu proposes nothing revolutionary or new, "but simply to renew and take up again a tradition which the Greeks, our masters and legislators in aesthetics, had imported from the Orient" (p. 167). Modern polychrome sculpture, as Laforgue observes, has, however, nothing to do with the old, neither Greek nor Oriental. The modern pieces are frequently sculpted and painted by different artists, and very often sink to the level of industrial production. Laforgue notes merely four interesting artists in the new genre, Kauer von Kreutznach, now dead, who was a precursor and had received the idea from an old painted way-side crucifix in his native region. Three other artists are represented by works "of good faith," a bust by Joseph

Kaffsack, another by Max Landsberg, and a woman's head by the well-known sculptor Albert Wolff. In general, however, Laforgue is not very impressed: "these curiosities prove nothing. It is in the more frankly natural efforts that one might find a fecund direction, like the two little wax statutes by Mr. Henri Cros, . . . two small, very modern women's heads," in modern dress, of course, "of the rarest and most exquisite reality, treated in the most refined processes" (p. 170). Thus, again the artistic light shines from France, to point the way to a new and modern form of art.

Notes

1 Cf. Chapter I, above.
2 Kahn, *Symbolistes et Décadents*, 27 and 182.
3 C. Chapter I, note 69.
4 Henri Monnier, creator of that nineteenth-century French version of Archy Bunker, had died in 1877.
5 *Pages de la Guêpe*, 150: "Taine's courses at the Beaux-Arts, those of M. Caro at the Sorbonne, Ch. Blanc and Paul Albert's, at the Collège de France are going to reopen. We are finally going to live. Hurrah for winter."
6 *Lettres à un Ami*, 30.
7 Cf. Chapter III, note 6.
8 Michele Hannoosh, "The Poet as Art Critic: Laforgue's Aesthetic Theory," *Modern Language Review*, (1984): 559.
9 These Laforguean texts have come down to us in the posthumously published fragments in *La Revue blanche*, 481–88, deuxième semestre, 1896, entitled "Notes d'esthétique." With Laforgue's other fragments on aesthetics, they were again published by Mauclair in the 1903 Mercure de France edition of *Oeuvres complètes de Jules Laforgue*, III, 133–218, *Mélanges posthumes*. Hannoosh takes issue with the faultiness of this edition in her above essay. Laforgue subsequently incorporated some of his notes against Taine into the first part of another group of texts on aesthetics, "L'Art moderne en Allemagne," *Mélanges posthumes*, 196–218, first published in *La Revue blanche*, deuxieme semestre, 1895, 292–300.
10 H. Taine, *Philosophie de l'art* (Heidelberg: Carl Winters Universitätsbuchhandlung, 1907), 23 and 27.
11 *Mélanges posthumes*, 141.
12 *The Ideal in Art* by H. Taine, transl. J. Durand (New York: Holt and Co., 1874), 25ff., 97ff., 143ff.

[13] Ernest Renan, *Dialogues Philosophiques* (Paris: Calmann Lévy, 1895), 82, 83–4.

[14] For example: "This is why you find in the lowest rank, those drawings, aquarelles, pastels, and statuettes, which in men do not depict the man, but his dress, and especially the dress of the day" (*The Ideal in Art*, 80). As I have noted above (Ch. VI, note 39), Laforgue's view here contrasts with Heine's.

[15] *Mélanges posthumes*, 146.

[16] *The Ideal in Art*, 124.

[17] *The Ideal in Art*, 118.

[18] *Mélanges posthumes*, 154. Laforgue here recalls the Hartmannian chapter of "Das Unbewußte in der Naturheilkraft" and the notion that "the Unconscious itself neither falls sick nor can produce sickness in its organism" (*Philosophy of the Unconscious* by Eduard von Hartmann, transl. W. Ch. Coupland; London: Kegan, Trench and Trübner, 1890), 165.

[19] In my "Laforgue and His Philosophers" (Chapter I, note 25).

[20] *Lettres à un Ami*, 18, 22–3, 59.

[21] Dennis N. Kenedy Darnois, *The Unconscious and Eduard von Hartmann* (The Hague: Martinus Nijhoff, 1967), 61.

[22] Hartmann, *Philosophy of the Unconscious*, II: 63.

[23] *Philosophy of the Unconscious*, II: 275.

[24] *Mélanges posthumes*, 147.

[25] *Mélanges posthumes*, 148.

[26] *Philosophy of the Unconscious*, I: 278.

[27] *Mélanges posthumes*, 149–50.

[28] Cf. Philippe Kolb et Jean Adhémar, "Charles Ephrussi (1849–1905) ses Sécrétaires: Laforgue, A. Renan, Proust 'sa' Gazette des Beaux-Arts," *Gazette des Beaux-Arts*, 126, (1984): 29–41.

[29] Arkell, *Looking for Laforgue*, 50. The poet's biographer continues: "On those summer mornings of 1881 Laforgue found himself living among Impressionist pictures that had only just been painted; like that Morisot *Hiver* of 1880, or Renoir's picture of a little girl, *La Bohémienne*, which had been done near Dieppe in 1879 and bought the same year by Ephrussi. Then there were Monet's *Pommiers* of 1878, Mary Cassatt's *Lydia* (1879) and the Degas pastel (1879) of Duranty. For the young man who, six months before, had wondered where he could see some Manets, it must have been a revelation" (51).

[30] *Mélanges posthumes*, 150–51, cf. note 14 above.

[31] *The Ideal in Art*, 93.

[32] *The Ideal in Art*, 105.

[33] We recall Laforgue's thirteenth Chronicle in *La Guêpe*, about the separation of art and morality, "place aux *Fleurs du mal*, *Mlle de Maupin*," p. 29 above.

[34] *Mélanges posthumes*, 151, 152.

[35] *Mélanges posthumes*, 153.

36 *Mélanges posthumes*, 154.

37 *Mélanges posthumes*, 155–56.

38 *Mélanges posthumes*, 165 and 157.

39 Mireille Dottin, in "Un Article retrouvé de Jules Laforgue," *Europe*, 673 (1985): 97–102, has introduced and presented the brief, essentially descriptive and insignificant piece. This issue of *Europe* is entirely devoted to Laforgue. Dottin comments: "Cet article, dont les platitudes conventionnelles viennent peut-être du rédacteur en chef Louis Gonse, n'a certes rien d'immortel; l'oeuvre d'Henri Daras—encore visible dans l'église—a sombré dans l'oubli, et le commentaire de Laforgue, aggravé de coquilles, paraît bien scolaire, guindé et maladroit" (97).

40 Laforgue, *Lettres* I: 42.

41 *Lettres* I: 58–9.

42 *Lettres* I: 81.

43 *Lettres* I: 204–5.

44 Cf. note 9 above.

45 Laforgue, *Lettres* II: 60–61.

46 Charles Henry, who remained Laforgue's friend throughout his life, was at the time developing his system of scientific aesthetics, well-informed by the German school of physiological psychology.

47 *Mélanges posthumes*, 196–218.

48 Laforgue, *L'Imitation de Notre-Dame la Lune*, 55–6.

49 Hartmann, *Philosophy of the Unconscious*, I: 269.

50 Cf. *System of Transcendental Idealism* (1800) by F. W. J. Schelling, transl. by Peter Heath (Charlottesville: University Press of Virginia, 1978), 219 ff., "Deduction of a Universal Organ of Philosophy, or Essentials of the Philosophy of Art according to the Principles of Transcendental Idealism." For von Hartmann's debt to Schelling, cf. Kenedy Darnois, *The Unconscious and Eduard von Hartmann*, 15ff.

51 As Warren Ramsey has pointed out, Laforgue here commits the error of attributing evolution to acquired traits, *The Ironic Inheritance*, 87.

52 Laforgue, *Lettres* II: 59–60: "I saw M. and Mme Bernstein again, who are not only the most artistic people here, but who, moreover, are so gracious as not to notice my unsociableness. We saw the Impressionists at Gurlitt's, very interesting if not the most significant ones. Pissarro is certainly solid; . . . Degas' *Jockeys* were marvelous with his saucy wallpaper effect, but no *Dancer*. Before the Renoirs always the same impression, that's fine, velvety and glistening like a pastel, the nude of his women is solid, expert and curious, but I don't like that porcelain-like glossiness. I have written a rather long review article, a physiological aesthetic explication of the Impressionist formula, which M. Bernstein translated for a review." This is the same letter from which I have quoted (p. 212) about the poet's night of aesthetic revelation.

⁵³ For a summary of contemporary German review articles of the exhibition, cf. the editorial, "A French Poet in Imperial Prussia," *Apollo*, 106, (1977): 88–97. Other commentators are Richard Shiff, "The End of Imressionism: A Study in Theories of Aesthetic Expression" in *The Art Quarterly*, (1978): 338–78; Laforgue's notions on Impressionism are briefly touched on in this piece. Jean Cassou, "Laforgue et l'Impressionnisme" in *Mélanges Cain* (undated), 111–115. Médéric Dufour, "Une Philosophie de l'Impressionnisme: Etude sur l'esthétique de Jules Laforgue" (Paris: Librairie Léon Vanier, 1904). The most perceptive and informed analysis of Laforgue's essay is that of Michele Hannoosh, in her article cited above, note 8. Laforgue's text appears in English translation in Linda Nochlin's *Impressionism and Post-Impressionism 1874–1904: Sources and Documents* (Englewood Cliffs: Prentice-Hall 1966), 14–20. Nochlin writes in her introduction to the text: "One can say that Laforgue's essay is the first coherent expression of the modern view of art, continuing in the path of Baudelaire, who had written as early as 1860, in *The Painter of Modern Life*: 'Modernity is the transitory, the fleeting, the contingent . . .'."

⁵⁴ *The Selected Writings of Hermann von Helmholtz* (Middletown: Wesleyan University Press, 1971). This is from the sub-chapter "The Perception of Sight," 194. Von Helmholtz says nothing at all about the "primitive state of the eye" in this connection, as Hannoosh also remarks.

⁵⁵ For example, "I have . . . found a similar hypothesis very convenient and well suited to explain in a most simple manner certain peculiarities which have been observed in the perception of musical tones, pecularities as enigmatic as those we have been considering in the eye," "The Perception of Sight," 181.

⁵⁶ Von Helmholtz, *Selected Writings*, "The Perception of Sight," 180: Dr. Young supposes that there are in the eye three kinds of nerve fibers, the first of which, when irritated in any way, produces the sensation of red; the second, the sensation of green; and the third, that of violet. He further assumes that the first are excited most strongly by the waves of ether of greatest length and the second . . . by the waves of middle length, while the last . . . are acted upon only by the shortest vibrations of ether.

⁵⁷ Von Helmholtz, *Selected Writings*, 306.

⁵⁸ *Selected Writings*, 307ff.

⁵⁹ *Selected Writings*, 316.

⁶⁰ Cf. note 50 above. *System of Transcendental Idealism* (1800), 222: ' . . . and as that power is called destiny, which through our free action realizes, without our knowledge . . . goals *that we did not envisage*, so likewise that incomprehensive agency which supplies objectivity to the conscious . . . is dominated by the obscure concept of *genius*. The product we postulate is none other than the *product of art*."

⁶¹ Th. Ribot, *La Psychologie allemande contemporaine* (Paris: Félix Alcan, 1909, 7th ed.), 174ff. For Ribot's importance in transmitting Schopenhauer's

thought to Laforgue, cf. "Laforgue and His philosophers" (Chapter I, note 25).

[62] Cf. Mireille Dottin, "Jules Laforgue, Salonnier," *Europe*, 673 (1985): 85–96. The author insists that Laforgue "fut poète *et* critique d'art" and that "il eut durant toute sa vie des rapports directs et constants avec les arts" (85). This article does not deal with Laforgue's aesthetic theories, but concentrates on his role as "salonnier."

[63] Laforgue, *Lettres* II: 29–30.

[64] *Lettres* II: 34 and 41–2.

[65] *Lettres* II: 80–81 and 90 and 91.

[66] In *Mélanges posthumes*, 174, Laforgue writes: "The only one who in his loose sketches of manners has accomplished something profound, sharp, compact, is the Englishman Charles Keene."

[67] The pagination of Laforgue's articles in the *Gazette des Beaux-Arts* is that of the volumes bound by year.

[68] In this connection it is interesting to note that Heine, the German poet, inspired musicians, cf. Chapter II, note 21; whereas the French poet, Laforgue, inspired painters, like Marcel Duchamp and Patrick Caulfield. Cf. Ronald Johnson, "Poetic Pathways to Dada: Marcel Duchamp and Jules Laforgue," *Arts Magazine*, (May 1976): 82–89. For Duchamp's compositions after themes by Laforgue's poetry, cf. Lawrence D. Steefel, Jr., "Marcel Duchamp's 'Encore à cet Astre,'" *Art Journal* XXXVI/1 (Fall, 1976): 23–30. For Laforgue's repercussions in Caulfield, cf. Timothy Hyman, "Caulfield's Laforgue," *Artscribe*, 24 (1980): 16–20.

[69] Laforgue, *En Allemagne*, 172–73.

[70] Henry Cros et Charles Henry, *L'Encaustique et les autres procédés de peinture chez les Anciens* (Paris: Ed. J. Pouam, 1884).

[71] *Lettres à un Ami*, 44.

[72] *Lettres à un Ami*, 51.

[73] Laforgue, *Lettres* II: 100.

Postscript

In the most recent collection of essays devoted to Laforgue, Jacques Gaucheron remarks that "Laforgue has much taste for Heine, and a comparison would be fruitful."[1] In the same volume, André Wurmser, deploring the poet's untimely death, describes Heine as "the only poet whom, by his tenderness and cruel clairvoyance, by his irony, and most of all by his self-mockery, his clever use of every-day words, he resembles *like a brother*."[2] In the foregoing essays I have attempted to examine for the first time in detail the kinship suggested by so many commentators over the years. In examining the poets' early literary journalism, their lyric poetry, their endeavors in the drama, and their art criticism, I have aimed at documenting Heine's influence on Laforgue, both direct and mediated, and at defining their resemblances, their affinities, and their differences.

Laforgue's earliest texts, both poetry and prose—his contributions to *La Guêpe* and *l'Enfer*—were already inspired by Heine (cf. Ch. I), and the reverberations of Heine's *Lyrisches Intermezzo* as well as some of his subsequent verse can be found in Laforgue's later poetry (cf. Ch. II). While direct Heinean echoes are rarer in Laforgue's mature verse, the younger poet's persona, however, continues to resemble his older brother. Pierrot and the "moi" of the posthumously published *Derniers Vers* reflect the image of a kind of French Heine of the *fin de siècle*. This profound kinship, I believe, owes much to the poets' historical situations, to the fact that each had arrived on the literary scene at the end of a period. Heine considered himself the last Romantic, one who could no longer be part of the

Kunstperiode ruled by Goethe. Laforgue felt the weight of Baudelaire—as Heine had felt that of Goethe—as one from which he had to liberate himself.[3] Heine, the post-Romantic, and Laforgue, the post-Symbolist, each had to create a new poetic idiom. We recall Laforgue's letter to his sister (p. 52 above), in which he tries to explain the new style of his "little poems of fantasy, having only one aim: *faire de l'original à tout prix.*" The young Heine, too, had stressed the originality of his poetry. Thus he wrote in a letter of 1821: "I . . . also know that experts . . . will not fail to recognize the study of the folksong, the struggle against customary poetry and a striving for originality in my verse." And in 1823, he describes the *Lyrisches Intermezzo* as "a strong cycle of humorous songs in the popular tone, . . . which by its originality arouses much interest, praise and bitter reproach" (HSA, XX: 47 and 63).

The two poets, as we have found, manifest another common trait, one for which both have incurred reproach: the relative thematic restriction of their verse. Heine himself was fully aware of it, as he wrote to his friend Immermann in 1823, when *Lyrisches Intermezzo* had first appeared: "I will gladly admit the main shortcoming of my poetry to you, by the reproach of which you probably believe you are offending me—it is the great onesidedness which my poems demonstrate in that they are all merely variations of the same little theme (HSA, XX: 91). The same criticism was launched against Laforgue in a now famous letter by Jacques Rivière to Alain-Fournier of April 23, 1906, in which he complains about Laforgue's "technical virtuosity and mastery over verbal pyrotechnics, with his egocentric concern with himself and the eternal misunderstanding between man and woman."[4] And Nerval in his enthusiastic presentation of the *Intermezzo*, while stressing Heine's originality, already pointed to the cycle's thematic restriction (p. 44 above): "All these disconnected stanzas have a unity,—love. . . . What is the subject of the *Intermezzo*? A young girl . . . loved by the poet . . . leaves him for some other lover . . . Nothing more, nothing less." It is the last point, the "nothing less," that is suggestive. For Nerval, himself a great poet, understood that

Heine's love poetry is much more than a vehicle for the expression of frustrated love, just as Laforgue's is much more than the expression of "the eternal misunderstanding between man and woman."

In the nineteenth century, such major critics as Elster set out to discover the "real" story behind the poetry: the young Heine's hopeless love for his cousins.[5] And this, ironically, in the service of a poet who had always been most elusive about his private life, and who had repeatedly and clearly spoken out against biographical criticism.[6] But at the end of the nineteenth century, the readers of the *Buch der Lieder* needed to be assured that the Jew Heine was indeed a true German poet, whose poetry was not the product of vain *Mache*, but *Erlebnisdichtung* inspired by the "true" sorrows of the heart.[7] David Arkell has traced Laforgue's amorous adventures at the Prussian Court and suggested their reflections in his poetry.[8] Yet a mere reading *through* the text for the story *behind* it would perforce exhaust itself soon. Heine and Laforgue came fully into their own only posthumously—"Tel qu'en lui-même enfin l'éternité le change"—as Mallarmé said it so beautifully of Poe. Thus, while the poets' loves may well be part of the stuff their verse was made of, more significant, surely, for each was a literary tradition, the vast intertext with which they had to come to terms. And they emerged from their struggles—both personal and poetological—each with a distinctly new voice, in which manner and *matière* cannot be divorced. Neither Heine nor Laforgue could have written "about something else" that same poetry which, a century later, we still read for *le plaisir du texte*.

The pervasive, romantically melancholy misogyny of the two poets is nevertheless striking, though it most often appears in comic trappings, sheltered by irony.[9] The somber figure of Schopenhauer (who in fact outlived Heine) here looms behind them both. But this misogyny, assumed or real, became in fact a poetic entrée for both poets to the inevitable lyric theme of mutability. At least for male poets, women's inconstancy was an image of the world's mutability as old as literature, along with the wilted rose, the waning moon, autumn with its falling leaves, twilight, and an almost endless procession of other representations of time's destructiveness. It could of course also be turned against male inconstancy with the sort of wry irony practiced by Heine and Laforgue, and it frequently was in the nineteenth century. "Souvent femme varie," sings (in 1832) the king of Hugo's *Le Roi s'amuse*, as his lover is faithfully dying for her love; "La donna e mobile," repeats the duke of Verdi's *Rigoletto* in 1852. The misogynic stance served the poet-ironists well.

In counterparting Heine's and Laforgue's attempts at dramatic writing, we have again found a remarkable affinity: as Heine's two youthful tragedies *Almansor* and *William Ratcliff*, his *Tanzpoem Der Doktor Faust* and the ballet *Die Göttin Diana* constitute a meager output compared with the poet's intense and high ambitions in the genre, so Laforgue's theatrical productions, the adolescent comedy *Tessa*, his scenario for the *Pierrot fumiste* pantomime and the playlet *Le Concile féerique* grafted from his lyric poetry, present, likewise, very little in view of his life-long ambitions as dramatist. Heine and Laforgue were above all poets and journalists, whose frustrated dramatic genius is reflected, however, in both their poetry and prose. I have pointed to the dramatic quality of Laforgue's verse in discussing *Le Concile féerique*, his only play(let) ever to be performed, in which the voices heard are reciting fragments from his poems. And multiple voicing is manifest in all of his lyric collections, while the dramatic quality of his prose, for example his legendary morality *Hamlet*, is as obvious as that of Heine's prose, for example in the Gumpelino episode of *The Baths of Lucca*. Barker Fairley has analyzed the theatrical nature of Heine's poetry in a celebrated essay: "What distinguishes the *Intermezzo* among books of songs," he says, "is its patent theatricality—. . . . Heine stages his lyrics as no other can. . . . One feels that each poem makes its bow, does it turn, and goes off, as in a vaudeville show. And in the songs themselves this imagery of the theatre insinuates itself continually." This tendency predominates also in Heine's later collections, where the staging, now no longer accessory, has been thoroughly internalized:

"The theatre imagery—all that we associate with vaudeville, circus, ballet, dance, orchestra, costume, chorus, pageant, masquerade, and such-like—has changed its position in Heine's mind. From being rather part of his technique . . . it has passed wholly into vision . . . The staging is inside the poems now. But the stage impulse is there throughout . . . In one form or another his theatrical mood was essential to his genius. It is unlikely that Heine knew how strong this bias was, how for him in very truth all the world was a stage and life a ballet."[10]

This deep-seated kinship between Heine and Laforgue led to another, closely related affinity: the poets' admiration for Shakespeare, who occupies a pivotal position in the work of each and thus constitutes a strong intertextual link between them. In examining Heine's Shakespeare and Laforgue's, we noted the frequency of the poets' quotations, direct and indirect, from the great dramatist's work, and especially their identification with the figure of Hamlet. Further, each poet paid Shakespeare the ironist's ultimate tribute: parody, Laforgue in a *moralité légendaire*, Heine in a *Reisebild*, each in his most characteristic prose genre.

Our exploration of Heine's and Laforgue's similarities has also revealed significant differences between the exiled poets. Most striking of these, perhaps, is the difference between their attitudes towards their exile. Heine embraced Paris and French culture far more rapidly than Laforgue embraced Berlin and the German. Of the several reasons for this difference the most important may have been the sheer magic of Paris, which has made her a refuge and *alma mater* for artists and intellectuals from the twelfth century's scholastics and cathedral schools to the present decade's linguistic and Deconstructionist gymnasts. Paris in the nineteenth century, as now, wore her culture out of ancient habit, with grace and sophistication, and treated the artistic and intellectual worlds as matters of great import. To Heine she was a garden of delights, while liberating him from the turmoils of Judaism in a Germany which denied him, a Jew and political revolutionary, full freedom to choose his profession and manner of life. She was likewise an escape from a Jewish burgher-family almost as oppressive in its dictatorial attitude as the Prussian state. And Heine's integration with French culture was undoubtedly made easier by his education in Düsseldorf during Napoleon's sway, where his formative years were touched by the French spirit. Thus he became immediately a member of the intellectual and artistic Parisian elite, and married a woman who—though certainly not part of that elite—was thoroughly French. Though he had moments of deep and genuine homesickness (cf. pp. 147 ff. above), he never seriously thought of returning to the land which would not tolerate his political stance, but where his poetry had already taken on the quality of a folk institution. Yet, Heine's "Exilsituation" in Paris was fraught with complexities; these have been well analyzed by Françoise Bech who attempts to explain Heine's reserve toward the greats of contemporary French literature, as well as their—frequently negative—attitude toward him.[11] Another commentator, in tracing Heine's notions of his poetic vocation, states: "In Paris Heine got into new contradictions, for he was a Jew among pagans, a Christian among Jews, a Romantic poet among Liberals, a Liberal among Romantics."[12]

Laforgue's exile, on the other hand, was dictated by economic circumstances. Simply put, he needed a job, reasonably suited to his talents, and his patron Ephrussi found him one. But in Germany, after the first few months, he never ceased to lament his absence from Paris. Berlin was hardly a substitute. The capital of a small state, suddenly in 1871 become a seat of empire, had the ponderous and awkward self-consciousness of the politically *nouveau riche*. The dreary heavy hand of the Prussian military was obtrusive. The intellectual and artistic life (with the exception of music) seemed thin, forced and gauche, cultivated out of a sense of imperial obligation rather than burgeoning as a reflection of life. And Laforgue was troubled by the language. Though he had studied German for several years at the *lycée* at Tarbes, he was not initiated into German letters until his encounter with Schopenhauer, von Hartmann and, most significantly, Heine during his autodidactic years after he had terminated his formal schooling. Laforgue felt exile as a penalty, Heine felt it as an escape.

We face also the difficulty—perhaps the absurdity—of comparing the work of an artist who had died in the flush of youth with that of one who lived through full maturity. Laforgue is of the romantically pathetic race of Mozart and Schubert, Seurat, Keats, and Shelley, treated abruptly by the ultimate "Spinner of Destinies" (Hardy), the "Director of the World" (Heine); brief, bright flashes of genius gone from the world before they had become a settled part of it. The disparity is especially obvious in the journalism of Heine and Laforgue. The former's texts cover many years, from youth to their author's full maturity, while Laforgue's cover barely a decade. Thus, while Heine was able to revise and publish his work himself, most of the Laforguean texts on the performing arts and art criticism were published posthumously, whence the frequently sketchy and unfinished quality of the work of the older poet's brilliant young disciple. As I have remarked earlier of their prose, in Heine we hear the voice of the mature writer, in Laforgue that of the brilliant beginner. What we have read, however, reveals also again a profound affinity between the two poets: that in exploring both their own and a foreign—each other's—culture, each remained deeply rooted in his own tradition. Witness Heine's disparagement of French classical theater and ballet, and Laforgue's comments on the German stage. Heine, as he frequently reminds his readers, is a *German* poet; and Laforgue, saturated with Schopenhauer, von Hartmann and Wagner, remains entirely French! In their journalism, each wears the mask of the *alien* observer.

Nothing will more clearly demonstrate the German-ness of Heine and the French-ness of Laforgue than excerpts from two texts, not *on* the performing arts, but in which one of these, the dance, is reflected in examples of their authors' most characteristic genres, a Heinean *Reisebild*, and a Laforguean *moralité légendaire*. In the second of the *Florentine Nights*,[13] the protagonist tells his beloved about a street dancer, Mademoiselle Laurence, whose act, accompanied by a dwarf barker, a trained dog, and her mother beating the drum, had so fascinated him several years ago in England that he followed the troupe through the London streets for months. He never forgot her dance. Before describing it, Maximilian tells Maria how little he likes French classical ballet, in almost the same terms we have read above: 'I detest nothing as much as the ballet of the Paris Opera, where the tradition of that classical dance has been preserved most purely, whereas in the remaining arts, in poetry, music and painting, the French have overthrown the classical system.'' He thinks that it will be difficult for them to bring about a similar revolution in dance. Mademoiselle Laurence, surely, was not a great dancer, but danced in the streets; ''she understood nothing of the art of dance as Vestris teaches it, but she danced as nature bids man dance: her entire being was in harmony with her steps; not only her feet, but her whole body danced, her face danced . . .'' This ''was indeed not classical dancing, but also not the romantic dance of the Eugène Renduel school'' (B, I: 592–93). It was wonderful, with enigmatic movements, ''a language which was saying something which I did not understand, that tossing back of the beautiful head, that listening bent toward the earth, the fear, trying to appease itself through the more and more frantic leaps . . .'' (B, I: 595). Later we learn what Mademoiselle Laurence was expressing with her dance: the story of her own life. She was, in fact, performing an expressionistic *Naturtanz*, or character dance, long before Isadora Duncan was heard of, or Martha Graham of our own day. And her unprecedented style would have been perfect for Heine's own *Tanzpoem Der Doktor Faust* or *Die Göttin Diana*.[14]

Laforgue's most famous dancer is Salomé, heroine of the legendary morality named after her.[15] In this exuberant parody of Flaubert's *Hérodias*, Salomé, daughter of the Tetrarch Emeraude-Archetypas of the Esoteric White Isles, entertains her father's guests, the Princes of the North—a parody of those Laforgue had seen in Berlin—during a national holiday celebration. The dancer appears before her courtly and aristocratic audience hermetically wrapped into jonquil-like arachnidean muslin with black polkadots which, fastened here and there by various fibulae, leaving her arms in their angelic nudity, formed between her hints of breasts, their almonds pricked by an eyelet, a sash embroidered with her eighteen years, and, attached a little higher than her adorable umbilical dimple in a belt of flounces of an intense and jealous yellow, adumbrated inviolably at the pelvis in the embrace of her thin hips, then came to a stop at the ankles, to come back up behind in two spread and floating sashes, finally fastened to the mother-of-pearl arm supports of the dwarf peacock's wheel, its background iridescent with azure, moire, emerald and gold, which formed a halo around her candid superior head (p. 225).

Salomé's "mystic delirium" is introduced by and set to the following choreography:

> . . . delicately poised on her right foot, her hip raised, her other leg bent Niobe-like, Salomé, giving in to a little coughing laugh, perhaps to inform her audience that above all one should not believe that she took herself seriously, plucked her lyre to the wood, and with the languished and sexless voice of a convalescent asking for his potion, which, fundamentally, he never needed any more than you or I, improvised thus (pp. 227–8).

She addresses her improvised harangue to "the latitudes, altitudes, Nebulae of good will" and to humanity, "oh passengers of this earth." And her long declamation, accompanied by the lyre, is not the story of her short life, but "a summary demolition of theogonies, theodicies, and formulas of the wisdom of nations," presented "in the name of the [Hartmannian] Unconscious." Her exhausting song and dance finally concluded, "the little yellow vociferator . . . broke the lyre across her knee and took up her dignity again," while "the intoxicated audience wiped their foreheads to keep their countenance" (p. 235). Surely, never has German philosophy been celebrated in a like performance; and surely, also, no one would have enjoyed it more than Heine.

In the art criticism of Heine and Laforgue the paradox of their inherent kinship and conspicuous difference is so profound that they could no longer be accommodated under one roof, as it were, but had to be housed in separate chapters. For while Heine, in politicizing the genre, appropriated it for his own ends, Laforgue mastered it, on his way to becoming a consummate art critic, his life-long ambition. Laforgue's remark that Max Klinger was "a poet gone astray" might well be applied to Heine's art criticism, except that there is calculation—method in Heine's straying.

For Heine, as he molds his *Salon* to his own social purpose, art criticism becomes a political instrument. Laforgue's *Salons* are propaedeutic, a young man's device to master the art criticism which concerned him so intensely. Political reformer and aesthete—two stances which continue to dominate today's criticism—stand opposed. While Heine, revolutionary dreamer, never experienced the realization of the promise with which he closed his 1831 *Salon*—"the new times will also bring forth a new art that will be in enthusiastic harmony with them"— Laforgue, aesthete, did. And when that renewal of both matter and technique occurred in painting toward the end of the century, the young poet-critic was among the first to understand it.

This major difference may be profitably—perhaps ironically— explored through Heine's insistence on and search for the Zeitgeist in the works of art he discusses, "all works of one and the same period have . . . the painted signs of the Zeitgeist." If Heine and Laforgue were alike in *Gemüt*, their divergences in the criticism of art reflect the broad fracture in Zeitgeist over the decades which separate them. The revolutionary fervor which gripped artists and intellectuals during Heine's maturity, with its call for human rights and the autonomy of the common man, had given way to a new fervor, also revolutionary, for the rights of the artist in the face of the academy, and for the autonomy of art without regard to politics or any other social factor. The artist as social motivator had given way to the artist as aesthete. The Zeitgeist, whether in the vision of Heine or of Taine, is a statistical construct which hardly touches the individual. If each artist is a keyboard played upon by "race, milieu, temps," Laforgue asserts that "my keyboard is perpetually changing, and there is not another identical to mine. All keyboards are legitimate." Laforgue gives voice to the individual's—the Impressionist's—rebellion against institutional Zeitgeist, which is the academy. Heine, Taine, Laforgue, are all thoroughgoing artistic relativists, but with what differences!

I have noted Laforgue's consistent denial of any artistic or aesthetic hierarchy, as against Taine. We may, if we wish, feed our own taste for irony by speculating how Heine, with his socio-political preoccupations and his moralizing hunt for principle in the program of each painting, might have received these denials. We may speculate further, imagining Heine's reception of Laforgue's hearty opposition to moral standards in art. Surely, Heine would have supported that!—except when the standards supported the social and political liberation of the oppressed. Laforgue in fact rejects all moral standards in art criticism in favor of aesthetic ones; Heine rejects one sort of moral standard in favor of another sort. The irony deepens. But Heine, like all great ironists, is yet ahead of us: he suspects his own standard of liberty, and the common man he would liberate. Yet further, and finally, he suspects his own suspicions. The perfect ironist is mercurial, and sees around corners.

Yet in this cleavage between kindred spirits we may find the earliest warning of this century's standoff between the New Criticism with its mutations on the one hand and Marxist criticism with its fellow travelers on the other. Of the two poet-ironists themselves, we may observe that Heine's irony extends to and turns upon the predicaments of societies as they deal with their peoples, and Laforgue's is more largely concerned with the private predicaments of the individual.

Thus for conspicuous differences. But the inherent kinship between Heine and Laforgue, at least in their art criticism, is that more fundamental one of one poet to another. Heine repeatedly poeticizes his *Salons*, especially in the service of rather unpoetic socio-political ideas, as in his celebration of Saint-Simonianism occasioned by Robert's painting, or his description of the Parisian reaction to the fall of Poland, linked to a painting by Delaroche. In Heine's disingenuous textual stratagem, the political event itself almost shatters his text, as he cannot continue writing on art with the shouting of the angry people under his windows in the street. Today we know that Heine was far from Paris, poeticizing in peace his political vision (Chapter VI, n. 48 above). Similarly, Laforgue's perspicacious remarks on German art frequently stray far, and poetically, from their alleged subject and occasion, from an exposition in Berlin to Wagner's "voices of the forest"! And while Laforgue's somewhat harsh and unjust condemnation of German art was, paradoxically, nourished and supported by German philosophy and science, its tone and style, with their witty irony, are thoroughly Heinean.

Although my studies have centered on the creative kinship between two poets of different nationalities, whose careers were separated by several decades, a few concluding comments on their common predicament—exile—and on the chief of their common model stances—irony—may be useful. Again, comparison is impeded and similarities obscured by the fact that one reached artistic maturity, with both its rewards and its disillusionment, while the other died on its threshold. "Laforgue dies just as . . . he is becoming Laforgue,"writes Wurmser. "The doors which he opened are closing behind him," as he rejoins Heine in death.[16] The broken column never achieves its florid Corinthian capital. Hence both exile and irony assume a depth more profound in Heine than in Laforgue.

Exile as such is always *thrust upon* the individual, whether by formal sentence of ostracism, as in classical (or current Soviet) times, or by economic circumstances—Laforgue—or by a combination of the hostility of family and national policy—Heine. It is in the most formal, external sense, *alienation*, the creation of an alien, and one is hardly surprised to find (as we have found) both Heine and Laforgue alienated subjectively as well as objectively. Laforgue occasionally views Berlin in the manner in which Ovid viewed Pontus. Yet, though Paris was Heine's home of choice, always a pleasure to him and an excitement to his genius, the stance of the exile paradoxically takes a more mordant form in his writing. Perhaps, as I have remarked, this was the result merely of disillusioned maturity. Perhaps it was the knowledge that the combined hostility of family and homeland made choice identical with necessity if he were to retain his freedom. Perhaps, we may speculate, it was the very dominance of exile in the annals of his ancient race, from the cherubim with the flaming sword, through the servitude in Egypt, to the captivity *super flumina Balylonis*. "By the rivers of Babylon," sang the Psalmist, "there we sat down, yea, we wept, when we remembered Zion . . . How shall we sing the Lord's song in a strange land?" (Ps. 137, i, 4). And from Babylon to the Roman destruction of Jerusalem and the Temple, which so hastened the Diaspora, thence to the seemingly endless succession of expulsions from the various states of medieval Christian Europe, which have kept Jews off balance for nearly two millenia, always, somewhere or at some time, figuratively *super flumina Babylonis*, Diaspora, wandering, expulsion, exile, have been the constant companions of the race. Whatever, then, the complex of causes, Heine's decision for exile had a finality, an irrevocability, which Laforgue's did not.

But the most terrible of all these sentences of exile was the first: in Jewish legend the flaming sword (Gen. 3:24) barring all humankind from access to the Tree of Life. This is mankind's exile into his very humanity, one of the most intensely tragic visions of all times, repeated by medieval Christendom, which saw the human race—to use the language of Bishop Amar's prayer of the eleventh century—as "poor banished children of Eve, mourning and weeping in this valley of tears." In medical terms, it is the sudden, unwilled exit from the blood-warm, paradisiac sufficiency of the womb into the chill, pitiless air, and the prime insult of the surgeon's slap which initiates the infant's adjustment, and maladjustment, to life as an individual. In Heine, the Fall is mythologized in the theme of the Exile of the Gods. With such a beginning, who could lack a sense of irony?

This ironic sense seems to develop early as a natural defense of the exiled/alienated. It forms a psychic insulation between the sensitive individual's perceptions and his feelings, for it subsists on perceived disparities—between expectation and result, promise and fulfillment, illusion and reality, ideal and actual, utterance and meaning, signifier and signified. Its literary expression is a terrain of semiotic quicksands, false narrative trails, logical potholes.

Recognition of these disparities is an exorcism of sorts: irony becomes a refuge, bitterly natural to the young, with their growing recognition of the manifold disparities in an alien, unparadisiac, extra-uterine world. But it can persist and intensify in old age, as the disparities themselves persist and multiply, unless the ironist finds the grace of benign acceptance. Exceptionally sensitive souls, such as Heine and Laforgue, take refuge in irony not only from an alien world, but often from an alien self. For this is the Fall, man's inescapable schizophrenia, that even the Self is a trash-heap of inexplicable disparities. Self-mockery was essential to the great ironists of the past, and is almost a part of daily life in today's irony-dominated world.

The literary products of this ironic sense, then, are sword and shield turned against both alien world and alien self. Heine's "Der Apollogott" from his late *Romanzero*,[17] and Laforgue's *Hamlet, ou les suites de la piété filiale* from his *Moralités légendaires* provide brilliant examples. Both are riots of the most mordant irony, and both among the most mature examples of their authors' work. I have discussed Laforgue's *Hamlet* at length, but "Der Apollogott" should be mentioned at least briefly. With complex, often difficult irony,[18] Heine tells of a young nun (thus exile from the world) who escapes from her convent to follow her magnificent vision of Apollo accompanied by the nine muses, who have passed by boat beneath her convent on the Rhine. With the help of a knowledgeable old Jewish peddler she finally locates them in Amsterdam, where the peddler has seen her Apollo "often enough . . . in the German synagogue." There the exiled Greek god was cantor and called "Rabbi Faibisch, which in *hochdeutsch* means Apollo." The god, then, is an exile both as Nazarene and as Hellene, Heine here yoking ironically the polar opposites of his own vision of world culture. But Apollo/Faibisch, moreover, is an apostate and freethinker, now exiled from the Jewish community—triply an exile. And he seems also to be a wencher and a pimp, now accompanied through Europe by "some wenches from the

Amsterdam cathouse," the fattest of which "grunts and squeaks especially well:" the muses, of course. By the time Heine closes, then, he has dissolved both his own career and culture, as well as the great cultural currents of all Western Europe, in scathing irony: romantic poetry (his and others'), the sentimental German burgher-public which reads it, his own Jewishness, the classical ideal, Judeo-Christian morality, modern commerce and industry. Irony can hardly reach further.

Here, then, are Heine and Laforgue at their most thoroughly ironic, full of savage mockery of the world, but equally so of themselves: Laforgue as the duplicitous Hamlet, not sure whether he is composer or composed, actor or act, untrusting in himself and untrusted by others; Heine as Apollo-Faibisch, and even as the romantic, escaped nun, false Hellene, Nazarene unbeliever in two faiths, literary pimp to the German burghers, who absorb his saccharine verse while indulging their digestion. Yet, behind all this ironic brutality in both poets, the reader discerns the thin skin, the lacerated sensibilities, of the sensitive artist.

Nor can we deny the adulterated pleasure, partly aesthetic, partly anaesthetic, which irony has offered both its readers and its writers from earliest times. Part of our fascination with irony is the complexity of the ironic experience, its subtle and elusive combination of pain and pleasure. How describe the pleasure offered by a bitter herb or a bitter incense—hysop or myrrh? But such is the savor of irony, bitterly satisfying, especially to the romantic sensibility. A. E. Houseman once wittily defended his own ironies by comparing them to the ever-larger doses of poison by which Mithridates inured himself to the effects of arsenic and saved his life from the poisoners around him ("Terence, This is Stupid Stuff")—incidentally, an ethical, not an aesthetic defense.

The ironies in Heine and Laforgue are more subjective, defenses against their own exile, both internal and external: Heine, triply an exile, and Laforgue, seemingly an exile from life itself. But for each, the greater exile was perhaps the internal, a sort of alienation from self, the curse of the artist or thinker whose vision penetrates beyond any single personal feeling or principle, and leads him to distrust his own beliefs and attitudes, his own logic, even his own integrity. This is the unstable equilibrium of the complete ironist, distruster and mocker of self. We see him most vividly in Heine, who without heart exchanges disbelief in one faith for disbelief in another, and who disbelieves himself in both apostasies. When he calls for order, he fears tyranny; when he calls for freedom, he fears license; when he calls for Zeitgeist, he fears chaos; when he calls for tradition, he fears stagnation. And he teaches his disciple Laforgue to cover with the masks of the ironist his fear of his fears. Like all great ironists, the two poets have left us the bitterly pleasurable experience of those masks.

Notes

[1] Jacques Gaucheron, "Laforgue au singulier," *Europe*, (1985): 12.

[2] André Wurmser, "Complainte du pauv' jeune homme, *Europe*, 19.

[3] For Laforgue and Baudelaire, cf. the perceptive study by J. A. Hiddleston, *Essai sur Laforgue et "Les Derniers Vers" suivi de Laforgue et Baudelaire* (Lexington: French Forum Publishers, 1980).

[4] Henri Peyre, "Laforgue Among the Symbolists," in Laforgue, *Essays on a Poet's Life and Work*, 44.

[5] The myth of Heine's unfortunate and frustrated love(s) as inspiration for his poetry has meanwhile been demystified by William Rose, *The Early Love Poetry of Heinrich Heine: An Inquiry into Poetic Inspiration* (Oxford: Clarendon Press, 1962).

[6] We recall the textual echoes of this Heinean attitude which I have noted above. Thus, for example, in the same letter to Immermann of 1823, from which I have quoted above, Heine writes: "Only one thing can hurt me most severely: when one attempts to explain the spirit of my poetry out of the history . . . of the poet. . . . One violates the poem, as it were, one tears its secret veil in revealing that influence of the story which in fact exists . . . And how seldom do the external aspects of our biography really correspond to our true, inner history! With me, at least, they *never* correspond" (HSA, XX: 92–3).

[7] Mayser, *Heines 'Buch der Lieder' im 19. Jahrhundert*, 208–16.

[8] Arkell, *Looking for Laforgue*, 119ff.

[9] What Sammons says about Heine's love poetry applies to Laforgue as well: "One wonders if there had ever before been a body of love poetry in which so much accusation is directed toward the beloved . . . The unity of unalloyed

feeling is broken up by his famous *Stimmungsbrechung*, the sardonic breach of mood . . . The tone shifts back and forth from the emotional to the conversational, from the delicate to the blunt, the setting from the realm of the imagination to the banal scenes of modern society. . . . the feeling and the frustration, the hope and the delusion . . . But there is no mediation between these contraries in the situation. The resolution is the poetry itself. Thus the poetry and what it is doing for the poet are ultimately the subject of the poetry rather than the beloved or the love story. The poet recovers his shaken dignity through the creative achievement" (*A Modern Biography*, 61–2).

[10] Barker Fairley, "Heine's Vaudeville," 200, 202.

[11] Cf. Françoise Bech, *Heines Pariser Exil zwischen Spätromantik und Wirklichkeit* (Frankfurt: Peter Lang Verlag, 1983), esp. the chapter "Die Exilsituation," 66ff. For a survey of the Jewish writer's prose "Exilschilderungen," cf. Irmgard Zepf, "Exilschilderungen in Heines Prosaschriften, *Emuna*, 10 (1975): 129–34.

[12] Ernst Feise, quoted by Paul Konrad Kurz, *Künstler Tribun Apostel: Heinrich Heines Auffassung vom Beruf des Dichters* (Munich, Wilhelm Fink Verlag, 1967), 14. According to Kurz, at all times, Heine is "in seinem Innersten Dichter" (140).

[13] B, I: 557–615. This work was first published in 1836; the same year, Heine published a French version in the *Revue des Deux Mondes*. *Les Nuits florentines* was finally included in the second volume of *Tableaux de voyage*, 291–375.

[14] Cf. Carl Enders, "Heinrich Heines Faustdichtungen: Der Tanz als Deutungs- und Gestaltungsmittel seelischer Erlebnisse," *Zeitschrift für deutsche Philologie*, 74 (1955): 364–92. The author likens Mademoiselle Laurence's dance to the "dramatic dance, as inaugurated in Heine's *Tanzpoem* and developed in Egk's *Abraxas*" (392).

[15] Laforgue, *Moralités*, 174–245.

[16] Wurmser, "Compainte du pauv' jeune homme," 19.

[17] B, VI: 32–36.

[18] Jeffrey L. Sammons, *Heinrich Heine, The Elusive Poet* (New Haven: Yale University Press, 1969) in his most pentrating commentary of the poem states: "*Der Apollogott* is one of Heine's greatest poems, although it is not altogether easy to understand and is so destructive of aesthetic idealism in import and so mean and violent in procedure that the reader is more likely at first to take offence than sense the pain and the wounded but surviving pride to which it gives expression" (364).

List of Works Cited

Heinrich Heine, *Sämtliche Schriften*, ed. Klaus Briegleb. Munich: Carl Hanser Verlag, 1968–1976.

——, *Historisch-kritische Gesamtausgabe der Werke*, ed. Manfred Windfuhr. Hamburg: Hoffmann und Campe, 1973–   .

——, *Säkularausgabe*, eds. Nationale Forschungs- und Gedenkstätten der klassischen deutschen Literatur und Centre National de la Recherche Scientifique. Berlin-Paris: Akademie Verlag & CNRS, 1970–   .

Heine, Henri, *De l'Allemagne*. Paris: Michel Lévy Frères, 1867.

——, *De l'Allemagne* II. Paris: Calmann-Lévy, 1891.

——, *Allemands et Français*. Paris: Calmann-Lévy, 1881.

——, *De l'Angleterre*. Paris: Calmann-Lévy, 1881.

——, *De la France*. Paris: E. Renduel, 1833.

——, *De la France*. Paris: Calmann-Lévy, 1884.

——, *De Tout un peu*. Paris: Michel Lévy Frères, 1867.

——, *Drames et fantaisies*. Paris: Michel Lévy Frères, 1886.

——, *Intermezzo*, trad. en vers français par Paul Ristelhuber. Paris. Poulet-Malassis, 1857.

——, *Lutèce*. Paris: Michel Lévy Frères, 1855.

——, *Poèmes et légendes*. Paris: Michel Lévy Frères, 1855.

——, *Poésies inédites*. Paris: Calmann-Lévy, 1885.

——, *Tableaux de voyage*. II. Paris: Michel Lévy Frères, 1856.

——, *Satires et portraits*. Paris: Calmann-Lévy, 1884.

——, "Les Nuits florentines," *Revue des Deux Mondes*, avril et mai, 1836.

Heinrich Heine, Dichter über ihre Dichtungen, 3 vols. ed. Norbert Altenhofer. Munich: Heimeran Verlag, 1971.

Heinrich Heines Zeitungsberichte über Musik und Malerei, ed. Michael Mann. Frankfurt: Inselverlag, 1964.

Heinrich Heine über die französische Bühne und andere Schriften zum Theater, ed. Christoph Trilse. Berlin: Henschelverlag Kunst und Gesellschaft, 1971.

The Complete Poems of Heinrich Heine: A Modern English Version, transl. Hal Draper. Boston: Suhrkamp/Insel Publishers Boston, Inc., 1982.

Oeuvres complètes de Jules Laforgue, ed. G. Jean-Aubry. Paris: Mercure de France, 1920–1930.

Jules Laforgue, *Oeuvres complètes* VI, *En Allemagne: Berlin la Cour et la ville*. Paris: Mercure de France, 1922. Slatkine Reprints, Genève: 1979.

———, *Les Complaintes*, ed. Michael Collie. London: The Athlone Press, 1977.

———, *Chroniques parisiennes, ennuis non rimés*, ed. Malraux. Paris: La Connaissance, undated.

———, *Les Complaintes, L'Imitation de Notre-Dame la lune*, ed. Pierre Reboul. Paris: Collection de l'Imprimerie Nationale, 1981.

———, *Les Complaintes et les premiers poèmes*, ed. Pascal Pia. Paris: Gallimard, 1970 and 1979.

———, *Dragées, Charles Baudelaire, Tristan Corbière, textes inédits* II. Paris: La Connaissance, undated.

———, *Les Pages de la Guêpe*, ed. J. L. Debauve. Paris: Nizet, 1969.

———, *Moralités légendaires*, ed. Daniel Grojnowski. Paris-Genève: Droz, 1980.

———, *Oeuvres complètes* IV, *Lettres I*; V, *Lettres II*. Paris: Mercure de France, 1920–1930. Slatkine Reprints, Genève: 1979.

———, *Lettres à un Ami*. Paris, Mercure de France, 1941.

———, *L'Imitation de Notre-Dame la lune, Des Fleurs de bonne volonté*, ed. Pascal Pia. Paris: Gallimard, 1979.

———, *Mélanges posthumes*. Paris: Mercure de France, 1903.

———, *Stéphane Vassiliew*. Genève: Club des Bibliophiles, 1946.

———, "Le Public des dimanches au Salon," *La Vie moderne*, 21 mai, 1881.

———, "Plans de Nouvelles et Notes," *La Revue blanche*, deuxième semestre 1896. Slatkine Reprints, Genève: 1968.

———, Posthumes, "Feuilles volantes," *La Revue blanche*, X, premier semestre 1896. Slatkine Reprints, Genève: 1968.

———, "Salon de Berlin," *Gazette des Beaux-Arts*, 1883, 170–81.

———, "Albrecht Dürer et ses Dessins," *Gazette des Beaux-Arts*, 1882, 608–16.

———, "Exposition de M. Ad. Menzel," *Gazette des Beaux-Arts*, 1884, 76–84.

———, "Exposition du Centenaire de l'Académie Royale des Arts de Berlin," *Gazette des Beaux-Arts*, 1886, 339–45.

———, "Exposition de Sculpture Polychrome à la National-Galerie," *Gazette des Beaux-Arts*, 1886, 166–70.

———, "Tessa, comédie en deux actes et en vers," ed. David Arkell, *Revue des sciences humaines*, 1980–II: 93–129.

Poems of Jules Laforgue, transl. Patricia Terry. Berkeley: University of California Press, 1958.

Baudelaire, Charles, *Curiosités esthétiques, L'Art romantique*, ed. Henri Lemaitre. Paris: Classiques Garnier, 1962.

Cros, Henri et Charles Henry, *L'Encaustique et les autres procédés de peinture chez les Anciens*. Paris: J. Pouam, 1884.

Diderot, *Oeuvres esthétiques*. Paris: Garnier Frères, 1959.

Freud, Sigmund, *Der Witz und seine Beziehung zum Unbewußten*. Frankfurt: Fischer, 1958.

Gide, André, *Romans, récits et soties*. Paris: Gallimard, 1958.

Hartmann, Eduard von, *Philosophy of the Unconscious*, transl. W. Ch. Coupland. London: Kegan, Trench & Trübner, 1890.

——, *Philosophie de l'Inconscient*, trad. D. Nolen. Paris: Germer Baillière, 1877.

Hegel, G.W.F., *Werke in zwanzig Bänden, XV Vorlesungen über die Ästhetik III*. Frankfurt: Suhrkamp Verlag, 1970.

——, *Cours d'esthétique*. Paris: Joubert, 1850–51.

——, *Esthétique*, trad. française. Paris: Germer Baillière, 1875.

——, *La Poétique*. Paris: Ladrange, 1855.

Helmholtz, Hermann von, *The Selected Writings*. Middletown: Wesleyan University Press, 1971.

Huysmans, J.-K., *Oeuvres complètes*. Paris: Cres & Cie., 1928.

Kahn, Gustave, *Symbolistes et Décadents*. Paris: Librairie Léon Vanier, 1902.

Nerval, Gérard de, *Faust, tragédie de Goethe: nouvelle traduction complète en prose et en vers*. Paris: Dondé-Dupré, 1828.

——, *Poésies Allemandes: Klopstock, Goethe, Bürger, morceaux choisis et traduits par Gérard*. Paris: Méquignon, Havard, Bricon, 1830.

Renan, Ernest, *Dialogues Philosophiques*. Paris: Calmann-Lévy, 1895.

Sainte-Beuve, *Oeuvres I, Premiers Lundis*. Paris: Gallimard, 1956.

Schelling, F.W.J., *System of Transcendental Idealism (1800)*, transl. Peter Heath. Charlottesville: University Press of Virginia, 1978.

Schlegel, August Wilhelm, *Die Kunstlehre*. Stuttgart: Kohlhammer, 1963.

——, *Sämtliche Werke IX*. Hildesheim: Georg Olms Verlag, 1971.

Taine, H. *The Ideal in Art*, transl. J. Durand. New York: Holt & Co., 1874.

——, *Philosophie de l'art*. Heidelberg: Carl Winters Universitätsbuchhandlung, 1907.

Littré, E., *Dictionnaire de la langue française*. Paris: Librairie Hachette, 1863.

Bech, Françoise, *Heines Pariser Exil zwischen Spätromantik und Wirklichkeit*. Frankfurt: Verlag Peter Lang, 1983.

Becker, Heinz, *Der Fall Heine-Meyerbeer*. Berlin: Walter de Gruyter & Co., 1958.

Boeck, Oliver, *Heines Nachwirkung und Heine-Parallelen in der französischen Dichtung*. Göppingen: Kümmerle, 1972.

Deblüe, Vera, *Anima naturaliter ironica: Die Ironie im Wesen und Werk Heines*. Bern: Verlag Herbert Lang & Cie., A.G., 1970.

Fendri, Mounir, *Halbmond, Kreuz und Schibboleth: Heinrich Heine und der Islamische Orient*. Hamburg: Hoffman und Campe, 1980.

Geldrich, Hanna, *Heine und der spanisch-amerikanische Modernismo*. Frankfurt: Verlag Herbert Lang, 1971.

Grésillon, Almuth, *La règle et le monstre: le mot valise. Interrogation sur la langue, à partir d'un corpus de Heinrich Heine*. Tübingen: Max Niemeyer Verlag, 1984.

Gutjahr, Herbert, *Zwischen Affinität und Kritik, Heinrich Heine und die Romantik*. Frankfurt: Peter Lang, 1984.

Hirth, Friedrich, *Heinrich Heine und seine französischen Freunde*. Mainz: Kupferberg, 1949.

Jost, Hermand, *Der frühe Heine: Ein Kommentar zu den "Reisebildern"*. Munich: Winkler Verlag, 1976.

Kircher, Hartmut, *Heinrich Heine und das Judentum*. Bonn: Bouvier Verlag Herbert Grundmann, 1973.

Kurz, Paul Konrad, *Künstler Tribun Apostel: Heinrich Heines Auffassung vom Beruf des Dichters*. Munich: Wilhelm Fink Verlag, 1967.

Lea, Charlene A., *Emanicipation, Assimilation and Stereotype: The Image of the Jew in German and Austrian Drama (1800–1850)*. Bonn: Bouvier Verlag Herbert Grundmann, 1978.

Lehmann, Ursula, *Popularisierung und Ironie im Werk Heinrich Heines*. Frankfurt: Peter Lang, 1976.

Mann, Michael, *Heinrich Heines Musikkritiken*. Hamburg: Hoffmann und Campe, 1971.

Mayser, Erich, *H. Heines "Buch der Lieder" in 19. Jahrhundert*. Stuttgart; Akademischer Verlag Hans-Dieter Heinz, 1978.

Mutzenbecher, Heinrich, *Heine und das Drama*. Hamburg: Verlag Lucas Gräfe, 1914.

Oehler, Dolf, *Pariser Bilder I (1830–1848) Antibourgeoise Ästhetik bei Baudelaire, Daumier und Heine*. Frankfurt: Suhrkamp Verlag, 1979.

Pabel, Klaus, *Heines "Reisebilder."* Munich: Wilhelm Fink Verlag, 1977.

Paucker, Henri Roger, *Heinrich Heine, Mensch und Dichter zwischen Deutschland und Frankreich*. Bern: Verlag Herbert Lang & Cie, A.G., 1967.

Prawer, S. S., *Heine: Buch der Lieder*. London: Edward Arnold Publishers, Ltd., 1960.

———, *Heine's Jewish Comedy*. Oxford, Clarendon Press, 1983.

———, *Heine's Shakespeare*, Inaugural Lecture, Univ. of Oxford, May 5, 1970. Oxford: Clarendon Press, 1970.

Rose, William, *The Early Love Poetry of Heinrich Heine: An Inquiry into Poetic Inspiration*. Oxford: Clarendon Press, 1962.

Rosenthal, Ludwig, *Heinrich Heine als Jude*. Frankfurt: Verlag Ullstein, 1973.

Sammons, Jeffrey, L., *Heinrich Heine, the Elusive Poet*. New Haven: Yale University Press, 1969.

————, *Heinrich Heine: A Modern Biography*. Princeton: Princeton University Press, 1979.

————, *Heinrich Heine: A Selected Critical Bibliography of Secondary Literature, 1956–1980*. New York: Garland, 1982.

Sandor, A. I., *Exile of the Gods: Interpretation of a Theme, a Theory and a Technique in the Work of Heinrich Heine*. The Hague: Mouton, 1967.

Sternberger, Dolf, *Heinrich Heine und die Abschaffung der Sünde*. Hamburg: Claassen Verlag, 1972.

Voigt, Jürgen, *Ritter, Henker, Harlekin: der junge Heine als romantischer Patriot und als Jude*. Frankfurt: Peter Lang, 1982.

Wadepuhl, Walter, *Heine-Studien*. Weimar: Aron-Verlag, 1956.

Weinberg, Kurt, *Henri Heine "Romantique défroqué" héraut du symbolisme français*. Paris: Presses Universitaires de France, 1964.

Wiese, Benno von, *Signaturen zu Heinrich Heine und seinem Werk*. Berlin: Erich Schmidt Verlag, 1976.

Zepf, Irmgard, *Heinrich Heines Gemäldeausstellung zum Salon 1831*. Munich: Wilhelm Fink Verlag, 1980.

Arkell, David, *Looking for Laforgue*. Manchester: Carcanet Press, 1979.

Betts, Madeleine, *L'univers de Laforgue à travers les mots*. Paris: La Pensée universelle, 1978.

Caprio, Dana Carton. "Jules Laforgue's 'Le Concile féerique': A Stylistic Structurl Analysis." Diss. Columbia University, 1973. (Ann Arbor: University Microfilms International 8220467).

Debauve, J. L., *Laforgue et son temps*. Neuchatel: Baconnière, 1972.

Guichard, Léon, *Jules Laforgue et ses poésies*. Paris: Nizet, 1977.

Hiddleston, J. A., *Essai sur Laforgue et les "Derniers Vers" suivi de Laforgue et Baudelaire*. Lexington: French Forum Publishers, 1980.

Mélim, José, "Another Study of the Irony of Jules Laforgue." Diss. University of Oregon, 1966. (Ann Arbor: University Microfilms International 167–1869).

Ramsey, Warren, *Jules Laforgue and the Ironic Inheritance*. New York: Oxford University Press, 1953.

Sakari, Ellen, *Prophète et Pierrot: Thèmes et attitudes ironiques dans l'oeuvre de Jules Laforgue*. Finland: University of Jyväskylä, 1974.

Behler, Ernst, *Klassische Ironie, Romantische Ironie, Tragische Ironie: zum Ursprung dieser Begriffe*. Darmstadt: Wissenschaftliche Buchgesellschaft, 1972.

Bloom, Harold, *The Anxiety of Influence*. New York: Oxford University Press, 1973.

Cornford, Francis Macdonald, *The Origin of Attic Comedy*. New York: Anchor Books, 1961.

Darnois, Dennis N. Kenedy, *The Unconscious and Eduard von Hartmann*. The Hague: Martinus Nijhoff, 1967.

Dédéyan, Charles, *Gérard de Nerval et l'Allemagne*. Paris: SEDES, 1957.

Dorr, Milo and Reinhard Federmann, eds. *Der politische Witz*. Munich: Verlag Kurt Desch, 1964.

Dubruck, Alfred, *Gérard de Nerval and the German Inheritance*. The Hague: Mouton, 1965.

Furst, Lilian R., *Counterparts: The Dynamics of Franco-German Literary Relationships 1770–1895*. London: Methuen, 1977.

———, *Fictions of Romantic Irony*. Cambridge: Harvard University Press, 1984.

Genette, Gérard, *Palimpsestes, littérature au second degré*. Paris: Editions du Seuil, 1982.

Glicksberg, Charles I., *The Ironic Vision in Modern Literature*. The Hague: Martinus Nijhoff, 1969.

Guillén, Claudio, *Literature as System*. Princeton: Princeton University Press, 1971.

Hohendahl, Peter Uwe und Egon Schwarz, eds. *Exil und innere Emigration*. Frankfurt: Athenäum Verlag, 1973.

Jankélévitch, Vladimir, *L'Ironie ou la bonne conscience*. Paris: Presses Universitaires de France, 1950.

Japp, Uwe, *Theorie der Ironie*. Frankfurt: Klostermann, 1983.

Jones, Louisa E., *Sad Clowns and Pale Pierrots*. Kentucky: French Forum Publishers, 1984.

Knox, Norman, *The word Irony and its Context, 1500–1755*. Durham: Duke University Pess, 1961.

Niehaus, Max, *Himmel Hölle und Trikot*. Munich: Nymphenburger Verlagsbuchhandlung, 1959.

Nochlin, Linda, *Impressionism and Post-Impressionism 1874–1904*. Englewood Cliffs: Prentice-Hall, 1966.

Prang, Helmut, *Die Romantische Ironie*. Darmstadt: Wissenschaftliche Buchgesellschaft, 1972.

Radkau, Joachim, *Die deutsche Emigration in den USA. Ihr Einfluß auf die amerikanische Europapolitik*. Düsseldorf: Bertelsmann Universitätsverlag, 1971.

Ribot, Th., *La Psychologie allemande contemporaine*. Paris: Félix Alcan, 1909.

Starobinski, Jean, *Portrait de l'artiste en Saltimbanque*. Genève: Skira, 1970.

Storey, Robert F., *Pierrot: A Critical History of a Mask*. Princeton: Princeton University Press, 1978.

———, *Pierrots on the Stage of Desire*. Princeton: Princeton University Press, 1985.

Strohschneider-Kohrs, Ingrid, *Die Romantische Ironie in Theorie und Gestaltung*. Tübingen: Max Niemeyer Verlag, 1960.

Tabori, Paul, *The Anatomy of Exile: A Semantic and Historical Study*. London: Harrap, 1972.

Zagona, Helen Grace, *The Legend of Salomé and the Principle of Art for Art's Sake*. Paris: Minard, 1960.

Anonymous, Editorial "A French poet in Imperial Berlin," *Apollo*, 106 (1977), 88–97.

Berendsohn, Walter A., "Heines 'Buch der Lieder,' Struktur- und Stilstudie" in *Heine-Jahrbuch* 1962. Düsseldorf: Hoffmann und Campe, 26–38.

Block, Haskell M., "Laforgue and the Theatre" in *Jules Laforgue: Essays on a Poet's Life and Work*. Cabondale: Southern Illinois University Press, 1969, 76–92.

———, "Heine and the French Symbolists: in *Creative Ecounter: Festschrift for Herman Salinger*, ed. Leland R. Phelps. Chapel Hill: University of North Carolina Press, 1978, 25–39.

Brooks, Peter, "The Rest is Silence: Hamlet as Decadent" in *Jules Laforgue: Essays on a Poet's Life and Work*. Carbondale: Southern Illinois University Press, 1969, 93–110.

Büchner, Wilhelm, "Über den Begriff der Eironeia," *Hermes*, 76 (1941): 339–58.

Cassou, Jean, "Laforgue et l'Impressionnisme" in *Mélanges Cain*. Paris: undated, 111–15.

Challemel-Lacour, P., "Un Bouddhiste contemporain en Allemagne, Arthur Schopenhauer," *Revue des Deux Mondes*, XCVII (1870): 296–332.

DeGraaf, Daniel H., "Quelques rencontres avec Henri Heine dans la littérature française," *Les Langues modernes* 59 (1956): 140–44.

Destro, Alberto, "Das *Buch der Lieder* und seine Leser: Die Prämissen einer mißlungenen Rezeption" in *Zu Heinrich Heine*. Stuttgart: Ernst Klett, 1981, 59–73.

Dottin, Mireille, "Jules Laforgue, salonnier," *Europe* 673 (1985): 85–96.

———, "Un Article retrouvé de Jules Laforgue," *Europe* 673 (1985): 97–102.

Dufour, Médéric, "Une Philosophie de l'Impressionnisme: Etude sur l'esthétique de Jules Laforgue." Paris: Librairie Léon Vanier, 1904.

Enders, Carl, "Heinrich Heines Faustdichtungen: Der Tanz als Deutungs- und Gestaltungsmittel seelischer Erlebnisse," *Zeitschrift für deutsche Philologie*, 74 (1955): 364–92.

Fairley, Barker, "Heine's Vaudeville," *University of Toronto Quarterly*, III (1934): 185–207.

Franklin, Ursula, "Laforgue and His Philosophers, or the 'Paratext' in the Intertextual Maze," *Nineteenth-Century French Studies*, 14 (1986): 324–40.

———, "Reverberations of Heine's *Lyrisches Intermezzo* in the Lyrics of Laforgue, *Comparative Literature*, 39 (1987):115–38.

————, "Heinean Inspirations in Laforgue's Early Literary Journalism," *Canadian Review of Comparative Literature*, 13 (1986): 350–374.

Frye, Northrup, "The Road of Excess" in *Myth and Symbol*. Lincoln: University of Nebraska Press, 1963, 3–20.

Galley, Eberhard, "Heine und der Kölner Dom," *Deutsche Vierteljahrs-schrift für Literaturwissenschaft und Geistesgeschichte*, 32 (1958): 99–110.

Gaucheron, Jacques, "Laforgue au singulier," *Europe*, 673 (1985): 3–15.

Hannoosh, Michele, "The Poet as Art Critic: Laforgue's Aesthetic Theory," *The Modern Language Review*, 79 (1984): 553–69.

————, "The Early Laforgue: *Tessa*," *French Forum*, 8 (1983): 20–32.

Henning, Hans, "Heines Buch über Shakespeares Mädchen und Frauen," *Shakespeare Jahrbuch*, 113 (1977): 103–17.

Hilscher, Eberhard, "Heinrich Heine und Richard Wagner," *Neue deutsche Literatur*, 4, No. 12 (1956): 107–112.

Hofmann, Werner, "Heine und die Malerei der Zukunft" in *Heine-Jahrbuch* 1981. Düsseldorf: Hoffman und Campe, 71–89.

Höltgen, Karl Josef, "Über 'Shakespeares Mädchen und Frauen'; Heine, Shakespeare und England," *Heine-Studien*, ed. Manfred Windfuhr, Internationaler Heine-Kongreß 1972. Hamburg: Hoffmann und Campe, Heinrich Heine Verlag, 1973, 464–88.

Hyman, Timothy, "Caulfield's Laforgue," *Artscribe*, 24 (1980): 16–20.

Janet, Paul, "La Métaphysique en Europe depuis Hegel, un philosophe misanthrope," *Revue des Deux Mondes*, XXI (1877): 269–87.

Johnson, Ronald, "Poetic Pathways to Dada: Marcel Duchamp and Jules Laforgue," *Arts Magazine* (1967):82–89.

Kanowsky, Walter, "Heine als Benützer der Bibliotheken in Bonn und Göttingen" *Heine-Jahrbuch* 1973. Düsseldorf: Hoffmann und Campe, 129–53.

Kolb, Jocelyne, "Heine's Amusical Muse," *Monatshefte für deutschen Unterricht*, LXXXIII (1981): 392–404.

Kolb, Philippe et Jean Adémar, "Charles Ephrussi (1848–1905) ses Secrétaires: Laforgue, A. Renan, Proust 'sa' Gazette des Beaux-Arts," *Gazette des Beaux-Arts*, 126 (1984): 29–41.

Lehmann, A. C., "Pierrot en fin de siècle" in *Romantic Mythologies*. New York: Barnes and Noble, 1967, 209–223.

Maynard, Louis de, "Des Peintres avant David," *L'Europe littéraire*, 2 (1833).

Peyre, Henri, "Laforgue Among the Symbolists" in *Jules Laforgue: Essays on a Poet's Life and Work*. Carbondale: Southern Illinois University Press, 1969, 39–51.

Pfrimmer, Albert, "Heine et les musiciens romantiques allemands," *Europe*, 125–126 (1956): 115–20.

Rasch, Wolfdietrich, "Die Pariser Kunstkritik Heinrich Heines" in *Beiträge zum Stilpluralismus*. Munich: Prestel-Verlag, 1977, 230–45.

Richard, Jean-Pierre, "Le Sang de la complainte," *Poétique*, 40 (1979): 477–95.

Robert, Frédéric, "Heine et ses musiciens," *Europe*, 125–126 (1956): 121–24.

Rose, Margaret, "The Politicization of Art Criticism: Heine's 1831 Portrayal of Delacroix's *Liberté* and its Aftermath," *Monatshefte für deutschen Unterricht*, LXXIII (1981): 405–14.

Schalles, Ernst August, "Heins Verhältnis zu Shakespeare," Inaugural-Dissertation Königl. Friedrich-Wilhelms-Universität zu Berlin, 13. Februar 1904.

Schiff, Richard, "The End of Impressionism: A Study in Theories of Artistic Expression," *The Art Quarterly*, I (1978): 338–78.

Söhn, Gerhard, "In der Tradition der literarischen Kunstbetrachtung Heinrich Heines 'Französische Maler'" in *Heine-Jahrbuch* 1978. Düsseldorf: Hoffmann und Campe, 9–34.

Sonnenfeld, Albert, "Hamlet the German and Jules Laforgue," *Yale French Studies*, 33 (1964): 92–100.

Steefel, Lawrence D., Jr., "Marcel Duchamp's 'Encore à cet Astre' ", *Art Journal*, XXXVI (1976): 23–30.

Stiefel, Robert E., "Heine's Ballet Scenarios, an Interpretation," *Germanic Review*, 44 (1969): 186–98.

Taillandier, Saint-René, "Les Débuts d'un poète humoriste," *Revue des Deux Mondes*, XLVII (1863): 497–529.

Turóczi-Trostler, Jósef, "Heine und Faust," 203–207 in Turóczi-Trostler, "Faust-Studien" *Acta Litteraria Academiae Scientiarum Hungaricae* 6 (1964): 203–19.

Weiss, Gerhard, "Heinrich Heines 'Französische Maler' (1831)" in *Heine-Jahrbuch* 1980. Düsseldorf: Hoffmann und Campe, 78–100.

Wiese, Benno von, "Mephistopheles und Faust. Zur Interpretation von Heines Tanzpoem 'Der Doktor Faust'," in *Herkommen und Erneuerung: Essays für Oskar Seidlin*, eds. Gerald Gillespie und Edgar Lohner. Tübingen: Niemeyer, 1976, 225–40.

Windfuhr, Manfred, "Heinrich Heines deutsches Publikum (1820–1860). Vom Lieblingsdichter des Adels zum Anreger der bürgerlichen Intelligenz" in *Literatur in der sozialen Bewegung. Aufsätze und Forschungsberichte zum 19. Jahrhundert*, eds. Alberto Martino, Güther Hentzschel, Georg Jäger. Tübingen: Martino, 1977, 260–83.

Wurmser, André, "Compainte du pauv' jeune homme," *Europe*, 673 (1985): 16–28.

Zepf, Irmgard, "Exilschilderungen in Heines Prosaschriften," *Emuna*, 10 (1975): 129–34.

**North American Studies
in Nineteenth-Century German Literature**

is a series of monographs on post-Romantic literature of the nineteenth century in the German-speaking lands. The series endeavors to embrace studies in criticism, in literary history, in the interdependence with other national literatures, and in the social and political dimensions of literature. Our aim is to offer contributions by American scholars to the renovation of literary history, the reformation of the canon, the rediscovery of once significant authors, the reevalutation of texts and their contexts, and a renewed understanding and appreciation of a body of literature of acknowledged international importance in the nineteenth century.

Jeffrey Sammons
Yale University